Agnessa

From Paradise to Purgatory. A Voice from Stalin's Russia

The Allan K. Wildman Group for the Study of Russian Politics, Society, and Culture in the Revolutionary Era has established its *Historical Series* to promote research into the history of the workers, peasants, and intelligentsia in Late Imperial and Soviet Russia.

The Allan K. Wildman Group Historical Series

1. Michael Melancon and Alice K. Pate, eds., *New Labor History: Worker Identity and Experience in Russia, 1840–1918* (2002)

2. Page Herrlinger, *Working Souls: Russian Orthodoxy and Factory Labor in St. Petersburg, 1881–1917* (2007)

3. Jeff Jones, *Everyday Life and the Reconstruction of Soviet Russia during and after the Great Patriotic War, 1943–48* (2008)

4. John W. Steinberg and Rex A. Wade, eds., *The Making of Russian History: Society, Culture, and the Politics of Modern Russia. Essays in Honor of Allan K. Wildman* (2009)

5. Rose Glickman, trans., *Agnessa: From Paradise to Purgatory. A Voice from Stalin's Russia*, by Agnessa Ivanovana Mironova-Korol', as told to Mira Yakovenko (2012)

Series General Editors: Michael Melancon (Auburn University), Alice K. Pate (Columbus State University)

Editorial Board: Diane Koenker (University of Illinois, Champaign-Urbana), Daniel Orlovsky (Southern Methodist University), Henry Reichman (California State University, East Bay), William G. Rosenberg (University of Michigan), Mark Steinberg (University of Illinois, Champaign-Urbana), Gerald Surh (North Carolina State University), Isabel Tirado (William Patterson University), Rex Wade (George Mason University)

AGNESSA

FROM PARADISE TO PURGATORY
A VOICE FROM STALIN'S RUSSIA

By Agnessa Ivanovna Mironova-Korol',
as told to Mira Mstislavovna Yakovenko

Translated by Rose Glickman

Bloomington, Indiana, 2012

© 2012 by Rose Glickman. All rights reserved.

Library of Congress Cataloging-in-Publication Data

Mironova-Korolí, Agnessa Ivanovna.
   [Agnessa. English]
   Agnessa : from paradise to purgatory : a voice from Stalin's Russia / by Agnessa Ivanovna Mironova-Korolí as told to Mira Mstislavovna Yakovenko ; translated by Rose Glickman.
      pages ; cm. — (Allan K. Wildman Group historical series ; 5)
   Includes bibliographical references.
   ISBN 978-0-89357-394-2
  1. Mironova-Korolí, Agnessa Ivanovna. 2. Mironov, Sergei Naumovich--Family. 3. Iakovenko, M. M. (Mira Mstislavovna) 4. Soviet Union--Biography. Iakovenko, M. M. (Mira Mstislavovna) II. Glickman, Rose L., translator. III. Title. IV. Series: Allan K. Wildman Group historical series ; 5.

DK268.M58A313 2012
365'.45092--dc23
[B]

2012038269

Slavica Publishers
Indiana University
1430 N. Willis Dr.
Bloomington, IN 47404-2146
USA

[Tel.] 1-812-856-4186
[Toll-free] 1-877-SLAVICA
[Fax] 1-812-856-4187
[Email] slavica@indiana.edu
[www] http://www.slavica.com/

To Evie, Dario, and Leila

—Rose Glickman

Table of Contents

Acknowledgments ix

Translator's Introduction xi

Time Line xiii

Agnessa

Part I 1

    Grandfather 3

    Father 6

    Mama 10

    Zarnitsky 13

    Mirosha 35

    Zarnitsky Again 44

    Karaganda 48

    My Life with Mirosha, 1930–39 57

    After Mirosha 132

Part II 155

    Slavery 157

    Return 181

    Last Party 206

Epilogue 207

Appendix A: Stenographic Report of NKVD Meeting
    Conducted by Mirosha, July 25, 1937 215

Appendix B: MEMORIAL: International Historical, Educational,
    Human Rights And Humanitarian Society 219

Bibliography 223

Acknowledgments

The opportunity to publically thank my friends and colleagues does not come as often as I would like. It gives me great pleasure to do so now.

Gabriel Burton, my best writing buddy, for her reliably great insights; this time suggesting ways to make this translation clearer to the "non-expert" in Soviet history

Heart to Heart International Medical Children's Alliance: for giving me, among other incomparable things, the opportunity to keep my Russian life alive and robust.

Nelli Lipskaya, for indispensable help as my St. Petersburg courier, advisor, and—since *obshchezhitie* days in Leningrad—for indestructible friendship.

Mary McAuley, for decades of support, intellectual and otherwise; this time for giving me *Agnessa* to read and for predictably interesting and useful comments on the manuscript when I most needed them.

Agnessa Sergeevna Mironova-Korovicheva (Agnessa's daughter "Agulya"), who took me into her home and heart and graciously bestowed on me her memories and her archive.

Anna Ryabkina, for helping me to better understand Russian, Russians, and Russia—past and present—and always at a moment's notice.

Jerry Surh, for decades of friendship and collegiality; this time for reminding me that it was time to take the *Agnessa* project out of "the drawer" and for encouraging me to do so.

Lena Traer, for her amazing agility in the cyber world, her good-natured tolerance in guiding me through it without making me feel as if I were five years old; for her unflappable kindness, good sense, and generosity at many stages in the preparation of this book—and in other situations as well.

Alla Volovich, for the deep, sensitive knowledge of her own language and literature as well as of her adopted language and literature that made her the most enjoyable partner in sorting out my own dilemmas in both languages.

Olga Yakovenko, the daughter of Mira Yakovenko, for her whole-hearted generosity and support in this project, for her ability to guess what I needed, for offering me valuable insights and materials.

Arseny Roginsky and Irina Shcherbakova of *Memorial* for their inspired devotion to the project of preserving the history of Soviet repression, lest it be repeated, and to advocating for human and civil rights in their country in the present. Their work in *Memorial* helps me to believe that there is balm in Gilead.

Translator's Introduction

This is a unique voice of a vain, flamboyant, irritating, complex, and amazing woman whose life spans most of the Soviet epoch. Agnessa, a small-town beauty, married a high-ranking NKVD operator, "Mirosha," who was the great love of her life. Her family referred to Mirosha as an executioner—and he was. Young, restless, and naive when she met him in 1926, she reveled in the life his position provided for them. While the vast majority of Soviet citizens were living through famine and every manner of deprivation, Agnessa reveled in pleasures, amenities, unimaginable luxuries that were reserved for the highest party and secret service elite—and that, to this day, have rarely been glimpsed by the public. But just like hundreds of thousands of Soviet citizens, innocent and not so innocent, Agnessa experienced the fear and then the reality of "repression." In 1940 Mirosha was shot in the purges of high-echelon secret service and party officials. Two years later Agnessa was arrested and sentenced to five years in the Gulag. She willed herself to survive, emerging chastened (somewhat) but unbroken. She negotiated her way through the pitfalls of rehabilitation into a still dangerous post-Gulag life with a new husband who was serving his own term in the Gulag. She did everything with a spirit and a spontaneity and an irreverent gaze that will either charm or irritate the reader—or both.

I love the title page of *Agnessa* in the original Russian. It looks like no other I have seen in a serious Russian publication. But how apt it is.

AGNESSA

Narrated by Agnessa Ivanovna Mironova-Korol
Tales about her Youth
About the Joys and Sorrows of Three Marriages
About Her Boundless Love for the Well-Known Stalin Chekist
Sergei Naumovich Mironov
About Fabulous Resorts and Receptions in the Kremlin
And…
About Prisons, Prisoner Transports, Prison Camps
About Life Lived on the Roller Coaster of Soviet History

In 1997 I was in Moscow working for the Ford Foundation, a major supporter of *Agnessa*'s Russian publisher, the human rights organization Memorial. Mary McAuley, the head of the Ford Foundation's project in

Moscow, was my boss and my dear friend since our first scholarly trips to the Soviet Union in the early 1960s. She gave me a copy of *Agnessa* hot off the press, so to speak, and promised me that I would love it.

I read it, I loved it, I was hooked. What I would have done to have a book like this for my students (not to speak of myself) in the twenty-five years that I taught Russian and Soviet history—in the bad old days when a book like this could never have been published. It probably took me five minutes after I set it down to decide that it should be translated.

Agnessa is also about Mira Yakovenko, to whom Agnessa told her story—stories—in the course of a twenty-year friendship. "I did not encourage her to write out her stories," writes Mira. "I feared that if she knew her words were being taken down she would censor herself and would begin to pick and choose and that her spontaneous recollections would turn into something contrived and lifeless." According to Mira's daughter Olga, Mira had a phenomenal memory: "Each time I left Agnessa" says Mira, "I would write down what I remembered and then I augmented her own words with what I learned from (talking to) her friends and relatives." But Mira Yakovenko, a near contemporary of Agnessa's, had something she too wanted to say about the "roller coaster of Soviet history." A talented listener and experienced writer, she shaped Agnessa's narrative. This book, then, was a collaboration between two remarkable women.

Mira Yakovenko was a volunteer at Memorial. I was able to talk with her a few times (too few, alas) that year and later. She died in 2005. But her daughter Olga Yakovenko answered many of the questions I would have asked Mira—and then some. Olga Yakovenko has been so generous and helpful in helping me clarify and enrich Agnessa's story that she is part of the story as well. Among the many ways she befriended and helped me was to put me in touch with Agnessa's adopted daughter, who is a character in the story—then and now. I spent several days with Agulya, as everyone calls her, in her St. Petersburg apartment, plied with lunches, teas, and her own recollections and clarifications about her mother's life, with pictures, documents, and now friendship.

Memorial is also part of Agnessa's saga. Irina Shcherbakova, who worked closely with Mira on the production of the book, tells that Mira "was hard pressed to fit this book into a genre. Of course, it is not exactly a memoir in the purest sense of the word, neither is it a work of literary transcription nor a novel... It is a bit of all those things."

The text's great virtue, says Irina, "is that it gives us what can never be conveyed in documents: the characters, feelings, sensations, and finally, the myths of another era."

Time Line

1902: *Agnessa is born in 1902 in Maikop, a city of 22,000 in southern Russia, about 75 miles from the Black Sea. She always gave her birthday as 1903. I will thus date her age at the important moments of her life from 1903.*

1914–18: World War I and the Russian Revolution
Russia is allied with England and France against the Central Powers (Germany, Austria-Hungary, Italy) from 28 July 1914. Russia is both poorly equipped and incompetently led. She suffers huge losses in soldiers dead, wounded, or captured and equally huge losses in territory. The civilian home front, grows increasingly volatile.

February 1917: The February Revolution. Strikes, food riots, and military mutiny force Tsar Nicholas II to abdicate. A Provisional Government is formed, dominated by liberals.

October 1917: The Bolsheviks, supported by soldiers, sailors, and Petrograd workers, seize power from the Provisional Government.

November 1917: Bolshevik troops disband the Constituent Assembly formed in Russia's first national democratic election.

December 1917: The Bolsheviks create the Secret Police, known by its acronym CHEKA (All-Russian Extraordinary Commission for Combating Counter-Revolution and Sabotage). **The Bolsheviks now call themselves the Communist Party.**

1918–21: Civil War
A loose alliance of anti-Bolshevik elements coalesce into the White Army and take up arms against the Bolshevik Red Army for control of the country. During the war the Bolsheviks impose an economic policy in the areas they control called War Communism. It is a draconian expropriation and requisition of private business and agricultural production. The result is great hardship: uncontrolled inflation, decline in agricultural production, and labor productivity.

1921–28: The Bolsheviks win the Civil War and Lenin acknowledges that War Communism was a disaster. In 1921 he introduces the New Economic Policy (NEP), a modest form of private entrepreneurship and trade, assuming that the modernization required for communism could be achieved gradually. But, the atmosphere of siege did not abate. The Bolshevik government and the Party continue to seek out and punish "anti-revolutionary" individuals and enemies of the people.

1918: The White Army takes Maikop, the city of Agnessa's birth.

1920 (March): The Red Army takes Maikop from the Whites and remains in control.

1920: Agnessa graduates from a gymnasium for girls. Her older sister Lena marries a White Army soldier.

1921: Agnessa meets her first husband, Ivan Aleksandrovich Zarnitsky, head of the staff of the Red Army's Border Patrol.

1922: Agnessa marries Zarnitsky, at the age of 19 and moves to Rostov. Her mother, sister, and brother join them in the city of Rostov.

1924: Agnessa meets Sergei Naumovich Mironov (1894–40). Mirosha has a brilliant record with the Red Army and is already making his way up the ladder of the CHEKA. Agnessa and Mirosha carry on a clandestine love affair until 1930.

1924–25: Agnessa completes a two-year course at a school in Rostov that gives her the credentials to work as a paramedic and midwife.

1927: Agnessa's husband Zarnitsky is made head of a shoe factory. He is accused of sabotaging production and faces prison. As the son of a priest—an enemy of the

1929–35: When Lenin dies in 1924, the ruling members of the Communist Party vie for power. Stalin is victorious and jails or executes his opponents. He plunges the country into industrialization at break-neck speed. The First Five-Year Plan (1929–35) abolishes all forms of private property; the state controls planning, distribution, and payment for labor. Production for consumer well-being is starved of resources. All peasants are forced onto collective farms; the fruits of their labor are paid at government controlled prices.

1932–33: Food production drops calamitously and famine rages in the grain growing areas in 1931–32. Although the famine ends, the Soviet Union remains a society of chronic shortages.

1932–33: Several million kulaks, prosperous peasants regarded as exploiters, are expropriated and deported to Siberia and Central Asia. Class enemies or all those regarded as "anti-revolutionary" are subject to arrest, torture, and exile. The Secret Police burgeons in size and power to handle perceived opposition or dissent. The Gulag system is established.

1934: Sergei Kirov, head of the Leningrad Party Organization, is assassinated. This event escalates the tempo and intensity of what is now known as The Great Terror. Trials, arrests, and executions begin to define the culture, and the Gulag is be-

people—he is especially vulnerable. But he conducts a courageous and brilliant defense and is judged innocent.

*1930: Mirosha convinces Agnessa to leave Zarnitsky and run away with him to his new post in **Alma-Ata** where he has the post of deputy to the Plenipotentiary Representative of the OGPU (State Political Directorate) in Kazakhstan. The OGPU is successor to the CHEKA.*

1933–36: Mirosha is advanced to the position of head of the GPU (successor to the OGPU) of Dnepropetrovsk Province, and he and Agnessa move to Dnepropetrovsk in the south-central region of Ukraine. On the eve of their departure, Agnessa and Mirosha adopt Agulya, the one-and-a-half-year old daughter of Pukha, Agnessa's brother.

coming the fate of millions of Russians.

1934–36: The GPU is renamed NKVD. Genrich Yagoda is appointed head and remains in charge until 1936.

1936–39: "The Great Terror." Sometimes referred to as the Great Purges. Waves of arrests now include members of the Communist Party, the military, the professions, the intelligentsia, and the Secret Services themselves.

1936–38: Nikolai Yezhov is head of the NKVD.

1936: Agnessa and Zarnitsky are officially divorced. Agnessa and Mirosha are officially married.

December 1936–August 1937: *Mirosha is appointed head of the NKVD (successor to the GPU) of Western Siberia. Agnessa and Mirosha move to Novosibirsk.*

August 1937: *Mironov is appointed Soviet Plenipotentiary to Mongolia. The family moves to Ulan Bator.*

1938: Mironov is appointed deputy to the Supreme Soviet. Agnessa and Mironov move to Moscow. They are given an apartment in a building that houses the Soviet elite. It became known as the House on the Embankment.

1939: In August Stalin and Hitler sign the Nazi Soviet Non-Aggression Pact. The Soviet Union agrees not to come to Poland's aid if Germany attacks. In return, Germany essentially gives the Soviet Union the Baltic States, and the Soviets occupy Latvia, Lithuania, Estonia, half of Poland, and part of Romania.
The Soviet Union attacks Finland on November 30 1939. The Russo-Finish war ends on March 12, 1940.

1939: On January 6, Mironov is arrested. The apartment in the House on the Embankment is searched, the Mironovs' possessions are confiscated, and the family is confined to one room in the six-room apartment.

1940: Mironov is shot on February 22.

1941–May 1945: World War II. Germany invades Russia and Russia joins the Allies. Twenty-seven million Soviet soldiers and civilians die in WWII.

July 1941: *Agnessa marries Mikhail Davydovich, Mirosha's cousin. They live in Moscow.*

June 1941: Operation Barbossa is put into effect—the German invasion of the Soviet Union. Key Soviet cities are quickly invaded. By midsummer the German encirclement of Soviet forces is completed.

September 1941–January 1944: The German armies encircle and blockade Leningrad for almost 900 days. Roughly one million civilians perish.

1945–53: Soviet prisoners of war returning from Nazi captivity are sent to Soviet prison camps. New waves of mass arrests

1953: Stalin dies in 1953.

1954: The slow process of "rehabilitating" some victims of the Great Purge begins.

October 1941: Agnessa, Agulya, and Mikhail Davydovich's daughter Maya are evacuated from Moscow to Kuibyshev.

1942: Agnessa is arrested. She spends eight months in the Butyrka prison and is then sent to the Gulag in Kazakhstan until 1947.

1944: Mikhail Davydovich is arrested and imprisoned in Lefortovo.

1945: Mikhail Davydovich is sentenced to five years in the Gulag.

1947: Agnessa is released from the Gulag. She (illegally) joins her sister Lena, her adopted daughter Agulya, and other relatives in Klaipeda, Lithuania.

1949: Mikhail Davydovich is released from the Gulag and sent into exile in Northern Kazakhstan.

1950: Agnessa prepares to join Mikhail Davydovich in his place of exile. However, he is re-arrested and sentenced to ten years of a strict regime in a Gulag in Karaganda. Agnessa goes to Bogorodsk to live with a friend from the Gulag. Her daughter Agulya enrolls in a chemistry institute in Moscow.

1956: Mikhail Davydovich is finally released and joins Agnessa in Moscow.

December 1959: Mikhail Davydovich dies. Agnessa remains in their Moscow apartment until her death in 1981

Part I

Paradise and Purgatory—Side by Side

My Grandfather

You know, I love Chekhov above all other writers. Only now have I begun to value him. He is also interesting to me because he was on Sakhalin at the very moment that my maternal grandfather was released from penal servitude on the island of Sakhalin. I think Chekhov knew him. I told my grandfather's story to the Lenin Library and they let me go into the manuscript division. I found a card index of prisoners that Chekhov compiled. He included a card about each prisoner for whom he could glean some information.

I found a card for Ivan Zelenov—a native of Tomsk, like my grandfather. Everything matches including the birth date. The only thing is that Grandpa's surname was Zelentsov. Did Chekhov make a mistake? Or was Grandpa known as Zelentsov on Sakhalin?

Grandpa Ivan and Grandma Anisya had been living in Barnaul, Siberia. Grandpa was a simple Russian man. Grandma was a Yakut, and she was illiterate. They had many children and Grandpa worked day and night to support the family.

They lived opposite a rich Polish family that was probably sent into penal servitude after the Polish rebellions of 1863 or even as far back as 1830. They actually grew rich in Siberia and had several houses that they rented to the locals. And when the landlord, the old Pole, was already in his eighties, he says to my grandfather, "I am old and weak. I can't do much except sit and look out the window. I see your house and I watch your life. I see how your children run barefoot in the frost, how you leave early every morning to earn money. You are never drunk and you go to church. I know from this that you are honorable and industrious. My wife and I have nobody—no children, no grandchildren, but death is just around the corner. I would like to bequeath to you all my property, and in exchange you will look after us as if we were kin."

Grandpa didn't agree immediately. He said he had to consult with his wife. He did and they accepted the offer. The old Pole did not live long. When he died Grandpa took good care of his wife: he called doctors when she needed them, he bought medicine, and looked after her. Often he would sit with her and chat and she treated him like her own son.

In the house there was a maid and two Poles who sponged off the family. They had probably dreamed of inheriting everything, and suddenly here comes this poor guy without relatives, without a tribe. So when the old lady died they began to spread rumors that Grandpa poisoned her, and they spoke as if they had seen him give her poison from a spoon with their own eyes. The rumors continued even after the old woman was buried. There was a trial. The local priest was the main witness; his word was worth the word of twelve witnesses. He said that in the coffin the deceased had yellow spots, which means that she was poisoned. And then the maid and those two Poles testified and repeated that they had seen Grandpa give the old woman poison from a spoon.

They dug her up, opened her stomach and sent it to Tomsk to be examined by experts. The answer was that traces of arsenic had been found. But arsenic was one of the ingredients in a medicine that had been prescribed for the old woman to encourage her appetite. That was not taken into account. Everyone knew that arsenic is a poison. And that means that my grandpa was a poisoner.

He was sentenced to twenty years of penal servitude. It was already winter. He was supposed to travel down the river Ob, but all the boats had left for the year. So Grandpa went to prison in Barnaul for eight months. Grandma and the children were allowed to visit him. They set up a samovar in the prison and everyone sat around the samovar and talked and drank tea with buns that the family had brought. And, by the way, the guards drank tea with them.

But when spring came, a boat came for Grandpa. He stood on the deck in handcuffs. He had iron chains around his waist and his head; the prisoner's hat. Tears rolled down his face.

After he was arrested, his oldest daughter, Mama's sister, went out to work. Mama went to a sewing workshop as an apprentice. She washed floors, did the shopping, and helped the cook. But no one taught her how to sew. Why is that, she asked. The owner answered that the machines were all busy during the day and no one had time to teach her. Learn by yourself at night. Every day she got two pieces of sugar. She hid them in a little bag and brought them home to her little brothers and sisters.

While Grandpa was waiting to be sentenced some clever people taught Grandma to pilfer small silver things from the Pole's house. Grandma went to Tomsk and other places and sold them. This helped the family to make ends meet.

Mama had four years of school. She left the sewing workshop. Her older sister had already been working as a cashier in a store and was able to find a place there for Mama. That's how eight years passed. Suddenly a telegram arrives: "Praise be to God, I have been acquitted."

And there he is again on the deck, a skinny man with a long white beard, tears streaming down his face. But he is not being seen off, he is being greeted. Why was he acquitted? Grandpa told us that on Sakhalin he told his story to a very intelligent and good man. That man immediately discovered a detail: when Grandpa was allegedly poisoning the old women, he was already the legal owner of everything. There was no reason to get rid of her.

That man soon left Sakhalin and turned in a request in St. Petersburg for Grandpa to be pardoned. And he was.

Who was that? Chekhov, perhaps? There is a photograph of Chekhov standing with a skinny man with a long white beard. I think that was my grandpa, but there's no way to find out.

When Grandpa returned the head of the town and other important people came to see him. Only the priest who had accused him didn't come. He had gone crazy. The town dignitaries presented Grandpa with gold and a check and said that all the years Grandpa had not been in his home, it had been rented to other people, and this was the profit—it belonged to Grandpa.

My Father

Greece! It is the homeland of my forebears. My father, Ivan Pavlovich Agripopulo, was an ethnic Greek born in Turkey. The tsarist government had permitted a certain number of Turkish Greeks to settle in Russia to save them from Turkish savagery, so Papa came as a very small child with his parents to Anapa on the Black Sea. When he was a young man, for some reason he moved to Barnaul in Siberia.

Of course, in a Siberian city like Barnaul, he was like a miracle—a southerner, a Greek. My mother's girlfriends ran to her at work. "Don't you know that a new salesman is working at Prokhorov's shop? A Greek! So handsome. All the girls are gaping at him."

Mama went to have a look, too. And, indeed, Papa was handsome, dark-eyed and dark-haired. He had a very large aquiline nose, but it didn't spoil his looks. And it was not just his face that made him interesting. He was much more cultured than the Barnaul youths, he loved books, knew literature. To Mama he was like a prince from distant exotic lands. They met at a masquerade ball where Papa went dressed as Pierrot, and there he began to court Mama.

My grandfather said to her, "Listen if you marry him he'll take you away to the other end of the world."

Mama said that she would not marry him and he would not take her away, but that is exactly what she hoped for.

They married.

The local priest refused to marry them. "You are of different faiths," he said.

Papa exploded, "And where do you think your religion comes from? From Greek Orthodoxy!"

In fact, the priest did not know that and he stubbornly refused to marry them. So they had to find another place with another priest who was more knowledgeable and educated.

Grandpa gave my mother a dowry of several thousand rubles and Papa immediately took her away to Maikop, the town on the Black Sea where we children were born and grew up. Papa had many Greek relatives in Maikop who rejoiced at Mama's dowry and dreamed of using it to get rich. Papa was easily seduced into their various shady deals.

The first scheme was to get rich selling lime that one could procure almost gratis. They acquired the lime, rented some railroad cars to transport it for five hundred rubles, filled them with lime—but nobody wanted lime. The railroad got tired of waiting and demanded that they return the cars. They ended up having to dump the lime in a field just at the moment when it poured rain. They lost everything. His relatives were a bunch of schemers, and bad ones at that. All of their schemes failed.

But Papa was capable of harebrained projects of his own. While the White Army still occupied Maikop during the Civil War, we took in boarders to help with expenses, one of whom was the father of a White officer—the very White officer who eventually married my sister Lena. The father was also an operator. He and Papa concocted a plan to buy a mill. The mill venture ruined them both. Although Papa was incapable of calculating, he was convinced that his partner had swindled him.

My memories begin before that time, when Papa worked as a manager for a very rich Greek. This man had a plantation that grew tobacco and grapes and he had warehouses, stores, and a cinema. Papa managed the store and the cinema and earned seventy-five rubles a month. At the New Year, his boss gave him an envelope with only fifty-five rubles (he couldn't even give him his entire pay, the skinflint). But they had a very close relationship. They were both Greeks. They spoke to each other in their native tongue and used the informal "you."

The boss's wife, Klio Fyodorovna, was pock-marked and plain but very well built, tall and shapely. She also treated us like family. Once she came to chat with Mama. When she made to leave, she tripped over the door mat and fell. We picked her up immediately. She didn't even have a scratch.

Suddenly the boss, very upset, told Papa that Klio Fyodorovna had lost a very valuable diamond from her ring, a gift from her deceased brother-in-law. Had we found it? Papa said no. We began to search. At first we didn't find anything, then Mama told the maid to turn all the rugs over and she began to carefully pick at the fiber with her fingers. She found the diamond. Papa's delighted boss called him to the telephone. He gave Papa some time off, thanked and praised him: "There, that means that you are honorable people." This was before the New Year.

The boss invited our entire family to the New Year's dinner. We children played with the boss's children. My girlfriend was Galatea—the boss gave his children Greek names. The dinner was lavish.

At the beginning of the meal Klio Fyodorovna rose and said, "Do you know what this dinner is about? This dinner is in honor of that diamond." And she proposed a toast to honest people. But they didn't thank us in any other way.

When the Soviets came to power and took everything away from our family, Mama said, "What fools we were, Ivan. We should have kept the diamond. We could now have bought ourselves a house."

I remember the wedding of Klio Fyodorovna's sister. The bride in a long veil, the groom a tall man who looked like Stolypin.[1] Two little girls, Agrippina and Medea, carried the bride's train. The wedding took place in a Greek café. The chairs were set up in the shape of a horseshoe. At first they didn't seat us children. My sister Lena and I were dressed in very simple white dresses. Our hair was tied back with blue ribbon.

After the holiday dinner there was a ball. Our father introduced it, so tall and handsome was he. He had a big black mustache. He danced beautifully. He invited the bride to dance. Everyone was looking at them. Papa conducted the ball and danced without stop—with Mama, with Klio Fyodorovna, and with others. We watched and admired and were so proud of Papa. This was how we felt: that is our papa dancing. Do you see what kind of papa we have? You may be rich and we may not be, and we may be simply dressed, but we are not beneath you. Our papa is better than anyone here.

Then they seated us at a table.

During the civil war (1918 to 1920) we did not have our own house. We rented an apartment in the mansion of a retired general who worked in his garden from morning until night. It was a gorgeous English garden with a perfect green lawn, the plants beautifully arranged and meticulously pruned. The general knew the names of all the trees and told us kids stories about them.

When the Red Army came they killed him, impaling him as if on a spit on the garden fence. He hung there for some time.

Papa was in Makhachkala, the capital of the Dagestan Republic, separated from us by the front. When he returned, by coincidence it was just when the Reds came to the mansion to requisition the contents of the mansion.

Papa said, "This is not our place."

Just the same, they took everything. Later they came for our own things. They found my sister Lena's new little boots.

"They say that the bourgeoisie had diamonds in their heels." And they wanted to remove the heels.

Lena implored them not to destroy the shoes. "And what if we find something, what then?"

"And if you don't find something," said Lena, with her characteristic passion, "I won't have anything to walk in."

They left the shoes.

There was nothing else to take from my family.

Soon after the Reds came to town in 1920, a rumor circulated: there was to be free love and no girl had the right to turn down any man. Papa begged Mama not to let us leave the house. Lena comforted us. She did not believe a word of it.

---

[1] Pyotr Stolypin was a major statesman in the reign of Nicholas II. He served as prime minister from 1906 to 1911.

The world we lived in turned upside down. Papa didn't like that at all. And then suddenly his relatives began to make a case for returning to Greece. Even before that the relationship between my mother and father had begun to sour. I often overheard Mama burst out with the accusation that his relatives had squandered her dowry. It was true, but my father was very devoted to those relatives, who, in turn, were hostile to my mother. Finally he left us and lived apart from the family. But he loved us, the children, very much. At that point we were no longer children.

My father had long dreamed of Greece, of a native land that he did not know, the homeland of his forebears. That dream grew stronger. And around 1920, when his relatives began to discuss returning, he found himself torn apart by the conflict. He came to us and tried to convince Mama and us to go to Greece with him. Mama didn't want to hear about it, and Lena and I already had our own lives; Lena was married, and although I hadn't told anyone, I was getting ready to marry. I lived with the expectation that my fiancé would come for me. We refused.

At that time the relatives got an answer from Moscow. Lenin gave them permission to go to Greece. Papa was torn in pieces. To go? To stay with us?

The relatives had already gone to Novorossiisk from where they were to leave by sea. Father came to us completely distraught. I remember how we tried to comfort him.

"Why are you so miserable, Papa? You want to go? Go to Novorossiisk. The boat probably hasn't left yet. And if it hasn't then go to Greece. You'll write us. If it's good there, then send for us."

He went to Novorossiisk and found the boat still in the harbor, the relatives ready with their suitcases. There was no time left to ponder. He decided. He left.

He vanished without a trace. We received no news.

We learned of his fate much later when my brother Pavel made inquiries. He wrote to a rich Greek in Athens who found Papa's cousin Alkiviad. Alkiviad told what happened.

It was very crowded on the boat, everyone went to the deck. At last they saw the Greece they had dreamed about for so long. But they were not permitted to go ashore. They were from Bolshevik Russia, so they were considered "Bolshevik agents." They were taken to an island and put into unending quarantine. It went on and on, they knew only cold and hunger. An epidemic broke out. Aunt Liza and her husband and children died. The brothers and sisters and other relatives also began to die. He held out, he swam in the sea to stay strong, he tried not to surrender. But the epidemic swallowed him up as well. He was terribly ill, he wept; he thought of his children and never stopped looking at a photograph of us. He said, "If Aga was with me I would recover." I was his favorite.

Of the entire family only Alkiviad survived.

Mama, My Sister Lena, and My Brother Pavel

Oh, how I want to live until 1986. Can you guess why? Because that's when Haley's comet will appear again. It returns every seventy-five or seventy-six years. I saw it in my childhood. As it came closer and closer to the earth, growing larger and larger in the sky, lots of people believed that the world was coming to an end. Some people in our town even dug huge pits to save themselves should the comet collide with the earth.

I know it was in 1910, because I saw the comet on a day that a neighbor boy at the well told me and my sister that Tolstoy had just died. We had no idea who Tolstoy was, but Papa explained that he was the greatest of all Russian writers. Papa took Tolstoy's death very hard, for he loved him. Now I know that Tolstoy died in the autumn or winter of 1910, and that's exactly when I saw Haley's comet.

I want to live to see the comet's return. The comet returns, but one's youth—never.

We were three children in my family: Lena the oldest, then me, and then my brother Pavel, whom we called Pukha.

Papa was very well-read. He put a lot into our education. Mama taught us a lot as well. She taught us to be kind—to help the poor, to pray to God, to care for people. "For every good deed," she would say, "You will be repaid with a good deed."

Once a kid instructed me on how to tease Jews: you stick your thumb in your ear, spread your five fingers apart and wave them. This was called "pig's ear" and was meant to mock Jews for not eating pork. I was delighted with this trick and as soon as I got to school I showed the "pig's ear" to the little Jewish girl who sat next to me. She had absolutely no idea what I was doing. I was bitterly disappointed.

At home I described to Mama how I had teased the little girl with the "pig's ear."

Mama was furious. "My mother, your grandmother, was a Yakut.[1] Your father is Greek. Should you be teased for that?"

Well, in fact, the kids taunted Greeks, too. When Pukha got a bicycle and rode through the town's streets, the kids yelled after him, "Pindos, he rides around on a pair of wheels."[2]

---

[1] Yakuts are an Asiatic ethnic group living in Eastern Siberia.

[2] *Pindos*—an ethnic slur against Greeks that was common in the south of Russia.

My sister Lena was the eldest, two years older than I and five years older than brother Pukha. She was the ringleader, the boss. She was hot tempered, accustomed to being the first, and convinced that she was the best.

When we were children she concocted a game—she was a queen sitting on a throne. But if Pukha and I were not obedient, she would beat us with her fists. And we tolerated everything because we were afraid that she would stop playing with us. She thought up very interesting games in which we agreed to be her slaves. She had to have all the power so that everyone would obey her without question. Pavel and I were small fry. She wouldn't hesitate to kick us out of a game.

Lena liked to mock people, she could make you laugh until you cried. Once, when I was already married, an Armenian came to pay a call. He was vapid and wishy-washy, boring and uninteresting. Lena pretended to be in love with him, she fawned all over him, she served him, and he didn't understand that she was playing a role and laughing at him. Well, we knew and had to restrain ourselves from bursting out in laughter. But it got worse. She went behind his back and made horns over his head with her fingers. My girlfriend Verochka was living with us at the time, and she couldn't contain herself. She had to run away from the table to hide her laughter.

Lena was very beautiful. Our Mama had something Mongol in her features from her own Yakut mother. Lena resembled Mama but had only a tiny touch of Mongol, which gave her face a sort of sneering expression. In all other ways she was a typical Russian beauty. Blond, blue eyes, thick braids, rosy cheeks. So rosy that she would run to Mama in tears: "Mama, they're teasing me, they say I've put rouge on my cheeks." Mama comforted her. When Lena was older Mama advised her to apply a thick layer of powder. It didn't help. The red color would eventually show through the powder.

When Lena was blooming, I was still a little girl. I wore all her hand-me-downs. It went like this: Lena bought something new and I wore it out. My mother was forced to buy me new clothes only when I began to grow and gain more weight than Lena. I became a "bombshell." Everyone around me said, "fat is not pretty." I believed them and grew self-conscious, shy. Lena said that my legs were fat, too, like bottles. I believed them until I began to notice that men greatly preferred "bombs" like me to skinny women. But Lena was very popular with men. She was always the outstanding one in any company, the life of the party. And she spared no one her sharp tongue.

When the White soldiers came to Maikop in 1918, many of them courted my sister Lena. A certain General Kalmykov held a ball. He wore a dark maroon beret and carried a riding crop. All the men vied for Lena's attention. But the general edged them all out. Although it was not the ball that interested him. His interest was carnage. Another of her admirers was a White officer, a nobleman from a well-known family. One day he invited her to take a ride to the railroad station on his splendid horses. He wanted to impress her, to show her the corpses that the Whites had hung. Men are always like that: they *must fight, kill, destroy*, and then boast about their accomplishments. As soon as Lena understood where he was taking her, she ordered him to turn back.

In general the Reds shot their victims; the Whites hung their victims. They hung them at the railroad station and in the town square. They announced that the corpses would be cut down and stored in the basement of one Sazontsev. The relatives could fetch them for burial.

Lena wanted to really shine, to be independent, to be the mistress of her home, the mistress of a salon. She wanted to have receptions. She was nineteen years old. She married a White officer and fulfilled her dreams. She was the mistress of her own household and didn't have to account for herself to anyone.

Two gymnasium students were in love with Lena, the brothers Rogov. Once the older brother met me on the street.

"Is it true that Lena got married?"

I didn't answer.

"Why couldn't she wait? I'll be finished with gymnasium soon and we could have married," he said bitterly.

Did Lena love her husband? No.

She lived with him exactly one year.

When the Reds came to Maikop, the Whites left without a fight, just as they had agreed. Those who wanted to remain in Maikop gave up their weapons because the Reds had promised not to touch them. They stayed and worked at various things.

Everything was quiet for a year. And suddenly an edict was issued: all the former White officers were to register and to be at the Tikhoretsky Station at such-and-such a time on such-and-such a day.

Lena went to the station with her husband on horseback. They parted. He wept. Lena went home. She told me that when she went home she suddenly realized that she was completely free. Free! What joy.

Her husband sent several postal cards from the road, telling her that they were being taken to Arkhangelsk, a city in the far north. Then—nothing.

One of the Whites who had been taken away managed to return. He told her that her husband had a serious case of typhus, that he laid on his bunk with his face to the wall. The others believed he was dying and just left him. All the other officers were taken out and shot.

That's how Lena found out that she was a widow.

Zarnitsky, My First Husband

The Whites had been in Maikop for several years. When the Reds came in March of 1920, I was seventeen years old, almost eighteen, and I was just finishing gymnasium. The Reds told us that we must now pass an exam in political economy, and they sent a lecturer to our school. He was a small, scraggly man. But he was so passionate about all that stuff—"communism and the dictatorship of the proletariat"—he was such a fanatic that one could only marvel at the ardent spirit in such a puny body.

This is the essence of what he taught us. "Imagine," he said, "that I have a jacket and you have none. Well, I must give you my jacket, and I must give it with pleasure. Or a shirt which, as they say, is closer to the body."

We young ladies of the gymnasium thought he was out of his mind.

CB 80

It was summer and the heat was terrible. I was at home. Suddenly my girlfriend Lilya came running.

"Agnessa, why are you sitting around? Don't you know what's happening? Last evening a Bashkir brigade came to town and you're just sitting here locked in the house.[1] It's a cultured, interesting brigade. The soldiers are Bashkirs and the officers, well, they're like the White officers. Honestly, come quickly to the city gardens where they're strolling. You'll see for yourself."

I quickly drew two buckets of cold water from the well and took them into the shed. I stood on planks that were laid cross-wise on the ground and rinsed myself off. Then I put on a white dress, stockings (one did not go without stockings in those days) and black patent leather shoes.

Lilya hurries me along. "Why are you dawdling, they'll leave!"

We left and on the way she told me in whispers about something that happened the day before. She was clearly embarrassed. "We really put our foot in it yesterday," she said. "In the evening Ira and I were in the gardens and we saw a Red commander, it was written on his cap. So I spoke to Ira in French, loud enough so that he could hear that we were speaking a foreign language that he, of course, didn't know. I say to her, scornfully—'Red,' I say, 'only fools like red.' And he, imagine this, says to us in French, 'Dear young ladies, you are mistaken. Red is the color of freedom.' Oh, I almost fainted.

---

[1] The Bashkirs are a Turkic people living mainly in Bashkiria, which lies between the Volga River and the Ural Mountains.

We immediately ran off. What do you think of that? Now I'm afraid we might run into him. True, yesterday it was dusk, he might not recognize us."

We got to the gardens and sat on a little bench where the ground slopes to the river. We watch and wait. The sun is setting. A fresh breeze blows from the river. We can hear the sound of a band playing somewhere in the valley.

We see three men approaching along the alley. The one in the middle was tall, well built, interesting, and wearing a Circassian coat. An older man stands on one side of him, a very young man on the other side. I watch the one in the middle, and suddenly he so pleased me that I thought—when I get married, it will be only to him.

There is a gust of wind and the silk kerchief that I have thrown over my shoulders is blown off. I run, chasing it down the slope to the river and catch it. I return breathing heavily, and Lilya whispers to me, "Why did you run after it? They all rushed after your kerchief. If you hadn't caught it, they would have brought it to you."

And they stand at some distance looking at us. I quickly understand. Another gust of air and I let my kerchief fly away again. I do not rush to catch it. And that very one who so pleased me brings it back to me.

"Why are you sitting here in such a wind. You could catch a cold!" And he looks at me.

"Perhaps it's cold for strangers, but we're used to this climate."

That's how the conversation began. The oldest one left. As we soon learned he was the commander of the Bashkir brigade. He was married and had a child.

The other two, they sat down on the bench on either side of us. The one I liked sat down beside me. His name was Zarnitsky. The very young one sat on Lilya's side. He told us his name was Zhenya, and then corrected himself: Ageev. He was clearly only recently away from home and not accustomed to using his surname.

I remember exactly what we talked about that first time. A story was circulating in Maikop at that time. When the Reds pursued the White prisoners through the town, one of them slipped through and approached a girl who was watching. He handed her a thick walking stick, "Here, take it, keep it for me. And tell me quickly, who you are."

"I live right here," she answered, pointing to a house.

She took the stick and examined it. It was a stick like any other. Why did he ask her to guard it? Later the prisoners were released and he came back. He turned the knob of the stick and pulled out money. A lot of it, tightly wadded up. He got that money when the Whites held the town and he was hoping that they would return.

Our young men laughed. "They won't return! Of course, the intervention, the Entente.² But, we'll beat them up, we'll definitely beat them!

And suddenly Ageev—Zhenya—says to Lilya, "And I thought that you spoke only French!"

She looked up and recognized him. She was about to run off, but I stayed where I was. And Zhenya said to her, "Please, don't run away, like you did yesterday!"

So we began to keep company. Zhenya had just finished the gymnasium and enlisted in the Red Army "to join the battle for the people's freedom." Before then, even in the gymnasium he was a member of illegal circles. He and Lilya began to have a romance, but he was soon posted elsewhere.

There was a theater in Maikop called "Twentieth Century" that was part theater and part cabaret. You could sit at little tables and eat while you watched a play. Then the tables were removed and the audience could dance. Ivan Aleksandrovich (that was Zarnitsky's name and patronymic) danced the tango very well. He was ten years older than me.

Once, the three of us—he, Lilya, and I—went for a walk. Suddenly thunder, followed by a cloudburst. We took shelter under a dilapidated lean-to. In a brilliant flash of lightening that was like a shard of shining glass, we could see the rain streaming through the chinks of the roof. Finally we found a protected spot, but not before we were soaked. When the rain stopped, Zarnitsky accompanied me home. I was wearing a red hat. Zarnitsky, in civilian clothes, wore a white shirt. He took my arm and I leaned toward him; the color from my hat ran on to his shirt. He didn't notice until the morning that his white shirt was striped red.

Strange, how one remembers such details. But everything is significant at the beginning of a love affair.

A cloud burst and a hat—this was already after Ivan Aleksandrovich clearly wanted to propose to me. I knew that right away, but he was educated and courteous. So after Zhenya left, he was equally attentive to both Lilya and me.

But it became perfectly clear which of us he really wanted. Once we three sat in a darkened cinema, Zarnitsky sitting between me and Lilya and holding both our hands. But then he raised my hand to his lips and kissed it.

"What powerful teeth," I cried.

"Whose teeth?" Lilya asked. She had not seen him kiss my hand.

"Mine, of course!" I answered.

At that moment Zarnitsky and I felt a kind of secret bond as if we were enclosed in a magic circle that excluded Lilya. But Lilya soon caught on. She was not offended. Zhenya returned and their romance picked up where it left off.

---

² The Entente was an alliance of fourteen nations that intervened in the Civil War on the side of the Whites against the Bolsheviks.

At that time in my life I could not have fallen in love with a man of my own age who, like me, had just finished gymnasium. I was attracted to older men who had already seen something of life. And later as well. I wanted someone whom I could respect for his intelligence and authority or strength and valor. Zarnitsky was like that.

We often strolled around the town, most often in the evening when we could sit under shady trees or in some secluded corner where one could kiss. I was surprised at Zarnitsky's restraint. Other men had tried to kiss me. I had to forcibly push them away. Zarnitsky was not like that.

When we took walks it was always he who decided when the rendezvous was over. He would say, "It's bedtime." He would kiss me passionately, but it was always he who broke away first. Then he would leave. I was confused. I wasn't accustomed to that. And we spoke to each other using the formal pronoun.[3]

Just before the brigade was to leave, he proposed to me. There was no time for me to think it over. I accepted. He said, "I'll come for you as soon as we have a base."

I began to get thick letters in blue envelopes. I would answer.

In our younger days Lena did not think much of me and she laughed at my admirers. But Zarnitsky—one did not laugh at Zarnitsky. She understood his worth and couldn't figure out how I had "nabbed" him. She and her girlfriend Tanya Kaplan would tease me.

"What are you waiting for? He's surrounded by other women and you sit here and wait? We heard that in Petrograd he has a fiancée, a city girl. You can't compete with that! You wouldn't even know how to conduct yourself in Petrograd."

I would only bite my lips—I never said a word. But I answered them in conversations in my head. "Well, if you want to know, I could easily even sit at table with a king and conduct myself properly. And if he had a girlfriend, if he didn't need me anymore, then why would he so often write me such long letters? If he wasn't interested any more then he could cut it off."

I could convince myself in my thoughts as long as he was writing. Suddenly his letters stopped coming. Lena and Tanya laughed at me.

"Well, Lady Zarnitsky, where is your fiancé now? We told you—don't bother waiting for him. He stopped thinking of you long ago."

Why was Lena so cruel? She loved to mock people, it was her character. But how could she, a woman, not understand what I was going through? Or perhaps at that moment, she was envious of me?

---

[3] In Russian, as in many other languages, there is a formal and an informal second-person pronoun. The informal is used generally among people very familiar with each other, by superiors to inferiors, elders to younger people. The formal pronoun is polite, normally used between people who would use surnames in English and between people with a formal relationship of any kind.

When the postman brought the mail, I gave him every penny I could scrounge as a tip. Seeing him approach, I would call hysterically to him, but he'd tell me, "I have no letters for you, young lady." I stopped running to meet him—I was so embarrassed.

At that time three of us were living together—Mama, Pukha, and I. Papa had already left for Greece in June. Lena was living with her husband, free and independent, the mistress of her apartment, squandering whatever money he gave her.

Then Abram Ilyich began to pay us visits. He was fiercely courting me. He was a military man, too, wearing a military uniform. He was always giving me small gifts, for example black gloves that fit my hand tightly. I would go to the cinema and the theater with him, but after Zarnitsky no one pleased me.

After Abram Ilyich would drink tea with us, Mama would say, "Listen, he's not bad, you know." She thought I was waiting for Zarnitsky in vain.

"O.K., so he's not bad. But he's boring."

Once Mama, Abram Ilyich, and I were walking down the street when some kind of a man of the "former people" approached us and tried to convince Mama to buy a Persian rug.[4] He was so insistent—"Buy it, buy it, you won't regret it"—so we unrolled the rug to have a look at it. It really was beautiful.

"How much does it cost?" asked Mama.

"One hundred and fifty million."

"I don't have that much."

"How much would you pay?"

"I have only fifty million."

"No, that's too little."

Suddenly Abram Ilyich broke into the conversation.

"I'll give you one hundred million. Then, Maria Ivanovna, will you have enough to buy it?

"Thank you, thank you very much. I'll pay you back."

Abram Ilyich hung the rug for us over the couch.

But none of that was what I wanted. I waited. I couldn't believe that after such rendezvous and such letters it could be over between me and Zarnitsky. It just couldn't be.

Finally I couldn't restrain myself. I asked Lilya, "Does Zhenya write to you?"

"Yes. Why do you ask?"

"Give me his address."

---

[4] Under the Bolsheviks *former people* identified groups of individuals who were disenfranchised and deprived of many other rights and opportunities: the royal family, the nobility, the bourgeoisie (broadly defined), clergy, anyone who hired labor. In other words, people from the "exploiting" strata of society.

"What for?" Lilya was suspicious.

"I want to ask him something."

Reluctantly, she gave it to me. I don't know what she suspected. I wrote to Zhenya and asked about Zarnitsky. He answered, "I don't know anything about him. We have been apart for two months, we are not in the same place."

How I suffered!

And suddenly—I see the mailman walking toward our house, waving a blue envelope. I begin feverishly to look for change to give him a tip. What joy, how light everything seemed, how happy I was. It was good to be alive.

Zarnitsky wrote that he had suffered a bout of typhus for three months. He was still weak, but mending.

And soon after, another letter saying that he would be based in Rostov again for a long time. "I will come for you on August 16."

"Who kept saying that I was waiting in vain?" I said to Lena and Tanya. They didn't answer.

And then August 16 was upon us.

We lived near the railway station. I look out of the window and see the wagon drivers driving their horse-drawn carriages to the train bound for Rostov. In my mind's eye I see the train arriving and the carriages returning with passengers. One train came and left. Then another, and another. And still no Zarnitsky.

I sat like that all day. There were other trains, I waited for each one, perhaps he'll be on this one or that one.

He just didn't come.

"Hey, Madam Zarnitsky. Where's your groom?" Lena said the next day. This time I said nothing.

A few days letter I wrote Zarnitsky: "You didn't come for me. Obviously you aren't interested in me, and we may both consider ourselves free."

No answer. Now when the mailman came to the courtyard he either ignored me or said jokingly, "Don't worry, you'll get a letter." That was not much consolation.

I still can't believe that Zarnitsky won't answer such a letter. And, indeed, a letter arrives. "You wrongly felt betrayed by me," Zarnitsky wrote. "I couldn't come for you. Now I am the chief of staff of the People's Border Patrol. As the commander I could not leave the staff. I will send my adjutant to get you on October 20."

But he did not come on October 20. A day or so later I left the house. Mama was at the bazaar. We got home and a neighbor says, "A soldier came to see you. He waited for you all day and said that he would come tomorrow morning sometime before noon."

She described him—it was not Zarnitsky. The next day a very young rosy-cheeked man appeared. Among ourselves we began to call him "piglet." He was a Tatar with a Tatar surname, which I have forgotten. Later he was the People's Commissar of the Tatar Republic on the Volga. Evgenia Ginzburg refers to him in *Journey into the Whirlwind*.[5]

He brought with him a letter from Zarnitsky. The letter said that "Piglet" would bring me to him in Rostov. I got very excited, I invited "Piglet" to dinner and then ran to the bazaar to fetch Mama, who was selling things. That was our only source of income. She was just leaving the bazaar, carrying a perch. I was so happy to see that we had something to serve our guest. We prepared borscht for the first course and the perch in a sauce for our main dish. Mama was happy and flustered.

"But, listen Aga, how can you go? You have nothing, not even bed linens. And I wonder, will you take your houseplant with you, the Latania?"

Well, this is how we resolved the problem: I would write to Zarnitsky to say that I was not ready. I would be ready in a month, so send someone for me then. And so I was.

We began to frantically collect things for my dowry. We had to sell the piano. When we were thrown out of the general's mansion, we found an apartment that was too small to keep the piano. So we had stored it with a friend.

We bought fabric and sewed sheets. We sewed a quilt cover for an old cotton blanket. We sewed dresses for me—black, blue, white. We bought cutlery at the second-hand market. Mama still had some silver that she gave to me. And we had a large, ancient mirror from the house in Barnaul that the rich Poles bequeathed to my grandfather.

Lena said, "And me? Nothing for me? Give the mirror to me, it should be for me."

Usually it was Lena who got everything. But this time Mama reminded Lena that when she married she had a dowry, too. That's when Papa still lived with us, and her dowry was larger and better than mine.

Mama lay down two conditions: first, that we would marry in the church and, second, that Lena would accompany me to Rostov. Lena insisted on accompanying me because she really wanted to go to Rostov, and Mama was happy because it was better to be accompanied by a sister.

಄ ಅ

In exactly one month "Piglet" came for me. This time there were no delays. This was November 20, 1922. I was nineteen years old, almost twenty. And so

---

[5] See Evgenia Semyonovna Ginzburg, *Journey into the Whirlwind* (New York: Harcourt Brace Jovanovich, 1967). This memoir of the author's eighteen years in the Gulag is a major document of the Soviet period. Written in the 1950s, it circulated underground (in handwritten and retyped copies) for many years in the Soviet Union. It was finally smuggled to the West. Volume 1 was published in English translation in 1967, volume 2 in 1981. In 1989 it was published in the Soviet Union.

we went on the road—"a picture, a basket, a box."[6] We had no trunks, only a small suitcase that I carried. It contained the most valuable things: silver forks, for example, that did not leave my hand. And we had bags and bundles packed with straw and covered with burlap.

The station. The train. Embarkation.

Embarkation! What a horror! At that time people even traveled on the roof. And we, with such baggage, were in a train car. Lena and I would never have found a place to sit if it weren't for "Piglet" and another soldier, an artillerist, who straightaway offered to help us. Pushing and scrambling, they managed to shove our stuff onto the train, and then they grabbed Lena. I was the last and I jumped on the step as the train was already moving. I had not pushed ahead. I behaved modestly, because in my heart I knew that, as the most important person, I had a right to be on that train. But because I remained polite, I was almost left behind. As soon as I jumped up on the step I heard the wailing and sobbing of a Maikop neighbor who was left behind in the crowd. "Lena! Aga! You got on the train, but I'm here with a baby." There was no way I could help her.

Boarding was terrible, but once on the train I saw that it was more peaceful and roomy that I had expected. Of course, there were no seats, but at least one didn't have to stand packed together.

I pushed forward and saw that our escorts were on the lower bunk and our things were strewn all over the floor and the bunk. In those days there were no compartments for luggage. It wasn't possible to lift the baggage on to the third shelf—people were in the way. The artillerist—he was from Odessa—warned us to keep our eyes on our stuff: "Otherwise someone could take a knife and cut your bags open."

We checked constantly. In those days thievery was rampant.

And so we went.

On the middle and upper shelves there were some people of the intelligentsia, and, as it turned out, there were engineers and a musician.[7] As soon as they set eyes on Lena and heard her speak, they stepped down and set our things on their shelves. They also kept watch with us on two bundles that

---

[6] This is a quote from the poem "Luggage" (1926) by the children's poet Samuil Marshak written in the 1930s: "A women boarded a train with a picture, a basket, a box, and a little puppy" (Дама сдавала в багаж: / Диван, / Чемодан, / Саквояж, / Картину, корзину, картонку / И маленькую собачонку).

[7] The term *intelligentsia* was, so to say, invented in Russia in the 1860s. It passed from Russian into other languages. It refers, roughly, to a social stratum of educated people, usually engaged in mental work and dedicated to "culture." Depending on time, place, and point of view, it can include people in the sciences, the humanities, and the arts, regardless of their class origins. It often, but not necessarily, connotes an anti-establishment cast of mind.

were too heavy to lift. As always, these men only had eyes for Lena. I was left with "Piglet." Lena shone at the center of our group.

My darling sister always forgot about me, I was always the last thing she considered. But I was used to it. Suddenly she condescended to me, saying, "You lie down behind us, Aga, and try to sleep. I'll cover you with my coat." I lay down, but I couldn't sleep. There was so much noise. All night bursts of laugher shook our compartment.

Lena told them that we were going to Rostov for a wedding. And when she said that I was the bride, not her, they didn't believe her. They thought that she was teasing them.

At each station again people poured in with suitcases and packages. We tried to keep more people from installing themselves in our compartment. When we were accused of holding places in the compartment with our baggage, we insisted categorically that these were our berths and then immediately lay down. I must admit that our intelligentsia very aggressively stood their ground—who would have expected that! "Piglet" and the artillerist did not hesitate to defend our place either. Another thing that helped us was that our compartment was almost the last one from the door. Before they even got to us, new passengers were often able to find places. In general, I can say that for those times we traveled in relative comfort.

We came to a transfer station in Armavir. We spread out on the platform with all of our junk. We sat on our things and decided to wait for the next train. But suddenly we were presented with a marvelous alternative. A handsome soldier, who would have been more interesting without his pimples, appeared on a sleek white horse. He called out, "Who among you is Agnessa Agripopulo?"

Someone had called from Rostov to tell the local Cheka[8] that Zarnitsky's fiancée would be arriving and to please receive her kindly. After all, Zarnitsky was a highly placed official. That soldier immediately fell for Lena and fluttered around her asking if she was Ivan Aleksandrovich's fiancée. "Not at all," Lena protested. "I am not a fiancée, she is," pointing to me. He laughed, because like the others on the train, he didn't believe her. But he took me, Lena, and "Piglet" to a requisitioned mansion. You walked into luxurious surroundings with old velvet-covered furniture. But like everything in Soviet times—mangy and neglected. But there was a supper on the table for us—fried eggs and cocoa. After we had eaten, some more Chekists arrived. As al-

---

[8] The Cheka (an acronym for Extraordinary Committee for Combating Counter Revolution) was the first official organ of the Soviet secret police. Established in 1917, it judged, sentenced, and carried out punishment for whatever the policy of the moment deemed to be a threat to the Revolution and, as often as not, used torture and summary execution. Its members were called Chekists. In 1922 it was reorganized and renamed the GPU—State Political Directorate.

ways, Lena reigned. I modestly held back. And again, the same old story. They couldn't believe that I was the fiancée.

The dining room in which we had eaten was on the second floor of the mansion. They took us downstairs to a luxurious bedroom with a large double bed. The sheets were clean and the blanket was excellent. But it was so cold! Then a woman appeared saying that she was there to help us. She bustled around, saying, "Now I will heat the room, young ladies." And she did. "And there is a chamber pot. I'll take it away in the morning." Of course, the plumbing didn't work—the water pipes had already been frozen since the previous winter.

Breakfast—again, fried eggs and cocoa. Then they took us to the train station in an open carriage. Today's boarding was like yesterday's. The Chekists fought to get a space for us. I remember the icy steps that we boarded with difficulty. The Chekists, having darted into the train car earlier than everyone, had already found us a good place in the depths of the train car. And again Lena attracted everyone's attention: "Lenochka, Lenochka!" And again, noise and laughter.

I sat on a small bench at the window and looked out into the blackness. I couldn't even make out the telegraph poles that flashed by. There was no electricity on the train. Someplace in the middle of the train car a candle burned. It wasn't cold. I sat lost in my dreams. I imagine how Zarnitsky will greet me, how I will stand before him in an elegant black coat and black hat, tight-fitting black gloves (a gift from Abram Ilyich), fragrant with French perfume (also a gift from Abram Ilyich). Mama had included in my dowry the Persian rug that had been bought with Abram Ilyich's money. I didn't want to take it.

"How can I take it, Mama," I yelled reproachfully.

"Never mind, take it, don't be shy. I'll settle with him."

The train comes into Rostov at 6 a.m. It is deep autumn, end of November, already dark. But I see fire before me. A whole sea of fire. The entire station is lit up with electric lamps. I have never seen illumination like that. Ah, so this is what the big city is like! I took it as a good omen.

We approached the Rostov station. I had already made myself pretty on the train. Oh, my heart—he will appear any moment, he will kiss me, inhaling my delicate scent.

But—there's no one there. No one. The platform is empty. Only us, with "a picture, a basket, a box." "Piglet" sees how upset I am and runs into the station to inquire. He calls headquarters. He returns and tells us that Zarnitsky knew that we were supposed to come and was terribly agitated. It turns out that he had come to the station to greet us yesterday and the day before. So today he didn't come. But now he would come immediately.

The clatter of hooves. A horse-drawn carriage. A figure appears on the brightly lit platform—quickly, quickly, almost running towards us—slender, wearing an overcoat with military patches, on his head a pointed cavalry cap with a red star. Panting and agitated.

"You see, I didn't expect you today, I haven't even shaved. Please forgive me."

He searched my face, but he didn't kiss me in front of everyone. He only gazed at me. At that moment the soldiers and "Piglet' caught up with us, carrying "a picture, a basket, a box." Zarnitsky took me firmly the hand and, forgetting about Lena, walked on. Of course, she was immediately insulted.

"And me," she hollered.

"Yes, yes," he said. "Lenochka." With his free hand he took her arm.

Here, for the first time I felt that from now on I would be—the first lady.

෮ ෨

Zarnitsky lived in a huge requisitioned mansion. This was the Cheka headquarters. Although he was the chief, he had only two rooms. His underlings and their families lived in all the other rooms. The mansion was like a big communal apartment.

Zarnitsky had warned me that all the neighbors knew he was expecting his fiancée and that a face would pop out from every door, curious to know what I look like. And so it happened. All the faces belonged to women.

Ivan Aleksandrovich took us to his room, to the bedroom, so that we could change our traveling clothes. His bed was in the room. As soon as he left, Lena pulled back the blanket, "Look here, this is what your fiancé sleeps on," she smirked, pointing to the torn sheet. How lucky that I had brought a dowry!

Then we had breakfast in his other room—fried eggs and cocoa. There was nothing else for the Chekists.

Until the wedding Lena and I lived with relatives, not Zarnitsky. I told him that I wouldn't have it any other way before our wedding.

"Well," he said. "We'd better get married."

He didn't protest. Probably because his father was a priest. "Piglet" told me that on the train. I was really surprised, I had thought he was Jewish.

We had to hurry up and get married because Lent was just beginning and it is forbidden to marry during Lent. So there was a huge rush to prepare the wedding and to paint our room. There were autumn chrysanthemums everywhere. And on our marriage bed—Abram Ilyich's Persian rug. On the eve of the wedding we had to register in a dark, dreary official building. They gave us a receipt to our registration in Rostov as husband and wife.

The next day we were married in the church. Before we went to the church Lena and I went to Ivan Aleksandrovich's mansion. I glanced into the cupboard and saw all kinds of cakes and pies that the neighbors had prepared for the wedding. Everyone loved Ivan Aleksandrovich. The neighbors came to ask to me whether I had a table cloth. I told them that I had sheets (again, I thought how good that Mama had taken so much care with my dowry). We covered the table with my sheets. True, afterwards there were many stains, but the Chinese laundry got them out. (At that time we had a very good Chinese laundry). Ivan Aleksandrovich said to me, "Aga, I've invited a hairdresser for you."

The hairdresser was late. We were so nervous. I was already in my wedding dress. Finally, he came. He made me a wonderful hairdo—a halo of curls around my head. Then my hair was a chestnut color, thick and shiny. No longer.

Then the hairdresser began to do Lena's hair (she had fashionably short hair), but Zarnitsky called out, "It's time to go!"

Lena was greatly annoyed. "And what about me?" She was so annoyed because she was accustomed to being the important one.

Ivan Aleksandrovich apologized. "Forgive me, Lenochka, but we were told what time to come and we cannot be late."

Lena had to go with an unfinished hairdo.

The priest married three couples at once, leading us around the lectern and singing "Isaiah exults." Then, the wedding dinner in the big hall in the mansion. It was noisy and joyful, and everyone ate and drank a lot. I could barely get to the food myself. Midnight—then 2 a.m., then 4 a.m., and there were still people there. They drank, danced, and yelled "Bitter!"[9] I was so tired. Ivan Aleksandrovich understood.

"Shall we go?" he asked me warily. We went to our room where we could hardly breathe for the masses of flowers. Lena accompanied us to the door and then left.

There is an Indian book called the Kama Sutra. It instructs men to carefully observe a woman's expression during intimate moments and to caress her in ways that seem to please her. Then, it instructs, it will be pleasurable for the man as well.

That is just how Ivan Aleksandrovich was, although he had never read the Kama Sutra.

We remained alone in the room. I saw myself in the mirror, white as death.

"Lie down," said Ivan Aleksandrovich. The bed was made with the clean new sheets that I had brought. I didn't see the old rug. Instead the bed was covered with a brilliant white blanket.

"I will lie down under one condition. That I'll sleep here and you there," pointing to a place near the door.

He burst out laughing. "OK," he said.

"Turn around so that I can undress."

---

[9] It is the custom at Russian weddings, to this day, for the guests to call out "bitter" (*gor'ko*), at which point the bride and groom must kiss.

He agreed to whatever I wanted. I turned around and lay down. My heart was beating like a hammer.

"Please, " I said, "can you prepare some valerian for me."

I was covered up to my chin. He lifted me up and gave me the glass of water with valerian drops. I was exhausted from the day: preparation, wedding, feast, but mainly—I had been anxious all day thinking about the night. I was a virgin. I couldn't stop thinking about what awaited me. During the wedding dinner I drank a lot of wine, hoping it would give me courage. Ivan Aleksandrovich kept saying, "Don't drink so much!" I didn't listen to him, I drank and drank. And now my heart was beating so. But—I drank the valerian and turned to face the wall. I fell asleep and slept as soundly as if I had fallen into a hole.

I woke up. It was light. People were already walking around. I was alone in the bed. Ivan Aleksandrovich was sitting on a chair by the door. That's good, I thought at first, and then I thought—but it was our wedding night!

I arose and approached him on tip toe in my long white nightgown. It was an antique that we had bought at the second-hand market, all lace with pink bows on the shoulders. I had worn it under my wedding dress, with the pink bows peeking out from under my décolleté. Lena had pushed them out of sight—in the church.

I approached him. He was sleeping. No, he wasn't sleeping. His eyes popped open and he laughed. I quickly kissed him and ran back to the bed. This was an invitation. He accepted it. Sitting at the edge of the bed he began to embrace me and kiss me, at first cautiously and then passionately. Later, he reminisced—"I'm embracing you and under my hands I feel lace, lace, only lace, I could hardly find you under the lace!"

Our neighbors delicately refrained from bothering us. But at noon, someone knocked.

"Are you alive in there?"

We went to the breakfast table. I was wearing a black dress with gold embroidery. I covered my neck with a little gold scarf to hide the traces of his kisses.

While I was preparing my dowry and then when I left to join Zarnitsky, Abram Ilyich was not in town. That was a great relief. He returned after my departure. Naturally, he was told about my marriage.

He went to our house and found Pukha in the kitchen.

"Greetings, lad," said a very grumpy Abram Ilyich. He abruptly left to the neighbors. Probably because he wanted to check whether the news was correct. The neighbors told him about the Persian rug. He came back to our house.

"Is Maria Ivanovna home?"

"Yes"

Then he knocked and opened the door.

"Hello, Maria Ivanovna. We have some accounts to settle. We have one bit of unfinished business."

Mama was hysterical (as usual, she had no money).

"I'll return everything to you. Everything. But just now I have nothing. I'll go and get some money and return. But wait a minute. Of course I'll give you back your money, even though you came to us to drink tea for a whole year. And I fed you even though times were so hard. Still, I'll give you money."

Abram Ilyich: "Never mind." And he left.

Many years later, after the war, my friend Tanya Kaplanova met Abram Ilyich in Moscow. She was on the tram when a chubby middle-aged man approached her. "Are you by chance from Maikop?"

"Yes, I'm from there."

"Aha, I recognized you. And weren't you acquainted with the Agripopulos?"

"Of course, I knew them."

"Which one?"

"All of them, the whole family."

He told her his name. Tanya remembered him. He began to ask her questions about me.

"What's her surname now."

"Mironova."

"Mironova! Why not Zarnitskaya?"

"She and Zarnitsky divorced."

"I thought so. I said it would happen. I had a premonition. You know, that I was hooked on that Agnessa Agripopulo."

Then he told her all about himself: married, children, manager of a fish store on Sretenka, one of Moscow's oldest and most charming streets. "Come there if you need something. Ask for the manager—that's me."

And Tanya went there. He took her bag, left, returned—and what wasn't there in the bag! Smoked sturgeon, caviar, preserved crab. And he said, "Go to the cash register and pay one ruble and eighty kopeks." Tanya went another time and the whole scenario was replayed.

"Come to his store with me."

I was dumbstruck: "Have you lost your mind?"

03 80

Oh, yes... smoked sturgeon. I remember how fed up Ivan Aleksandrovich was with smoked sturgeon. One of his underlings gave him a smoked sturgeon as a gift. The sturgeon is a huge fish. We hauled it to the shed where the coal was kept. The fish was as tall as me. Every day Ivan Aleksandrovich and I cut off a chunk for us and for others. But there seemed no end to it. Fat dripped from it and made the floor greasy.

Although we got sick of that fish, it was actually very useful to us. I couldn't do anything around the house. I can't even remember how we fed ourselves. Later Mama came to live with us. She brought some order to the house.

And soon Lena showed up in Rostov. This is how it happened.

In Maikop, Vasya Goncharenko was in love with Lena. And she loved him. Vasya was talented. He drew beautifully. He sang in a beautiful baritone voice. Sometimes he gave concerts. At one of them he sang a duet with a young soprano. Lena was sitting in the hall, and it seemed to her that the singer was behaving too intimately. Lena blew up. She decided that she hated him and would leave him. Quite simply, she was awfully jealous. She was, after all, very possessive. So she threw up everything in Maikop and came to me in Rostov.

In Rostov a handsome interesting man fell in love with her. They started keeping company, but she got angry with him about something or other and broke up with him, too. But he wanted to make up. Once I met him on the street and invited him to our house. He brightened up." Did Lena send you to invite me?

I had to admit that she had not.

Immediately after her quarrel she married the engineer Sukhotin, probably to take revenge. She did not love Sukhotin. But he was reasonably affluent and Lena could dress well and shine.

Sukhotin was thirty-six years old. Lena was barely twenty. She gave birth to a son, Borya. Sukhotin was the father. One day, when Borya was eleven months old, Lena and I were alone and I initiated a frank conversation on intimate subjects. Suddenly she said, "For over a year I have not actually had a husband. Earlier I had noticed that he took some kind of pills, but now it seems they don't help anymore." She said this with irritation and contempt.

At that very time Vasya Goncharenko showed up in Rostov. He probably came because of Lena. He began to spend time with Lena and Sukhotin and before long they were all three living together. Lena became pregnant and had an abortion. Vasya was very upset.

Although he kept his feelings from Lena, Sukhotin hated Vasya. Whenever they had guests, Vasya would sing and either Lena or I would accompany him (we had studied music in our childhood). Vasya sings, Sukhotin hides his face behind a newspaper, pretending to read. But whenever I pass by him he mutters, "And when will he stop howling?"

Sukhotin was absent-minded. Whenever he was taking his leave he would kiss the hands of all the women. Once Zarnitskii held out his hand for a handshake, and Sukhotin kissed his hand, too. He would put salt in his tea instead of sugar, and drank the tea without noticing. Lena, with irritation, "What are you drinking? It is salted."

Perhaps he was always distracted by his work. The house overflowed with books and foreign technical journals. He was a fine engineer. He was accused of sabotage, arrested, pronounced guilty, and taken prisoner to a camp. Lena—I must be fair to her—regularly sent him packages.

She was not mercenary. Quite the contrary, she was impractical and sometimes just threw money and things about. She was generous and would do anything for people that she loved. Some time after Sukhotin's arrest, she married Vasya. They had a daughter called Nika.

CB ŠO

Although I was a terrible, incompetent housekeeper, when we visited Zarnitsky's parents I tried hard to help them around the house. I insisted that Ivan Aleksandrovich introduce us. He tried to avoid it, he didn't want to mix with them. After all, he was the head of a troop of border soldiers in the North Caucasus. He really didn't want to advertise the fact that he was a priest's son. Even worse—during the famine in the Volga territory the newspapers wrote that all the priests, including Zarnitsky's father, had taken the great riches of the church and now didn't want to give anything to the starving.[10] It was all a lie, but it was in the newspapers—it could ruin Zarnitsky's career. So he had no contact with his parents.

But I insisted. What is that all about? He, the eldest son, had no idea of what was happening to his parents, his brothers and sisters? Ivan Aleksandrovich always did what I wanted. He never refused me anything. So we went to Murino, near Leningrad, where his parents lived.

His father's parish was the Murino church. The family was large, many children, among them some very small ones. I remember how well they greeted us. His father was so happy, so touched. His mother cried from happiness. Ivan Aleksandrovich was happy, too. He so wanted his parents to like me. On the very first day of our visit I was in the garden playing with the small children, when I overheard a conversation through an open window. I heard how he praised me.

"You know, Mama, she can do everything, she has such clever hands. Today shoes with glass beads are fashionable, and she can sew them on to her shoes, better than any you can buy in the stores. Just think! And a knitted hat with little balls, she can make those, too. That's very clever, don't you agree?"

I also wanted them to like me and I tried to clean and pick up all over the house. Once I was sweeping one of the rooms and one of Ivan Aleksandrovich's sisters said to me, "We don't sweep this room, we mop in this room."

---

[10] The devastating famine of 1921–23 in the Volga region was the result of natural disasters and ruinous social and political forces. Tsarist requisitions during World War I and the depredations of both Red and White armies during the civil war were exacerbated by severe droughts and locust infestations. Statistics are uncertain, but it is clear that several million people in the Volga and Ural regions were starving and dying.

They all liked me, and not only because I tried to please them. They had despaired of seeing their son and brother, and I returned him to them. After Kirov was murdered in 1934, all of the "former people" in the Leningrad area were arrested, exiled, and shot. That wave swept his family away, too.[11]

༺ ༻

Even though Ivan Aleksandrovich didn't see his family until he married me, he did not hide the fact that his father was a priest. The GPU inspector, Mikhail Frinovsky, was assigned to him.[12] Frinovsky had a face as flat as a pancake and small, cruel eyes. He was nobody's fool when it came to material possessions. Ivan Aleksandrovich couldn't understand people like that who grabbed everything in sight. These were completely unlike his former friends. He himself had slept on torn sheets before I came to Rostov.

In Ivan Aleksandrovich's study there was a lovely desk on lions' paws—requisitioned, of course. On the desk there were crystal writing implements. Ivan Aleksandrovich paid no attention to them. He just made do with whatever had been provided for him. Frinovsky badgered him—hey, make me a gift of that crystal set. Later, the desk as well went to Frinovsky.

Ivan Aleksandrovich said to me, "You know, he wants my position."

But Frinovsky pretended that he was very concerned for our welfare.

"Why in the world are you living in that communal apartment? A fine separate apartment on the third floor will soon be vacant. Petryakin lives in it, but he's about to be fired, and he'll lose the apartment. Come and look at it."

We didn't understand. Why should we look at it while someone else was still living in it? But Frinovsky was so insistent, assuring us that in any case Petryakin was being sent somewhere else. So we went. We went to the second floor with Frinovsky where Petryakin's wife greeted us coldly. I didn't like that.

---

[11] Sergei Kirov, a popular Leningrad party leader, was assassinated in 1934. Given his long, impeccable record in the Bolshevik party and state elite and his close relationship with Stalin, it was the most shocking political event in the history of the Soviet state to date. It was explained, perhaps correctly, as the act of a single emotionally disturbed man, Leonid Nikolaev. However, to this day there are conflicting theories of conspiracies, including one that accuses Stalin of engineering the whole thing himself. It was a defining moment, unleashing ever mounting waves of repression and terror between 1934 and 1938.

[12] Mikhail Petrovich Frinovsky (1898–1940). His entire career after the 1917 revolution was in one or another branch of the secret police, and he was responsible for massive acts of repression. When Yezhov was appointed head of the secret services, Frinovsky reached the pinnacle of success—and when Yezhov fell, he fell with him. He was arrested and shot in 1940.

Later I said to Ivan Aleksandrovich, "Do you really think we'll get that apartment? We won't get a damned thing!"

And that's exactly what happened. Zarnitsky lost his position, Frinovsky was appointed in his place, and the apartment—well, what right to that apartment did Zarnitsky have, now that he was jobless and penniless? We left the OGPU mansion and rented two rooms in another region.[13]

ଔ ଓ

During the time that Zarnitsky was still chief of staff, Frinovsky tried to seduce me. Once when Ivan Aleksandrovich was away on business, Frinovsky substituted for him as chief of staff. I went to staff headquarters to ask for some theater tickets. Frinovsky greeted me and he just about clicked his heels, just a minute, just a minute, I'll get them for you!

He returned with another man, Kogan, and they both began flirting with me, fixing their unctuous eyes on me.

"We're coming to drink tea with you."

"Oh no, I don't receive anyone without my husband."

And after that Frinovsky, the fat mug, took Ivan Aleksandrovich's job. Indeed, from the very beginning Frinovsky knew everything—that Ivan Aleksandrovich was a priest's son and that his father would be arrested. The reports Frinovsky made were meant to smear Zarnitsky. Rubbing his hands Frinovsky played with us like a cat with a mouse, thinking, "Soon I will have his job."

Still, because he was probably uncomfortable, he was fawning and obsequious to us to give the impression that "I, of course, have nothing to do with this..."

I will have plenty more to tell you about Frinovsky.

ଔ ଓ

Ivan Aleksandrovich went to work in the police department, wearing a black uniform with a red band around his cap. This was nothing like the Red Army. He had fallen many rungs; the police uniform was not particularly honorable. But at least the work was not dangerous. There were plenty of bandits around in those days, but "brother" Ivan Aleksandrovich did not arrest them. He was required to document everything in writing, like an employee in the Protocol Department.

My friend Verochka from Maikop came for a visit. Our families were friends. When Papa was the director of a store, her father was the senior salesman.

---

[13] The OGPU (Joint State Political Administration) was the successor to the GPU from 1923 to 1934.

View from the Outside: Verochka

I lived in Rostov with Agnessa for three months. I was paying for lessons and got money from home to pay two teachers and to contribute to Agnessa's household. They lived modestly. I remember once Agnessa found some black crepe de chine; it was like a holiday. She wrote ecstatically to her Maikop girlfriends about the crepe de chine and how she planned to sew it into a garment.

Ivan Aleksandrovich worked as a secretary for the militia. But he really wanted to get away from any kind of military work, so he took a night course in bookkeeping. Agnessa also took some kind of night course, but she never completed it. She had no patience for it. Then for a while she did some kind of work, but she left that too. She thought it was boring to work.

Ivan Aleksandrovich was very punctual, very orderly, and accurate. I remember how surprised I was when I chanced upon his diary. This is what I found: Verochka—5 kopeks for the tramway; Maria Ivanovna—10 kopeks for a candle; and so forth.

I was amazed that he so thoroughly accounted for such trivia. Was he stingy? I don't think so. I think that it was simply because his budget was so strained, it was so difficult to make ends meet that he took that small change into account.

He was tall and still quite fit, although he was beginning to put on weight. He tried to eat less and move more. It wasn't easy; he wanted to eat, and his work was sedentary. I remember how he stood before the mirror trying to fasten his army belt. He pulls, pulls and finally—victory! He crowed, "Verochka, today I was able to fasten my belt on the last hole!"

Evenings when he had no classes, we would stroll around the town. Ivan Aleksandrovich in the middle, Agnessa and I on either side. He wore his police uniform, so no one could bother us. From the back streets now and then we could see prostitutes looking over clients. Agnessa couldn't tear her eyes from them, they were very interesting to her.

It seemed to me that Agnessa and Ivan Aleksandrovich were soul mates. I would often hear her tenderly calling "Musha, Musha!" That was her pet name for him.

And suddenly she said to me in a conspiratorial voice, "I have a secret request to make of you. Please take this letter to the hotel—to room number 15 to Mi-ro-nov. Will you remember? And not a word to anyone, alright?"

Of course I promised to keep it to myself, but it was so strange, so awkward, so incomprehensible. I really did not want to go, I felt so ashamed. But Agnessa talked me into it. Fortunately the addressee was not in the room (otherwise I think I would have burned up with awkwardness) and I gave the letter to the porter to deliver.

Lena was also living in Rostov, but someplace in the country beyond a vacant lot—Nakhichevan. Once Agnessa said that she was going to spend the night at Lena's. But suddenly she appeared at 2 o'clock in the morning. I couldn't help thinking about the letter to the hotel. I was very upset. Now, I thought, everyone will wake up and guess that she was not at Lena's. But nothing happened. In the morning she said that she had been at a girlfriend's and was afraid to go to Lena's across that vacant lot. And that's why she came home. No one had the slightest doubt about her story. But she slyly winked at me and I understood that my uneasy guesses were correct. Oh dear, I thought, little by little something will come out and there will be a scandal and shame! But nothing was ever revealed.

C8 80

Ivan Aleksandrovich worked in the police department, but the Party said to him: "You have higher education, you are a knowledgeable person, competent. It would be better if you went into industry where we lack educated people."

So they made him assistant director of a shoe factory. In reality, he was the director and did all the work, because everyone else in the administration was illiterate. People were promoted to the directorate even though they didn't know anything, didn't do anything. All they did was make noise and swear.

Pretty soon Ivan Aleksandrovich became grumpy. Our *g-r-e-at g-e-n-i-u-s* (Agnessa referred to Stalin this way with scorn and hate) had just initiated a campaign against wreckers and saboteurs. "Saboteurs" were discovered at the shoe factory as well. They found some kind of rotten leather and from there cooked up a case. The leather had allegedly been sprayed with a solution that caused it to decompose, but laboratory analysis had falsely pronounced that the leather was in good condition.

They blamed Ivan Aleksandrovich and several other employees. Five years later with such an accusation he would have lost his freedom. But that was another time and they did not arrest him before the trial came up.

Ivan Aleksandrovich was the main culprit. Of course—he was not in the Party, he was the son of a priest and he stayed in touch with his father. How could he not be a saboteur?

The trial began. Ivan Aleksandrovich did not go to work. Ten days before the trial he said to me and Mama, "Don't bother me for ten days."

He sat at the desk, covered with papers, receipts, reports, and all the ten days he prepared to defend himself and the others. He was orderly and disciplined. They allowed him to defend himself. He gathered together all the papers, sorted them, distributed them, put them in order.

And then, the trial. Ivan Aleksandrovich was on the bench with his colleagues. He was clean-shaven, collected and erect, neatly dressed. He created an immediate impression.

The interrogation. The judge asks him his given name, his surname, and the occupation of his father. Ivan Aleksandrovich answers loudly and directly.

"Preacher!"

Notice: he not say "priest" (*svyashchennik*) but "preacher" (*pop*)—distinctly, it seemed to me, like a challenge. Or maybe just the opposite, using their language, not wishing to hide behind euphemisms, not wishing to cushion the effect.[14] At first there were accusations, all sorts of gibberish. All the "witnesses" for the prosecution corroborated the accusations.

Ivan Aleksandrovich asked for permission to speak. He read from an official document. "I, Ivan Aleksandrovich Zarnitsky, was fired from the factory in May 1927 (or 28?). The leather in question was already spoiled before that."

The prosecution didn't have a leg to stand on. Immediately all the drivel that the accuser and the witnesses had heaped upon him was smashed. It was all air.

The hall exploded.

The judge: "Order, order."

So the accusers countered by talking about how ignorant the laboratory personnel was and how they falsified analyses. This, of course, was their evidence of sabotage.

But Ivan Aleksandrovich again called out, "May I have permission to read?"

The hall fell instantly silent, waiting nervously for how he would get out of that one. Ivan Aleksandrovich read from an official document—"A Memo from the Assistant Director" (himself). He read slowly and precisely, sparing no words to demonstrate how this or that analysis had been made by unqualified workers. He explained how the work had been slipshod and ignorant, just to make money on the side. The result had been deficits for the factory. At the end of the memo were the recommendations that Ivan Aleksandrovich had made: to change the entire style of work in the laboratory, to do strictly proper analyses, in other words not to produce what we called in the Gulag "crap."

The judge: File a petition!

And he left. The accusation was a bucket of lying rubbish. Ivan Aleksandrovich had provided an official document, accurate and precise, and the filth was immediately apparent. Complete rot. The impression he made was dramatic. The audience was impatiently waiting, holding its breath as if

---

[14] Although literally *pop* and *svyashchennik* both mean "priest," *pop* is arguably the more conversational word, with a connotation of being somehow lower or perhaps cruder or less educated than a *svyashchennik*. According to one of my Russian advisors, one might (roughly) think of the *pop* as "preacher" and the *svyashchennik* as "priest." — Trans.

for a great actor or a warrior: how would Ivan Aleksandrovich continue to counterattack. I simply admired him—he was reason incarnate.

That is how Ivan Aleksandrovich fought them for three days while the judge malingered. He always spoke in a calm, formal voice, never loud, but, so to say, completely sincerely. The audience was silent.

On the first day the other defendants came unshaven and unkempt, cringing, stuttering. But as Ivan Aleksandrovich demolished one accusation after another, they raised their heads, mustered some courage and by the next day they were shaven, nicely dressed, heads held high.

It was clear to everyone that the director was skinned, guilty of ignorance, laziness, incompetence. But the court had no intention of accusing him. After all, he had worked himself up from the proletariat! How could he do evil? As for ignorance, well, he was exonerated because he was from the working class who had not the opportunity to attend an "academic institute." Where was he supposed to acquire the necessary knowledge?

Nonetheless, from the first day it was the accused who had the court's sympathy, and when they were acquitted, the hall resounded with applause.

The judge smiled at Ivan Aleksandrovich and then at me. He had already noticed me on the first day, slyly glancing over at me, as Ivan Aleksandrovich and I exchanged glances after the very first victory.

I was in awe of Ivan Aleksandrovich's intelligence.

When I told Mirosha about this with such rapture, he suddenly frowned, as if he had been slapped.

"I could have been just like that," he said with pride.

But now I will tell you about Mirosha.

Mirosha

His real name was Miron Iosifovich Korol. In those days it was fashionable to take a pseudonym, and he became Sergei Naumovich Mironov. His family and close friends called him Mirosha.

I saw him for the first time in Rostov in 1923 or 1924, when Ivan Aleksandrovich was still the chief of staff of border troops in the Northern Caucasus. It was at a rally to celebrate the anniversary of the Red Army. The speakers, our local Rostov party types, were philistines and bores. Suddenly an unknown figure mounted the podium, a man in black leather, an army cap, a revolver at his waist. He spoke about world revolution. We had conquered the interventionists, he said, but they were regrouping to attack us again. I scarcely heard a word he said, so enchanted was I by his strong, handsome face and his kind, endearing expression. He had the most beautiful brown eyes and amazing eyelashes—long and thick, like fans.

By and large I am suspicious of handsome men because they are excessively preoccupied with their conquests. Women fall all over them and spoil them. So I immediately lost interest in him. Still, at home I asked Ivan Aleksandrovich: "So, what kind of a man is he?" He answered, "He's one of the commanders who came along with E. G. Evdokimov, the head of the Cheka in southeastern Russia." I didn't give him another thought.

One day soon after the rally we military wives were called to headquarters. We were scolded for being concerned only with our clothes and our domestic affairs. Petty bourgeois, they called us. We must keep up with our husbands! We must become politically literate! So we were ordered to attend special classes on Tuesdays at five p.m. to study politics.

Don't be late! Bring copy books and pencils!

Since Ivan Aleksandrovich warned that if I didn't attend I would compromise him, I appeared promptly at five the following Tuesday.

We women sat around chattering, surreptitiously looking each other over, who was dressed how, who had some kind of a pendant around her neck, who wore a necklace—was it real pearl or artificial? Many of the women were dressed more expensively than I, but tastelessly. How wasted those costly things are on them, I thought. How marvelous I would look in those expensive clothes.

When the teacher entered, I recognized him at once as that very commander who had spoken at the rally! He wasn't wearing his cap this time, and I examined him more closely. A noble face, a high brow. His smiling eyes were unusual—the upper lids arched, the lower straight. And those amazing luxuriant eyelashes. His cheeks were dimpled; his powerful mouth beautifully formed over even white teeth, his thick wavy hair framed his face. Broad-shouldered, strong, his gait thrusting, powerful. His smile was so charming. I saw that our ladies were smitten.

He introduced himself as Mironov without his first name and patronymic—that's how it was done in those days—and explained that he had been assigned to discuss political issues with us.[1] It was our task, he began, to defend the revolution, the first and only revolution in the world. We must defend the Red Army with all our strength because the proletariat of other countries was somehow late with their own revolutions—and the capitalists were not drowsing.

Our ladies could not tear their eyes from him. They had all fallen in love with him. They were even trying to take notes. Alright, I thought, here's a job for me. I certainly did not intend to fall in the mud on my face. Am I worse, for example, than Nyuska with her white fox draped over her shoulders? In such a hot spring! Why don't these people understand that one must dress for the season?

I too began to take notes, sloppily to be sure. I was in such a hurry. But at home I asked Ivan Aleksandrovich to explain things better and to drill me. He was very pleased that I wouldn't shame him.

At the next session Mironov suggested that we review the previous discussion. He called first on Nyuska. I hear her babbling in fits and starts what she had memorized about world revolution and "Sicialism." I itched with impatience—why doesn't he call on me? I know it all. Finally, I couldn't contain myself and I raised my hand. Mironov nodded at me and I rattled off everything I had learned about the Allied Intervention and the evil Entente. He couldn't praise me enough. He set me as an example for the rest of our ladies. I outshone them all.

That's how I became his star pupil. From then on he kept his eye on me and as soon as the question period began he would call only on me, or if someone interrupted me during a discussion he would say, no-no, looking at me. For the only time in my life I became politically literate. My goodness, I couldn't have endured that boredom for anyone else. But Mironov could bring to life even that tedious material. Mirosha, Mirosha! How capable he was!

Then, somehow... In the warm spring dusk of our southern town, we disperse after class... Mirosha catches up to me and walks by my side. The weather is lovely, we don't want to go home, we walk to the park, he composes verses, just out of his head. We began to meet regularly.

---

[1] In Russian one has a given name and a patronymic, the name of the father with appropriate gender ending, indicating that one is "the son of" or the "daughter of." Name and patronymic is the common form of formal and polite address.

We had a favorite place. A young poplar grew at the end of the street beyond the bend in the road where it descended to the river. Every spring it was pruned to prevent its fluffy seeds from covering the street, and its branches puffed out into a prickly globe. In the quiet evenings we meandered through the sidestreets as far as possible from my house. Or we wandered through the groves beside the river or along the densely wooded paths of the park. Even in the winter when the nasty piercing wind blew, we didn't pay attention to the foul weather.

I already knew that Mirosha had fought on the Polish front in Budyonny's army,[2] and that when he became a Chekist he received an important medal from Feliks Edmundovich Dzerzhinsky, the head of the secret police. Indeed, for years afterward on anniversaries of the Red Army or the Cheka he always got a friendly letter from Semyon Mikhailovich Budyonny and on his name day he received gifts, a gold watch or a Mauser.

Over time Mirosha told me his life story. He was born in Kiev in a neighborhood called Shulyavka that was like Odessa's Moldavanka: thieves, bandits, black marketers, gold contrabandists. Who didn't live there! Even Jews—like Mirosha's grandfathers and great-grandfathers. When the family fortunes improved, thanks to the labors of his grandmother Khaya, they moved out of Shulyavka. Grandmother Khaya was highly regarded for her energy and her kindness to the needy. Everyone knew and respected her. They called her "shatym-malykh" which means guardian angel in Hebrew. She kept a dairy store on the Kreshchatka, Kiev's main business artery, that was famous for the freshness and excellent taste of her products. She arranged for Mirosha and his sister Fenya to attend one of the best gymnasia in Kiev. But Mirosha, capable as he was, wasn't fond of study. A holy terror in his childhood, he became a strong, handsome youth, a hero among his peers.

Before the Revolution it was difficult for Jews to attend institutions of higher education. One had to have won a gold medal and even then to fall within the limits of the quotas allocated to Jews. Again, thanks to Grandmother Khaya, Mirosha overcame these obstacles, and at the onset of the First World War he enrolled in the Commercial Institute.

In 1915 Mirosha was called up to the army. He burned with patriotism and the desire to fight for "faith, fatherland, and tsar." And, I think, to distinguish himself in battle. He began as a simple soldier and moved up rapidly. When the officers' ranks were opened to Jews in 1916—but only to the cream of the crop—he became a warrant officer and then, in 1917, a lieutenant.

---

[2] Semyon Mikhailovich Budyonny (1883–1973). A successful cavalry officer before the Revolution, when the civil war broke out in 1918 Budyonny organized a Red Cavalry force in the Don region which played an important role in vanquishing the White Army. He was not purged along with several other high-ranking military men in the Great Purges of 1937–38, and although Stalin blamed him for some of the setbacks in World War II, Budyonny died a natural death in 1973.

When the Revolution broke out he cast off his uniform and for a while was at loose ends. But it was not his nature to stand on the sidelines. In 1918 he joined the Red Army. He distinguished himself in Budyonny's First Cavalry, was appointed Red Commander, and joined the party in 1925.

For Mirosha, a Jew, the Revolution opened all doors. It was *his* revolution. He rose quickly. An adventurous, enthusiastic man, he was the child of fortune. He succeeded in everything.

His good looks no longer troubled me because I understood that he took little notice. It was not important to him. Of course, he knew that he was handsome, but it never occurred to him to use his looks to lord it over women. He didn't need that. His real passion was men's work.

We met as I have described for a whole year, but we did not consummate the relationship. I didn't want to become intimate too quickly. After he left he wrote me, "You probably took me for a school boy." Then—no more letters. I was confused; had he forgotten me, had he met another? A few months later, without warning, my friend Susanna quietly slipped me a note: "Come to our place at 6 p.m. Mirosha."

How can I describe that reunion? I remember every glance, every word. Mirosha stood under our poplar, smoking and looking off into the distance. I slowly approached him. He saw me and, flashing his happy laughing eyes, threw the cigarette away. Without a word, we walked to the river to our grove. I noticed that he was wearing the order of the Red Flag for service in battle. That was the most prestigious military medal and not easy to get. It made him into a hero in my eyes. How those medals appeal to the feminine imagination! Not the medal itself, of course, but the courage it represents.

Sitting on the bench in the shadow of the trees, I congratulated him and asked him what he had done to deserve it. He was flattered by my interest. He loved to show off to me. But at first he answered my questions evasively, as if to say this military business is for men. Of course, that only provoked my curiosity. But he didn't keep up that act for long. Soon he was telling me that he had commanded a unit of the Cheka. With Uborovich's infantry division, he suppressed an uprising in Ossetia and Dagestan led by the imam Gotsinsky, whom the British had supplied with arms.[3] Mirosha got his medal by capturing the imam alive and unharmed.

Not that it was easy. In fact, it was very difficult. The mountain dwellers in the ravines of the Caucasus were as agile as goats; our people were unaccustomed to the terrain and very awkward. They depended on a native guide who deceived them, leading them into a dead-end ravine where they almost perished. They all could have easily been shot to death. Mirosha himself interrogated the guide and shot him point blank.

---

[3] Ieronim Petrovich Uborevich (1882–1937). A member of the Russian high command, Uborevich was arrested and shot in 1937 in Stalin's campaign against–high ranking military personnel.

Mirosha profited from the experience. In a similar ravine his Chekists were able to quickly capture the imam. They offered the imam his life and a pardon if he would give himself up.

Once, in Rostov's bazaar, we saw the imam, a paunchy old man in a white turban, flanked by two Chekists. He would point to whatever he wanted and the Chekists would obsequiously buy it for him. Then they took him away to Moscow.

"What will happen to him?" I asked Mirosha.

"I don't know."

"Will they shoot him?"

"Maybe."[4]

ೞ ೞ

At that reunion, Mirosha and I became lovers.

Now he was in Rostov only on the fly.

He went from one success to another. At the ten-year anniversary of the Cheka he was given the medal of the Red Flag for his fight with bandits in the Caucasus and for great service during the Civil War. I understood how much this acknowledgement meant to him. He was very ambitious; his career — that was everything to him. He always had to take first place, even in such trivial matters as chess and billiards. I know how irritated he was when he lost a game to someone, but he played very well and rarely lost.

Zarnitsky was already working at the shoe factory. His salary was small and he was supporting Mama. And then when Lena's husband Sukhotin was arrested, Lena and Borya became his dependants. Later my brother Pavel joined us. There was never enough money. And even though NEP was still in effect and you could buy anything you wanted, I couldn't really dress stylishly.[5] We had to be good at "creating something from nothing." Lena and I had one fashionable hat between us. Lena said it looked better on her than on me, and I said it looked better on me. We just grabbed it back and forth between us.

I didn't work much. Ivan Aleksandrovich and I did not have children. I didn't want children. Mama took care of the housekeeping. My life seemed calm and happy, and no one guessed that I lived entirely in expectation.

---

[4] In 1925 Gotsinsky was, in fact, tried and shot in Rostov.

[5] NEP: New Economic Policy. In 1921 Lenin relaxed state control of the economy, imposed after the Revolution. This was an attempt to stimulate the economic revival of the country, exhausted by World War I, the Revolution, and the civil war. Market relations were restored, private property was legalized and entrepreneurs could hire labor. In short, NEP was a return to a form of capitalism, and goods and services became more abundant and accessible. It was, however, regarded by many as an unwelcome retreat from Communism.

Mirosha came to Rostov when he could. Whenever I knew he was in Rostov I was beside myself, nothing at home made sense to me, I lived only in the dream that soon I could tear myself away and go to him.

Sometimes the two of us, Mirosha and I, were in a hotel room with Lena. And although when she was with us she was gay, laughing and being silly, more and more frequently she counseled me to think it over. "It's time to put an end to it," she said, "before someone tells Zarnitsky." She thought that I shouldn't do anything to lose Zarnitsky. Indeed, I also asked myself—how long can I play a double role? And Mirosha had a wife—Gusta. There was a rumor that at the time of the imam's insurrection she came to Mirosha dressed in men's clothing.

And then we quarrel, part, and I tell him "This is fine. It's high time." And I pretend that I am in the seventh heaven of happiness that I was finally rid of him. But as soon as he leaves I am overcome with grief—jealousy, sadness, such pain that I would just as soon throw myself under a train. But I restrain myself, pull myself together, flirt with others. I do that for myself, to keep from feeling like a whipped dog. Mirosha doesn't come to Rostov. Where is he? What is he doing? I don't want to think, I don't want to know anything.

I even begin to get used to the parting, as if I had really calmed myself. And then the telephone rings. My heart leaps—can it be him? But I ask my girlfriend Susanna to say that I'm not at home. He calls again.

Susanna tells him, "She doesn't want to see you, she's busy, she's playing the piano."

He says, "I want to hear all of that from her!"

I run to the telephone, and without permitting myself to even hear his voice I scream three words into the receiver: "No, no, no!" and I fling down the telephone and in despair begin to furiously play the piano. In my soul I hear him jubilantly say, "Aga, you can't live without me."

The next day the phone rings again. I pick it up myself. "Is that you, Aga?" he says.

"It is I."

"Come to me."

But it is not I who answers. Throwing reason to the winds, it is my lips that whisper, "I'm coming."

"Oh, are you really coming? Really?"

I can't bear waiting until the evening. Oh, but finally it's evening. The household sits down to play Preference: Ivan Aleksandrovich, Mama, Lena and her suitor of the moment. I never played with them.

"Mama," I say casually, but softly so that Ivan Aleksandrovich can't hear. "I'm going to see Susanna." (Tomorrow, I must be sure to tell Susanna that I was supposed to be with her.)

Mama waves me away as if to say: go, don't interrupt me.

I put on Lena's fur coat and the hat that she and I share and I run out—quickly, quickly along the dark streets to the hotel.

Some friends of ours lived on the third floor of that hotel. I think, if someone were to whip me, I would confess that I went to him. Only please, not now! I quietly walk up the stairs. I get to the door of the second floor, I look around—there is no one, and I walk briskly down the corridor. Mirosha always left the door to his room slightly ajar, so that I wouldn't have to search for his room.

I quickly slip into the room and pulled the door closed. From the other end of the room he sees Lena's coat and the hat that we shared—his face darkens. "Where's Aga? Why hasn't Aga come?" I stand there smiling. And suddenly he recognizes me and exhales. "Aga, is that you?"

That's why I love to reread *Anna Karenina*. I recognize my relationship with Mirosha in that book. No, I'm not speaking of what Anna subsequently suffered. I recognize the beginning of their romance. Those secret meetings, those quarrels, those violent reconciliations.

⋘ ⋙

Mirosha was utterly devoted to Soviet power. Half jokingly, he would often call me his "little White Guard."[6] Once, to test the strength of his love for me, I asked, "And what if I really turned out to be a White Guardist, a *spy*? And what if they ordered you to shoot me, would you?"

I expected to hear him say that he would give up everything in this world for me, that he would defy everyone and everything. But without hesitating for a moment, his face white as a sheet, he replied, "I would shoot you."

I couldn't believe my ears.

"Me? You would shoot me? You would shoot … *me*?"

"I would shoot you."

I burst into tears.

Then he collected himself, embraced me, and whispered, "I would shoot you and then I would shoot myself." He covered my face with kisses.

I dried my tears, and although I said over and over, "How could you think such a thing even for a moment," I accepted the compromise: if he would then shoot himself that meant he truly loves me.

What Mirosha called our "underground apprenticeship" lasted for six years. Then he began to insist—"Aga, we can't go on like this. How long can we live like this—like thieves? We have to make a decision." I tossed it off with a joke.

Suddenly Mirosha was called to Alma-Ata, the capital of Kazakhstan. I accompanied him to the train and entered his compartment. He told me he had a stopover in Moscow on the way to Alma-Ata.

---

[6] Mirosha is referring to Agnessa's lack of interest, indeed disdain, for party politics.

"And what if I take you to Moscow?" he asked.

I laughed.

"Why are you laughing? I'm serious. Come to Moscow, have a look around. You've never been to Moscow. Of course, after a bit you'll come back here."

I was wearing a thin dress, a little jacket, and I carried only a small purse. "How can I go like this, with nothing?" That, I thought, was irrefutable.

"Don't worry, we'll buy you everything. You won't lack for anything."

A conductor appeared, calling "The train departs in two minutes. Everyone without a ticket—off the train." The bell sounded on the platform.

"I won't let you off, Aga," Mironov said, laughing and gripping my hand.

"Hey," I laughed. "You're hurting me."

The bell rang twice, the train shuddered, the railway buildings glided past the windows.

I imagined my family sitting down in the evening to play Preference—Mama, Ivan Aleksandrovich, Lena, probably a guest—without me. "Where's Aga?"

No one knows. They begin to play, and still I don't appear. Night falls. I still don't return. Ivan Aleksandrovich searches all of Rostov on foot.

I decided that I would get off the train at the next station and go back. But as we approached it, I began to think: if I leave now, I will not see Mirosha for a very long time, and if I continue on with him, we will at least be together in Moscow.

I didn't get off the train.

We went through the whole business again at the next station. Mirosha said, "If you're worried, we will send your family a telegram." So, at the very next station, afraid to let me off the train to send a telegram, he paid a guard to send it.

The only other passenger in our compartment slept on one of the lower bunks. I lay on the other. Mirosha covered me with his overcoat (in those days blankets were not provided on the trains) and sat beside me, his head close to mine, crooning a song. Do you know that old song "My cart glides through a sea of dust / Ketevanna sleeps in my cart"?

He sang it to me, changing the words:

Our train tears through the empty plains
Aga-vanna sleeps in my compartment
I took her from a little street in Rostov.[7]

He didn't sleep that night. Mirosha, who could drop off as soon as his head hit the pillow, who snores so loudly that only I could sleep through the

---

[7] This is loosely based on a poem by Mayakovsky.

noise. But he wouldn't let himself lie down on the upper bunk. He guarded me, so fearful that I would leave at some station.

In Moscow we stayed at the Metropole. In those days a couple didn't have to show their marriage certificate to get a room in a hotel. In general, it wasn't thought important to be officially married. On the very first day we went to a store and I chose everything that pleased me. He paid for everything. I wanted this, I wanted that—oh, how my desires expanded. Sometimes I felt a bit embarrassed, but he noticed what I liked and bought everything, although in those days there wasn't much to choose from.

As it got closer to the time Mirosha had to go to Alma-Ata, he said to me, "Think about this, Agneska. While I was stationed in the Caucasus I could frequently get away to see you in Rostov. You surely understand that from Alma-Ata you don't extricate yourself so easily. That means—either you come with me immediately to Alma-Ata or we will be separated forever, and it will be your fault. Make a final decision. I leave tomorrow."

Of course, I went with him.

And he, of course, counted on it from the moment he took me from Rostov.

For a long time he liked singing that song about Ketevan. He was so pleased with himself for taking me away.

Zarnitsky Again

I had left suddenly, without warning. Mama, my brother Pavel, and his daughter remained in Ivan Aleksandrovich's care for some time. I left all my things—excuse me, down to my brassieres—at home where they lay untouched. My underwear, my black gloves, the hat with little plumes that Ivan Aleksandrovich so proudly showed off to his mother, and all my other things lay in a box in the big armoire in the room that we shared.

Ivan Aleksandrovich was very gloomy and depressed. On my birthday he brought home a huge bouquet of red roses as he had always done. Somehow he had found them even in the winter. Mama saw how he went to the armoire, opened the box of my things, began to tear off the rose buds and threw them in. Then he threw in the open flowers. He stripped the stems, threw them in as well, and closed the box. Then he saw Mama standing in the doorway. His face was twisted and she was sure he was about to weep. That seemed a bad omen to her. Terrified, she yelled "What have you done? Are you preparing to bury her?"

"Yes, for me she has died." And he quickly left the house.

Mama threw open the box to look for his pistol. It was gone.

ଔ ଓ

About a year later, mid-1932, I came to Rostov to fetch Mama and Pavel's daughter Agulya. They had already moved away from Ivan Aleksandrovich's house and Mama was taking care of Agulya.

"Ah, what have you done, Aga!" Mama was grieving. "He almost shot himself."

"Let's go to see Ivan Aleksandrovich," I said gaily.

It was his birthday.

Ivan Aleksandrovich was shaved and nicely dressed, as if he had been expecting us. And really, he greeted me with a smile and calmly said, "I was sure that you would come."

While the table was being set, while Mama was busy arranging things and Pavel played with his little daughter Agulya, Ivan Aleksandrovich and I went to our former bedroom. Nothing had been moved. Everything was just as it had been on the day I left.

Ivan Aleksandrovich said to me, "Aga, it all happened too quickly to be solid, serious." And he began to ask me to return to him.

"I simply can't live this way; I didn't shoot myself because I believed that you would return to me."

Tears ran down his cheeks. He grabbed my hands and began to kiss them. He, who was normally so restrained, so proper.

At that moment I just couldn't say "no," I couldn't kick a person in that condition. I was also upset. I had stirred up the past. So I said, "I have to think about it, Musha. Maybe I'll come back."

He had said, "It all happened so quickly." So of course he thought it was a frivolous impulse, a whim. He knew nothing of my six-year "underground apprenticeship," of my six-year deception.

I left for Alma-Ata. I was pursued by a thick, pleading, passionate letter.

I didn't return. Once again I betrayed him.

Everything, everything, everything that I later suffered, that I endured—all of that paid me back for treating him so wickedly.

○ ○

Almost ten years later Mirosha was arrested. I carried packages to him in the notorious Lefortovo prison. Then they stopped accepting packages, we—a crowd of wives—spent the night waiting to hear how our husbands had been sentenced. All of us got the same news: "Ten years without the right of correspondence." In other words they were to be shot!

Suddenly I received a letter from Ivan Aleksandrovich. "I know that your husband was arrested, that you are alone. Come back to me! I live with another woman, but I love only you, I will leave her and we will be together again."

My old friend Susanna brought me the letter. I answered it through her, "How can I think about that when my husband is in prison?"

Once again I betrayed Ivan Aleksandrovich. I was already seeing Mikhail Davydovich, Mirosha's cousin.

Several years later I met with Ivan Aleksandrovich again. I was already married to Mikhail Davydovich, and I had come to Rostov to stay with relatives. He heard about it and came to see me. When he was preparing to leave I said, "I'll accompany you, Musha."

I tenderly took his arm and we walked through the evening streets. I whispered to him, "After all is said and done, real love happens only in one's youth."

"Yes," he reminisced.

Why in the world did I again stir up the past? But this time he didn't fall for it.

"Are you in a hurry?" I asked

"I'm in a hurry."

"Is someone waiting for you?"

"Yes, my wife is waiting for me."

He said that firmly. We parted amicably, even tenderly, but he never again asked me to come back to him.

In 1942 I was arrested and sentenced to five years in the Gulag. I wrote him from the Gulag. He was living in Tashkent, working as the chief engineer of a shoe factory. I gave the letter to Katya, a *zek* who had been released before me.[1] There was no answer. I wrote Katya. She answered that she had given him the letter with her own hands.

After I had finished my term in the Gulag and went to live in Bogorodsk in 1950, I wrote him again, recalling our past. I wrote that I was alone and miserable, that Mikhail Davydovich had received a ten-year sentence, and that there was no way he could survive it. And I really did believe that it was hopeless to expect him to return.

Yet again, Ivan Aleksandrovich did not answer me. I wrote another long letter to Katya explaining that he had told me he was living with another woman, but that he loved only me, that he had written poems to me. I repeated the poems in the letter. Why doesn't he answer, not even a word? The subtext of my letter was a reproach. It of course was a way of saying, "call me and I'll come to you."

I was in a very bad way then. I thought of him as a close, dear friend. You see, I cannot live without love... and I tried to revive it, to look for it where it had once been all-embracing.

Katya took the letter to the factory where Ivan Aleksandrovich worked. He read the letter in front of her and said sadly, "Yes, I wrote her such letters, it's true. But that was long ago and a lot of water has flowed under the bridge since then."

A year later I wrote another letter for Katya to take to him. She wrote back that he was dead.

I went to Tashkent to see Katya. I went to his factory and asked about him. Of course, everyone knew him, loved him, and mourned his death. I wanted to know all the details—where, how, when? They told me to go to the personnel department. I went and asked, "Do you know where he is buried?"

"You had better ask his family," they answered and gave me their address.

But I never went. I didn't want to meet his wife.

Last year—fifty years later—I was in the very area where we had gone to visit his parents. I was staying with my daughter Agulya in Leningrad and

---

[1] The gulag prisoner was referred to as a *zek* in both official documents and common parlance. The word derives from the initials "Z" and "K," originally an abbreviation for the "zakliuchennyi kanaloarmeits," the gulag prisoners who built the White Sea–Baltic Canal. This was one of Stalin's favorite projects; 126,000 Gulag prisoners constructed a 227 km. canal from the White Sea to Lake Onega in the record time of two years (1931–33).

had a bit of extra money. I was overcome with nostalgia, so I went there. You see, in my last years I walk "in the traces of my youth."[2]

I went to the local train station and asked for a ticket to Murino. The cashier said "There is no such station."

"Excuse me, please, but fifty years ago there was a station by that name."

"Now it is a city" said the cashier, and she explained how to take the electric train and get off at such-and-such a station.

So I went. Platform. No forest. No dachas, no fields. New little houses scattered about. I had no idea where to go. Then I saw the belltower of an old church. I went in that direction and found the church. One little old house was still standing. I looked in and saw a grey-haired woman.

"Excuse me. Have you lived here long?"

"I was born here."

"Then you probably knew the Zarnitsky family, a priest and his wife."

"Certainly I knew them. And who are you?"

"I was the daughter-in-law."

"Which son?"

"The oldest. Ivan Aleksandrovich."

"Ivan Aleksandrovich, I remember him perfectly. How is he?"

"He died."

She began to tell me about Ivan Aleksandrovich.

"He was such a good preacher. He would put on a cassock, go around to the believers, and speak to them of conscience and goodness. Today no one even knows those words. Everyone has turned into dogs. But we listened to him and our souls were easier. And his father, Batyushka, stood where he couldn't be seen, but he listened and rejoiced. Ivan Aleksandrovich was the eldest son and the parish should have passed to him."

"He joined the Red Army."

"I know, I know. Everyone talked about it. And you? Didn't you once come here with him? How time flies. You brought such joy to his family."

"What happened to them after they were sent away, did you ever hear?"

"I don't know anything, my darling. It was as if they drowned in the water. They took so many people from us, and it's the same with all of them. Not a word."

I found their house. It was bigger than the other little houses that had not yet been taken down. It was partitioned in two parts. Even a round stump in the garden was divided into two. Some people lived on one side and the other side was a kindergarten. I asked for permission to enter the kindergarten. Everything seemed to me even smaller than small. Where was the "honeymoon room"? I went through the whole place, but nowhere in the jolly pink and blue children's rooms did I find anything that looked like the "honeymoon room."

---

[2] This was probably around 1971.

Karaganda

> **Translator's Note:** Agnessa here interrupts the chronological flow of her story, as she probably did many times in the twenty years she told it to Mira Yakovenko. Her narrative in this section tells of her first sight of Karaganda when it was about to become the administrative center of a huge cluster of Gulags. A decade later she was a prisoner in one of those Gulags.

I was in Karaganda twice. The first time was in 1931 when Mirosha and I moved to Alma-Ata. Mirosha was named deputy to V. A. Karutsky, the plenipotentiary representative of the OGPU in Kazakhstan. (Before Karutsky the head of the OGPU was Danilov, who was removed for engaging in contraband.)

On the very first day the manager brought me a pile of crepe-de-chine, which I accepted. Mironov was furious.

"Get it out of here."

I had to take it to the manager's home. His wife was surprised? "You didn't like it?"

Karutsky—paunchy, swollen—was a big drinker. His wife had previously been married to a White officer and had a son from him. People began to throw this in Karutsky's face. So he said to his wife: "It would be better for the boy to live with your mother." They sent him away, but Karutsky's wife missed him terribly and not long after we arrived she killed herself.

Karutsky had a dacha not far from Alma-Ata where he built a bachelor's cottage. As soon as we arrived he invited us here. There I saw pornographic photos made by some famous French artist whose name I can't recall. I remember one to this day: it was of a church in Bulgaria and showed how Turks were raping nuns.

Karutsky loved women. He had an assistant called Abrashka who supplied Karutsky with women. He would look out for them, grab them, and procure them for Karutsky. As soon as Mironov left for work in the morning this Abrashka made a habit of dropping in on me. He would bring me one thing or another—grapes, melons, pheasant. What didn't he bring me! Mirosha was beside himself.

"Why do you accept these things? Get rid of him!"

One time Mirosha came home and found an ashtray full of cigarette butts. "These aren't mine. Who was here?"

"Abrashka."

"Him again? Why?"

"I don't know."

"Why do you receive him? I have already told you, get rid of him!"

He was furious and the next day he came home, dark as the night. "Now I know why Abrashka comes here. Karutsky is sending me away for a month to inspect the entire Kazakhstan. He is purposely sending me away so that you will be here alone. Maybe that's what you want, I don't know."

"Mirosha! That paunchy Karutsky?"

"Well, then. Let's trick him. They are giving me a whole train compartment. Will you come with me?" So I went with him on his business trip.

଼ ଼

So it was that in the winter of 1931 I passed through Karaganda with Mirosha. We traveled in a Pullman car that dated to the time of Nicholas II. The salon was all in gold velvet, the bedroom in red velvet. Two huge couches. The conductors (they were also cooks) fed us gloriously. Among us there was only one other woman—the engineer.

It was late autumn, but in northern Kazakhstan it was already as cold as winter and there were snowstorms with ferocious winds. The car was always well heated. But I am a woman from the south and I was always freezing. So they got me a thick, well-made fur coat. I wrapped myself in it and could wander out anywhere—into the storm, into the frost. I was warm!

Everything would have been fine, if Mirosha had not grown more withdrawn and grumpy by the day. Even I could not shake him out of his mood.

Then we come to some kind of a stop buried in snow.

"This," we were told, "is the village of Karaganda." It was actually just in the process of being built.

They uncoupled our car, and Mirosha's colleagues went to see what kind of a place Karaganda was. I wanted to go as well, but Mirosha wouldn't permit me. They were gone for a long time, so Mirosha and I went to our bedroom. Mirosha lay down on the couch, silent then asleep. I was bored and I went to look for the others. Some of them returned from the village.

"This Karaganda" they said, "is just a word." There are only temporary hovels built by exiled kulaks. There is nothing in the store but empty shelves. The saleswoman said, "I don't work, I don't trade because there is nothing to sell or trade. We have forgotten what bread looks like. What can I offer you? I think there is a tiny bottle of liqueur someplace. Do you want it?" They took it and continued to talk to her.

This is the story that the saleswoman in Karaganda's only store told us.

"The exiled *kulaks* that were sent here, they're all dying off because there is no food.[1] See that hut? The mother and father died, three small children remain. The youngest, two years old, died soon after. The oldest boy took a knife and cut the baby up. That's how he feeds himself and his little sister."

The group fell silent. It seems that Mirosha's colleagues were already acquainted with hunger. But after some hot tea, they revived and turned to other things. One of them began to "show off" to me and the woman engineer.

"Don't stare at me because I'm short," he exclaimed. "No woman has ever complained about me."

And he told about how he and a friend had gone to a photographer's house to have a picture taken. In the background of the photo they saw a pretty female face. That was the photographer's wife. When the photographer was not home, they returned to his house.

"May we wait for him?"

In the meantime the wife busied herself in the kitchen. They chopped some birch wood for her fire. Suddenly they heard the sound of heavy steps on the stairway—the husband's.

"What are you doing here? Get out of here!"

They ran down the stairs with the birch wood flying after them.

"Do you think that was the end of it?" asked the story teller, so self-satisfied. "She came to me later without being asked!"

Other stories in the same vein followed. Then they played cards. But I, I could not get those children out of my head.

When Mirosha awoke, I told him all about the children, thinking I would shock him.

"I know all about it," he said.

He usually kept his work affairs from me, but here I am telling him about his business.

"I know all about it. We went into one of the huts... full of corpses. That's a working trip for you."

At that time he suffered greatly about things like that, I could see it. But he was already beginning to push them out of his head, to dismiss them.

---

[1] A *kulak* was a peasant who hired labor and was, in principle, more affluent than the "average" peasant. The Soviet government considered these peasants to be class enemies, exploiters of the great mass of Russia's peasantry. In 1929 Stalin initiated the policy of collectivization, organizing peasants, their land, and animals into large collective units. By 1930 the state began a systematic elimination of *kulaks* as a class. The definition of *kulak* expanded to include peasants who, for whatever reason, resisted collectivization. The *kulaks*' land was expropriated (when they actually owned any) and millions were deported to distant places, sometimes to areas incapable of sustaining life, and/or imprisonment in the Gulags. Among many tragic consequences of collectivization was mass famine that ravaged Ukraine.

He was so dedicated to the party, he always believed that everything the party did was for a purpose. Early in our life together, I often said to him, "Mirosha, how can it be that they are all guilty?" Mama had put those ideas in my head, she was a clever woman.

"Of course you don't believe they are guilty. You are my little White Guard woman."

At the same time, in the midst of this dying hamlet, we had plenty of provisions in our velvet train car. We carried with us frozen ham, chickens, mutton, cheeses, just about everything you could want.

Petropavlovsk in northern Kazakhstan. As soon as we got there, the head of the Petropavlovsk OGPU came to see Mirosha. It was Mirosha's job to inspect the work of these officials, but you could hardly say that he was strict. On the contrary.

"Tomorrow, " he said to the head man, "we will start to work. But today bring your wife and have dinner with me and my wife. We are having roasted suckling pig."

They came. His wife Anya was pretty but fat. And, oh, her dress! How can a fat woman wear such a dress? An accordion pleated skirt—that makes one look even fatter. I remember how she tried to explain herself. "It's because we were in Central Asia where the summer is very hot. I drank water all the time."

The table in the salon was set unimaginatively, but sumptuously. The chef brings in the roast pig on a platter, cut into chunks in a sauce. He cautiously walked past us, probably trying to avoid Anya's luxuriant hair-do, but as he bent forward to set the platter down, the sauce spilled all over her dress. She jumped back and screamed, "What an outrage"... and she began to curse.

The cook almost expired. He looked terrible—what would happen to him now?

I tried to calm her down, called out for salt to be poured on the dress, but the joy of the meal was gone. Mirosha says to her:

"Can we let a dress spoil our pleasure in such a roasted piglet?"

Her husband frowned at her, as if to say—"enough." But she would not be consoled, and that's how the entire meal went.

The next day they invited us to their house. A feast—and what a feast! Many servants, many sycophants, many toadies. They served every kind of fresh fruit. Just imagine, even oranges. And what can I say about the grapes and the ice cream of all sorts.

Fifteen years later, I was once again in Karaganda. Mirosha had been shot long ago, Mikhail Davydovich, my third husband, was languishing in the camps. Behind me was the Lubyanka, then a terrible journey through the steppes in a snowstorm—and dystrophy from which I almost perished.[2] My sentence was nearing its end and I was attached to a hospital in Aratau, a three-day journey by horse from Karaganda. Panna, the wife of the camp commandant, had befriended me, and she helped me in any way she could. There was a jailbird in our hospital who had allegedly lost the use of his legs. But our chief doctor suspected that he was simulating because his spine was intact. It was decided to send him to the Karaganda hospital. The chief doctor said to the armed guards of the convoy, "I don't trust you to look after him, so I am sending a nurse with him. She will not run away, she only has three months left to freedom." I was that nurse.

It was said that our armed guards were the children and grandchildren of those dispossessed kulaks who had been sent here in the 1930s to die. They hated us—as intelligentsia, or more precisely, as the former authorities, the *party* types who had dispossessed and exiled their families. Perhaps among them was that little boy who had eaten his younger brother.

The guards were especially cruel and coarse, but mainly they were barbaric and boorish. For my part, I did not suffer from their cruelty. I had quickly understood this life and somehow taught myself to get along with them without behaving badly myself. And another thing that helped me. I never, not for a single day, wore prison or camp clothing. It seemed to me that once you wore those dreadful quilted trousers and jackets with cotton stuffing poking out of the holes you were no longer a human being. You turned into a slave in their eyes and in your own, a slave whom they could order around as they wished. It was important to guard one's human dignity. And I tried to hold my ground—not to cave in or discredit myself. That helped me to have a different kind of relationship with the people around me, even with the armed guards.

But I return to my story.

So, we set off as a convoy, a cart carrying two guards and a machine gun, with a wagon driving behind it, the patient lying on a bed of straw. I sat at his feet with my little bag.

June. Sunny. Steppe, high grass and flowers. At some point in the day we stopped. The guards built a bonfire and cooked a meal for themselves. The prisoner and I were given a bread ration. Then the guards began to call to me, "Hey, doctor lady. Come and eat with us!" But I was disgusted with them. I accepted only a boiled potato that I shared with the patient. We slept in huts. The two guards and I on benches, one of us at a time in the cart keeping watch over the patient. When it was the driver's turn to keep watch, the two guards were nervous. What if the patient escapes? I calmed them. "Don't worry, Vasily the driver is with him." "Oh yeah, Vasily, fuck your mother!

---

[2] The Lubyanka was the dreaded headquarters of the Soviet secret services in Moscow. After arrest, it was often the first venue of interrogation, often under torture, and imprisonment.

He's already snoring. Who can stand it?" They got up several times in the night to check on Vasily.

We came to the banks of a river. The machine-gun cart easily forded it. But our wagon was lower to the ground. As we started to cross, the water seeped into it. The guards and I were able to lift ourselves, but the patient was lying in the water. And suddenly the horses began to swim. God only knows how they pulled out of their harnesses. They swam with the current, but we were immersed in the water. I thought, "I know how to swim, but the patient?" He was already in the water, frightened out of his wits, his face contorted with fear. Afterwards, I said to the guards, "That proves that he really can't walk."

The horses emerged from the water and were once again harnessed to the machine-gun cart and attached to the wagon that pulled us out of the water.

It was warm. We dried ourselves in the sun. The patient cheered up, so happy that he hadn't perished. After we started out again, he told me why he was arrested.

Before he was arrested, he had lived well. He came to a town by a small arterial road of the Transiberian Railway and paid some woman three–four rubles for a place to sleep for a few days.

At a substation he walked slowly alongside the freight cars. The inspectors rapped on the cars, paying no attention to him. But, walking by a car, he sensed that it was full of fabric. He knew it by smell. When evening fell he dressed himself smartly, with an ax and a hammer hanging on the inside of his jacket and his pockets full of nails. He found the car on the dangerous rails and climbed onto the break platform. There, in the door to the car were planks which he pried open with his axe, leaving them hanging by a nail. He managed to squeeze into the car, replacing the plank so that no one would notice a hole. He walked through the car. It was packed with bolts of material. It was hard to push through. He sniffed the bales in the dark. He didn't take the cotton. He was looking for crepe de chine and silk. There were only a few bales of silk and he took two. Then he opened the hole and looked about him. Was it quiet? Usually there was not a sound to be heard at a substation.

He crept out, quietly closed up the hole, went to the woman with whom he was staying, and put the bales in a suitcase. In the morning he took the first train to his fence. She really knew how to make a profit. If a meter of crepe de chine was worth nine rubles, she gave him a ruble per meter. He got his money after he helped her cut the leavings into three-meter pieces. She gave the cuttings to her employees, women who would sell them at the flea market.

The fence was the cause of his ruin. She gave him up. She deliberately cheated him in the accounting. He went back to demand what was rightfully his, and the police were lying in wait for him. He was furious with her: "I'll be put away, but you will be, too." He told on her and she was arrested, too.

☙ ❧

And here, again, is Karaganda. The whistle of the train. I am looking at a train for the first time in many years. Trains, trams. Oh no, Karaganda was no longer that snow-bound, dying village of fifteen years ago. Now it was a real city. But a city of camps and exiles who remained here after being released from a camp. Only the very first exiles—repressed *kulaks*—were no longer to be seen. They were already dead.

The doctors who worked in the hospital here were first class and they treated the camp heads and the correctional officers. The camp bosses built houses here, some of them with columns. They raised cows, pigs, chickens. Prisoners worked the farms for them. If someone in the boss's household was ill, they called a professor to come to his house, to look at a child's throat or to treat the mother-in-law's backache. The most illustrious doctors took care of them at home.

Our escorts brought the prisoner to the hospital. "Now," they said to me, "we will get rid of you." But instead of putting me in the camp, they put me in a hotel because I had accompanied the prisoner. The hotel was an empty barrack except for bunk beds with straw mattresses and blankets, crudely stitched together like doormats.

The manager of this hotel was called Tatyana. We decided to go into the town together. She said that we could buy fizzy water and ice cream in the town. Ice cream! It had been years since I'd eaten ice cream.

I tried to dress myself somehow. I had a long black skirt—a gift from Panna. I walked to the exit alongside the grates that partitioned the male and female enclosures. On the men's side, a bunch of prisoners poured out to look at me and yell, "A new one! A new one!"

Tatyana told me her story. Her father had been a rich landowner on the Volga. In 1920 her two brothers were officers in the White army. They did not keep in touch with Tatyana. But under Yezhov, head of the NKVD between 1936 and 1938, she was arrested and given ten years because of her father's class status. Suddenly, just before World War II she was called out of the camp with her possessions. What could that mean? She is put on a train to Moscow—to the Lubyanka—and then taken to Beria himself. Beria, who had succeeded Yezhov, sat behind a desk in a luxurious office with a full-length portrait of Stalin on the wall.[3] He tells her to sit.

"Do you have relatives abroad?"

Tatyana swears that she has never had contact with her brothers.

"Too bad," says Beria. "How long is your sentence?"

"Ten years."

---

[3] In 1934 the OGPU was replaced by the NKVD (People's Commissariat of Internal Affairs). Lavrenty Beria replaced N. Yezhov as head of the secret services in 1938. He slowly became second in command to Stalin until his arrest and death in 1953.

"Well, that's a long one. Too long. Now I will explain why we have called you up. One of your brothers lives in Constantinople, the other one died in the United States and left behind sixty million dollars. He has no direct heirs. You and your living brother can collect that inheritance only if you go to the United States. We will put you on a plane with the appropriate documents. Two of our people will go with you. You will get the money and return."

She waited—can you imagine how agitated she was? She thinks, well if I go, won't I bolt? Won't I remain there? Of course, they could kill me. I'll bribe them with five million each.

She waited and waited, but the war broke out. She waited some more. They said, "The arrangement is still in place."

But here she is!

When I went into town, Tatyana asked if she could keep my lunch. "I'll keep your bread for you." I agreed. She ate my slop and my porridge.

In Karaganda I even got to the hairdresser and had my hair done. How long it had been since I'd been to a hairdresser.

The hairdresser was surprised: "I have never seen you before. Did they send you here to work?" I didn't want to tell him the real story. He made me look wonderful. I felt like a human being again.

When I went back the men again swarmed to the grates. I wore a long black skirt, my hair beautifully curled. I held my head high and didn't look at anyone. One of the men gingerly clapped and suddenly all the men applauded loudly, greeting me.

I was supposed to go back to the camp with the convoy. I was called to the car of women guards who came to Karaganda to go shopping. They looked me over and screamed, "What a hairdo! And we never thought about going to the hairdresser." As if to say, here we are, in command, and we are being made to look foolish.

I made an armature out of a piece of wire that I covered with gauze, and behold! I had made a hat to protect my face from the sun. The guard couldn't get over it, so irritated was he by my hat. "Take off that damned nest," he yelled.

What irritated him was probably that with my hat I was lording it over him, like a high-class person.

I calmly answered, "Why should I take it off. It isn't bothering anyone."

"Take it off, I said!"

But he didn't rip it off my head. The guards were not usually so rude, but perhaps the presence of the women guards restrained him.

When we got to the camp, all the others were very sunburnt with swollen red noses, and again they exclaimed, "Agnessa Ivanovna, how do you stay so white?"

And they call themselves women? They can't even understand that one must protect the face from the sun.

When I got back to the camp, I had the following conversation with Tatyana.

"When does your sentence end?" she asked.

"September 1947."

"Mine, too."

And we agreed to meet then. Tatyana said, "I'll wait for you. If you can't find me, that means that something happened."

She had become very attached to me, and after I left she fell into a deep depression. I got one letter from her and none after that. She did not turn up at the place we had agreed to meet and I couldn't stay to look for her. I never saw from her again and never had any news of her.

My Life With Mirosha, 1930–39

> **Translator's Note:** In these years Stalin and his government undertake the radical transformation of Soviet society: the first two Five-Year Plans for rapid industrialization and the transformation of agriculture in the form of collectivization. The raging famine of 1932–35 in the grain producing regions abates, but the Soviet Union remains a society marked by chronic scarcity of food, housing, and most goods for daily life and well-being. The burgeoning size of the secret police and its power to deal with alleged "enemies of the people" and "anti-revolutionary activity" creates a culture of fear and repression, random arrests, show trials, deportation, and the system of Gulag labor camps, peaking in the Great Purges of 1937–39.

When Mirosha and I lived in Alma-Ata from 1930 to 1933 and then in Dnepropetrovsk from 1933 to 1936, every year we took a holiday on the Black Sea and often jumped over to Grozny, Vladikavkaz, or Tbilisi, all places where Mirosha had many friends from previous work.

At that time Beria was secretary of the Regional Party Committee in the Transcaucasus. The assistant to the executive representative of the OGPU was Armen Gerasimovich Abulyan. So there you had two lords on one estate. Beria hated him.

Abulyan was Mirosha's friend. They fought together in Budyonny's army. Then, like Mirosha, he came to Rostov with Evdokimov, and from there they both got positions in various places in the Caucasus.

When Mirosha was already the head of the Dnepropetrovsk OGPU, we happened to read a note in a newspaper that Abulyan had died, allegedly in an automobile accident. Mironov's expression darkened and he said nothing, but I understood—he was very upset. A month and a half later we went to Tbilisi.

"We must visit his widow," I said.

He replied, "You go yourself, without me."

There was a good reason for that. I went alone.

Abulyan's wife was Russian, a red-head. She had two children.

I went to their house. No one was there. The doors were not locked. It seemed that the children had been sent away. I was greeted by an elderly woman, probably a dependent, who moved about the house like a shadow. Her finger on her lips, she pointed to a bedroom.

I looked into the room. Abulyan's wife, Valentina Vasilevna, all in black, hair disheveled, eyes red, half-mad, sat on the floor surrounded by piles of photographs. She saw me and began to sob. When she calmed down, she whispered, "You know, Aga, that Lavrenty [Beria] killed him. He is a murderer. He murders his own people."

This is what she told me.

It was a hot summer. They lived in a dacha in the hills. Abulyan was driven to and from work and was often very late coming home. Allegedly, his car and a truck smashed into each other. The car was found at the bottom of an abyss. Both Abulyan and his chauffeur were mutilated beyond recognition. Squeezed between two trucks to the edge of the precipice and then hit by them. Or Abulyan and his chauffeur were killed first and then thrown into the abyss? No one saw the accident, it was dark. Beria's people knew the road Abulyan took to get home, and they knew exactly when he usually left.

When I told the story to Mironov, he warned me: "If you want to live, keep quiet about that. Not a word to anyone."

The traces of the event disappeared, everything was kept in the dark, and no one was guilty of anything. It was an accident.

Several years later we found out that Abulyan's family was living in Moscow. I set out to visit them, but when I came to the address there were other people living there. No one knew a thing about Abulyan. That was when Stalin had already brought Beria to Moscow as an aide to Yezhov.

Abulyan had disappeared without a trace.

In general, Beria had no use for the Chekists who had worked in the Caucasus; they knew too much about him.

For Mirosha the move to Dnepropetrovsk was a rise in status. He was the plenipotentiary of the Dnepropetrovsk OGPU. In Alma-Ata he had been only the assistant to the boss. In Dnepropetrovsk we lived in a beautiful house.

View from the Outside: Leva (Mirosha's Nephew)

> *I remember an old two-story mansion, many rooms on the second floor for the family and guests, a viewing room for movies, a billiard room, and a toilet and bathroom in each wing.*
>
> *On the first floor lived Uncle's family and his personnel chauffeur. And also there was a huge study with an exit to a glassed-in veranda.*
>
> *When I was brought to Dnepropetrovsk I was enrolled in a kindergarten. As soon as I began to boast that Mironov was my uncle, everyone—the teachers, my playmates parents, and even my playmates—began to curry my favor and fawn on me. Everyone felt that I was special; and why not? After all, I was the nephew of a very powerful man, Mironov himself.*

03 80

For several years after Mirosha and I left Rostov, my husband Zarnitsky waited for me, believing that I would return to him. But after five years he asked for a divorce because he wanted to remarry.

Mirosha controlled all the branches of ZAGS, the civilian registry office, in the Dnepropetrovsk region. So, in 1936 a ZAGS employee came to our house and issued a divorce for me and Zarnitsky and married Mirosha and me. As for Mirosha and his wife Gusta—in those days one could divorce and marry by correspondence. So in a half hour there were two divorces and a marriage.

Mirosha had to go to Kiev and I always tried to travel with him. We came to Kiev to find that the rumor of our marriage had arrived before us. Everyone congratulated us. V. A. Balitsky, the plenipotentiary of the Ukrainian OGPU since 1933, laughed and shouted "a wedding, a wedding."

It all happened so quickly that I didn't even have time to have a white dress made for me. Balitsky provided the money to make the wedding—of course, it was government money and a lot of it, too. You can't imagine what was given away in envelopes! The wedding took place on the banks of the Dnieper in the People's Commissar's dacha. The event lacked for nothing! The employees of the Department of Internal Affairs did a brilliant job of organizing everything—they wanted to have a good party.

But what about the wedding dress? One woman there offered me her wedding dress, but it was second-hand. I politely refused.

I came in a light green dress trimmed with gold buttons. It didn't embarrass anyone. And how gay it was. Everyone shouted "Bitter! Bitter!" And when Mirosha said that we had been married for twelve years—six years without formally registering and, before that, six years of "underground apprenticeship," everyone began to shout "To the devil with the underground apprenticeship, we don't care about it! Today we want you to be newlyweds!" That meant that everyone wanted this event to be authentic. I passed around a tray with little glasses of vodka and went to each guest individually. When I stopped in front of a guest everyone sang "To Whose Health Shall We Drink?" ("Komu charu pit'?"), and that guest would drink up and leave money on the tray.[1] Then it was Balitsky's turn. Balitsky was very handsome—tall, blond, stately—a real Siegfried. Everyone had already drunk "To Your Health...," and was waiting expectantly: what would he do? I knew that Balitsky liked me, but his wife was sitting right there. She was small, pathetic, wicked and didn't take her eyes off of him. And he drank up in a flash, but with her glaring at him he did not dare kiss me. He left a silver ruble on the tray. At that time they were very rare.

After the banquet everyone began to holler "Lock them in the bedroom," and they did. But I prayed that as soon as Mironov's head hit the pillow he would fall asleep (he was very tired). I wanted to be with the guests and to have fun. So they released me.

---

[1] The origins of this wedding ritual are obscure. It is described in Dostoevsky's story "The Hostess" ("Khoziaika") and the verses appear in many Russian folk song anthologies.

That's how I became Mironov's legal wife in 1936.

☙ ❧

Mirosha's first wife, Gusta, forgave his infidelities. She believed that a wife should be a friend, a refuge to which the husband can always return. I didn't fancy that role. I didn't want to be beneath him in any way. When he entered a room everyone said, "What an interesting man, that Mironov!" I feared that they would say about me "He's so interesting, but his wife—well…" I succeeded in getting them to add "but his wife is his equal."

"It's not always easy with you," Mirosha once confessed. "Sometimes I'd just like to let myself go, to just give way and relax, and then I see how smart you look and what great form you're in, and I smarten myself up. With you, I can't let myself go."

"Are you dissatisfied?"

"No, no, how can you think that? I'm grateful to you." And he added, laughing, "Just think. We've been together for twelve years and I've not once deceived you. How can that be?"

How can that be? I'll tell you. From the beginning to the end our relationship was an unending, enduring romance. Never prosaic, never ordinary, never boring. Never that stultifying routine. Between us it was always games, mystery. We were like new lovers. We were forever in love, lovers, newlyweds.

And another thing. I was always on the alert. Women loved him! His men's business was, of course, always first, but he was not immune to female adulation. He basked in it.

Someone once repeated to me an intimate conversation among the women. One woman had confessed, "I would give myself to Mironov and then I would die."

"I, however, will not die," I responded sarcastically.

But I remained alert.

Normally, I tried not to be separated from Mirosha, but at one point I had to leave Alma-Ata to spend some time in Rostov—I went to fetch Mama and Agulya. When I returned I was told that at a picnic Mirosha had paired off with one of the women who worked for him. She was a pretty thing with a little face as white as porcelain, black hair to her shoulders and a fringe. I was immediately on my guard!

"Did they go off alone? No? Well, what did they do?"

"She gave him a pastry from her basket."

I didn't like that either. At exactly that time we were on the eve of a holiday and had arranged to give a party. I went into action.

I took great pains to keep my figure. If I were to eat everything I wanted, I would get fat in a few days. But I exercised my will power; I was always hungry because I scrupulously kept to a regimen. Everyone marveled at my slenderness. And so I had a dress made up for the party, I designed it myself. Imagine this—black silk (the color black is slimming) shot with multicolored sparks, the waist and hips close fitting with pleats like shining arrows—I have never since seen such a style. The top spilling over with these arrows, and the bottom, almost to my knees, the widest flounced skirt—fluffy, airy, like the spring fog at dusk. To the side a large buckle, iridescent with the all the colors in the rainbow, like colors of the fabric.

We had several servants. Maria Nikolaevna—she cooked for us and went everywhere with us like a member of the family. I couldn't have done without her. Irina—she brought us food, everything she could find at the special stores and dining rooms; a housemaid who cleaned and served at table; a laundress who washed and ironed and helped with just about everything else when there was no laundry to do. And then Mama came to live with us as well.

They all loved to dress me. They tighten up here, they buckle me there, and then they look and are carried way with admiration. On the evening of the party even Mama, who was more restrained than the servants, couldn't hold back. "Today you will outshine them all."

And that's exactly what I intended. To outshine everyone! To eclipse them all, to sweep away like dust anyone who would try to rival me.

When I appeared among the guests all eyes turned to me. And she, that employee with her black fringe and little porcelain face in a simple white skirt and blouse on the arm of a girlfriend. How, how could you compare her with me? I no sooner walked into the room than she was obliterated. Mirosha's own eyes convinced him who I was and who she was.

And she was finished off because of her felt boots. "Aga, can you imagine," Mirosha said to me with surprise. "Z. came to my office wearing felt boots!"

He found that amazing. I didn't ask him why she came to his office—I understood that those felt boots killed off any interest he may have had in her. You should have seen the expression on his face when he told me about the boots, as if it were something indecent, improper. I had taught him to understand and value the esteem in which a woman should hold herself. Felt boots—he would never see me in felt boots, and he understood that Z. was simple, dreary, cheap.

◌ ✿

When we lived in Alma-Ata first the exiled kulaks died off. Then the Cossacks perished. We, of course, had everything, so I knew nothing about the famine raging in the Ukraine as well until I learned about it from my sister

Lena.[2] I wrote her back asking what to send—silk, stockings, dresses…? She answered me in Russian interspersed with phrases in Greek, which our father had taught us to read and write, "Don't send clothing. Better to send food."[3]

But, you know, the satiated don't understand the hungry, and I didn't attach much importance to her words, casually saying to Mama, "Oh, send what you like." Mama was a simple woman, but she understood life well. At the same time we had a guest from the Ukraine who cried, "For heaven's sake, don't you know there is a real famine in the Ukraine?" Fortunately, some of Mirosha's employees were about to go to the Ukraine. We quickly snatched whatever came to hand—a bag of flour, millet, potatoes.

Later Lena told me: "I always gave my son Borya whatever I could get with my ration coupons. I myself was wasting away. The streets, the doorways were strewn with corpses. I kept thinking—soon I'll be among them. Suddenly a car stopped in front of the house and soldiers got out of it with huge bags. They called to me, smiling shyly. 'This is for you, from your sister it seems.' I couldn't believe my eyes. I opened a bag—millet! Of course, in my haste I spilled some, so I quickly-quickly threw the millet into a pot, poured water into it, cooked it. I couldn't wait until it was done, and while it was cooking, I gobbled it raw."

In the autumn I left the sanatorium in Sochi a week earlier than Mirosha to return to Alma-Ata because I wanted to make a quick stop in Rostov. In our eight days at the sanatorium the servants had packed for me boxes of food—roasted chickens, smoked fish, meat pies, pastries, fruit and other victuals, even oranges still on their green branches, and a bouquet of chrysanthemums.

I got to Rostov and burst into my relatives' apartment with the huge bouquet of chrysanthemums and the boxes. They were stupefied. I was especially struck by little Borya, my nephew. Somber, joyless, wordless, he only ate. He ate his way through everything I had brought.

Lena wept, "You have saved us, Aga."

They survived thanks to our parcels.

When we came to Dnepropetrovsk the famine was still raging. In the autumn Mirosha and I went as usual to Sochi, Gagra, or Khosta, resorts on the Black Sea, and in summer he took us to an official dacha in Berdyansk. Three times a day the police brought our food from a special sanatorium. Sometimes at dinner we had freezers full of ice cream.

A local woman who served us once asked, "May I take what's left over from your dinner? I have three children…"

"Of course," Mama exclaimed.

---

[2] The introduction of the first Five-Year Plan and collectivization resulted in a massive famine that raged throughout Ukraine in 1932–33.

[3] According to Agnessa's adopted daughter, Agulya, Agnessa and her sister Lena attended a Greek school for three years before they went to gymnasium.

Two days later the woman asked again, "May I bring my children to play with yours?"

And she brought her little boy and two girls. I was horrified at how thin her children were. The little boy, Vasya, was like a skeleton, his ribs protruding from his torso. Next to our Borya, who had grown quite chubby, little Vasya was like a representation of death. Someone photographed them side by side. I said, "Remember long ago there was an advertisement for rice flour? It was a before and after picture; a skinny person before she ate rice flour and a well-fed person afterward. This photograph reminds me of that picture—Vasya before and Borya after."

The woman, understanding that we felt sorry for them, brought her fourteen-year-old niece from Kharkov to live with us as well. She arrived so weak the wind could have blown her over.

By now we were nine people. The sanatorium fed us all, they didn't dare refuse. A tiny island in a sea of hunger.

Remember I told you that women have far greater fortitude than men? I observed this everywhere, not only in the camps.

When we were in the Ukraine, I began to take courses at the medical school.[4] I was almost thirty, older than the other students. But the students were very friendly, they looked out for me and shared their lecture notes with me (I frequently missed classes). Although I tried to avoid the anatomy laboratory, after all, it was obligatory. The laboratory was in the basement, with a big sign in Ukrainian—MORGUE. The shelves were heaped with corpses of men—or, more accurately—skeletons covered in skin. The skeletons were so thin, they couldn't even decompose. The corpses of little boys lay on the floor, crisscrossed over each other, and all bore a number written in aniline die. The anatomy teacher told the servant to bring us a woman's corpse.

The servant made a helpless gesture, answering, "There are none, only men."

> **Translator's Note:** To make her point Agnessa hear jumps ahead to 1943, when she was serving out her five-year sentence in the Gulag. Dolinka was one of hundreds of camps in the area of Kazakhstan called Karlag because of its proximity to Karaganda.

Later in the Dolinka camp in the winter naked corpses were stacked in the huge cold entryway to the hospital until spring. They were piled up so high that they would slip against the door. We had to press them together to

---

[4] An official document in Agulya's archive certifies that Agnessa had finished two years of a school in Rostov for paramedics (feldshers) and midwives in 1924. She would have been twenty-one. Curiously, the certificate calls her Agnessa Ivanovna Mironova: in 1924 she was still married to Zarnitsky. See figure 7 in the gallery of images following p. 154.

get out. We scarcely reacted to it—it was simply our lives. But when it got especially painful for me, I would reminisce about other things. I would take my thoughts to my former life, trying to conjure up my life with Mirosha. We are in the south in that paradise created for us by the special official sanatorium.

Do you remember Nekrasov's poem? "Oh, the south! / Yes, the south. / She dreams of the south! I'm with you again, dear friend / I'm with my beloved friend again / and he is free."[5]

But the one thing I expunged from my memory was how we ate! Our breakfasts, lunches, dinners. Had I not forbidden myself to remember the hunger would have been intolerable. But now I can speak about our meals.

We came to the sanatorium in the autumn when the south was bursting with fruit. October, beginning of November. Indian summer. The air was no longer sultry, but the sea was still warm, and there was every imaginable variety of grapes, persimmons, oranges, and not only our local fruits but imported exotic fruits as well in huge bowls on our tables. Once Mirosha and I bought nuts, and when we returned we found nuts on our tables, nuts on the branch, Greek nuts. Mirosha said jokingly to the manager, "What are you doing to us? You are depriving us of our last opportunity to spend money."

The manager laughed, "Forgive me, I forgot that you must spend money."

Oh, what chefs, what dishes they heaped on us! If only we could have indulged ourselves… But Mirosha, too, was inclined to put on weight. Following my example, he tried to restrain himself, to keep himself in good form. The doctor ordered fast days of toast and milk for him. Every one of those days Mirosha shed half a kilo. And, of course, we didn't take siestas. On the contrary, immediately after lunch we played billiards. Several hours of billiards kept us in good form. I encouraged Mirosha to take part in this regimen and he submitted, acknowledging that otherwise they would engorge us with their fantastic meals.

Before our departure for the sanatorium I would go to Kiev to buy fabric in the store reserved for people with foreign currency. Then I would have clothing sewn for me in Kiev or by my seamstress-magician in Dnepropetrovsk. Mironov constantly exhorted me to dress more modestly. He claimed that my extravagant style embarrassed him. But along with simpler garments to placate him, I sewed my elegant clothing as well—and I turned out to be right.

---

[5] The poem, written in 1871–72 by N. A. Nekrasov, tells the true story of two princesses who followed their husbands, participants in the Decembrist revolt (1825), into exile in Siberia. N. A. Nekrasov, *Russkie zhenshchiny*, in *Sobranie Sochinenii v semi tomakh* (Moscow: Knizhnyi Klub Knigove, 2010), vol. 3.

The autumn that we went to the sanatorium of the Ukrainian Central Committee in Khosta, all the young women strutted about, vying to be the best dressed. I said to Mirosha, "You see? Good thing I didn't listen to you!"

We showed off before each other, eyeing each other's toilet. Daniil Petrovsky's wife stopped us in our tracks. She wore a Venetian shawl, such a shawl! Black, with iridescent tassels of dark blue, azure, green, white, the colors blazing forth one after the other. She never removed it from her shoulders.

We sat there watching her from afar—bursting with envy, suffering. And then a functionary from the Central Committee ran over to us—I can't remember his name. He made an obsequious bow and whispered to us, "Do you know why she wears that shawl?" His eyes gleamed maliciously.

"Why?"

"Because dogs gnawed off her left breast."

All the ladies "ha, ha, ha" at his witticism.

That's how we passed the time.

It was the November 7 holiday, the anniversary of the 1918 Revolution. The manager said to us, "Now a car will come for you. Go to the hills and have a picnic. We will have everything ready for you when you return."

We sat in an open car that was already supplied with wine and containers of delicacies. Then we went to the market in Adler, another Black Sea resort town, then we swam, and then we hiked in the hills. It was an excellent day. We returned festooned with garlands made of cypress branches.

The holiday table was already set. There was a vase of flowers at each place and the forks and knives lay on a bouquet of flowers.

We rested and changed our clothes. I wore a white dress and a bow, white with blue polka dots, white shoes. In those days we didn't wear sandals.

That evening we had Postyshev, Chubar, Balitsky, Petrovsky, Uborevich, and finally Mikoyan came from Zenzinovko, where Stalin went on holidays.[6] Balitsky was master of ceremonies. Well built, lively, merry, entertaining. Seeing how we had distributed ourselves, he pretended to be shocked: "What's this? Why are the women sitting with the women and the men are sitting with the men? Up! Everybody up!"

And he took a woman by the hand, a man by the hand and sat them next to each other, then on to another pair. He ran over to me, but I played at being

---

[6] Vsevolod Apollonovich Balitsky, Pavel Petrovich Postyshev, Vlas Yakovlevich, Daniil Ivanovich Petrovsky, Ieronim Petrovich Uborevich, and Anastas Hovhannes Mikoyan were all long-time high-level officials in the Soviet secret service organs and/or members of the Politburo of the Communist Party. Postyshev and Petrovsky had taken part in the 1905 revolution. The others became members of the Bolshevik Party between 1916 and 1921. Only one person in this group, Mikoyan, died a natural death (1958). The rest were shot in the Purges of 1937–38.

capricious. "I don't want to sit next to just anyone. First I want to see who you will put next to me."

He thought for a while, faltered for a moment and then raised his eye brows and quietly said to me, "You'll sit beside me."

And he turned to the others to seat them. He sat me down, but didn't yet sit down himself. His wife was sitting across the table, screwing up her eyes and looking at me suspiciously. Everyone started to laugh because Mirosha brought a chair and slipped between me and Balitsky. He said, "I don't like this."

Balitsky whispered something in the ears of two servants. They picked up Mirosha's chair with Mirosha on it and sat him down next to the woman who had been chosen for him. Everyone laughed until tears ran down their faces.

Finally Balitsky sat down and began to flirt with me, but not for long. The master of ceremonies must make toasts and conduct the meal. I tried not to look across the table. I didn't want to impale myself on the thorns of the evil looks his wife was shooting me.

After the supper—dancing. And who didn't I dance with! While Balitskii and I danced, everyone else danced, but when I began to dance the tango with Daniil Petrovsky, the people formed a circle around us. Everyone stopped dancing to watch us. We really laid it on—he flings me away with his arm and I pretend to be falling, he pushes me away, I spring up and we are side by side again with our arms stretched. Do you actually think anyone knows how to dance the tango properly these days? Well, Daniil knew how, we understood each other without words. Postyshev is sitting in a chair, dying of laughter and his wife is laughing, too. When we stopped, we were greeted with applause.

I was hot, so I ran into the vestibule where I sat down at the piano and pounded out the melody, still keeping the rhythm of the tango .

I look up and see Uborevich. In a pince-nez, thin, well-groomed. He never takes his burning gaze off of me. I stop playing for a moment, and he says ecstatically, "How you danced!"

I played some more chords. And there is Balitsky coming into the vestibule, Balitsky and Petrovsky. Balitsky says jokingly, "Her again! She is everywhere," as if he had come upon me by accident. But he had come on purpose. He had come after me.

Mirosha suddenly appeared, whispering in my ear as soon as the chords ended.

"Stop it! Snap out of it." He really didn't appreciate my success.

I got up from the piano and very quickly walked down the stairs to the entrance and explained to the people who were gathered there. "Oh, I'm so hot."

An unknown man ran after me down the stairs, saying "How you danced!"

He approached me and whispered, "I see that you are hot. I have a car here, if you like I'll take you for a ride in the breeze. No one will know, ten minutes and you're back. Don't be afraid, I'm only offering you a ride."

Although I had had quite a bit to drink, my sense of self-preservation was very acute. I refused, of course.

This is what I think about it now.

Zenzinovko, where Stalin was vacationing, was seven kilometers from us. Allilueva had already shot herself, and he was alone.[7] That unknown man in uniform with his stupid, dense face... Mirosha taught me to recognize them. They come to all the receptions, mix with the guests, modest and unnoticed... Who was he? A procurer? Or simply a bodyguard who wanted to eavesdrop or to get a woman like me, who had such success with the men that night? To carry her away—and in the morning my corpse would be found in the hills. I can only guess.

A few days later Balitsky invited us to his house. He lived not far from the sanatorium in a mansion that had once been some rich person's dacha. He had invited only a small group. And, as usual, wherever Balitsky was, it was gay. We drank champagne and danced. I danced with Balitsky again. As a joke I opened a little Chinese parasol and hid our faces with it.

Later Mirosha was angry.

"You drank again. What was that business with the parasol? It was simply tactless."

He was jealous of course.

The Balitskys left before us. They had a train car to themselves. Several couples, husbands and wives including us, accompanied them.

This was the farewell ritual: the woman shook Balitsky's hand, gave his wife flowers, and hugged her.

When my turn came I shook Balitsky's hand, gave his wife flowers, and was about to hug her, but she abruptly and demonstratively pushed me away.

I bit my lip. It was embarrassing in front of everyone. I thought maybe Mirosha wouldn't notice, but as soon as they departed he spitefully whispered in my ear, "Well, are you satisfied?" Balitsky probably also got scolded. Remember, he wouldn't kiss me at my wedding.

CR 80

In the camp I reminisced, reminisced, to distracted myself. But there were moments when I couldn't reminisce, when memory shut down from hunger.

---

[7] Nadezhda Sergeevna Allilueva was Stalin's second wife. Their volatile marriage is often attributed to her alleged mental illness. The cause of her death in 1932 is not clear. Perhaps it was a normal death, perhaps a suicide (a gun was found by the side of her dead body). Many scholars speculate that Stalin may have killed her.

It was only when I got to the farm, where I had a bit to eat from the summer pastures, that my memory grew stronger. Then, in difficult moments I distracted myself most often remembering that time—my native south, the Black Sea, the cypress, palms, our beautiful clothes, our carefree diversions. But, of course, I could never tell anyone about my memories. What for? So they could have laughed at me, as they laughed at that prostitute in Maxim Gorky's play *The Lower Depths*. We in the camps were so ragged, so pathetic, hungry, demeaned. The way we looked, it would have been simply ridiculous to recount my triumphs. I was so yellow from everything I had suffered in prison that the others nicknamed me "the Japanese."

I remember how in one barracks in Kazakhstan the "ladies" swore at me up and down because of my fur coat.

"Hey, what's this, a new arrival?"

"Yes, a new one—ta-dum! And with such a fur coat, ta-ta-ta-dum. Full of fleas, they love fur, tra-la-la..."

I tried to reason with them: "That's not correct, fleas love bodies, not fur."

"Who cares, mother fucker, as soon as you lay down here my whole body began to itch. Fucking fleas attacked me from your fur coat."

That's how they greeted me in that barracks. They were just calming down when a woman guard came. She was not entirely in her right mind, but she came right to the point.

"A newcomer?" she asked. "What's your surname?"

"Mironova."

"Mironova? I knew a Mironov, he was a big boss in Alma-Ata. What a handsome guy. And his wife was a regular princess, and even more interesting, she was a beautiful woman. Are they relatives of yours?"

"No," I answered softly and pulled the stinking sackcloth that served as a blanket up around my face. I could hardly tell her that it was I—this woman in filthy clothes that showed only a nose.

ॐ ॐ

I have already told how I went looking for clothes in Kiev. I couldn't trust Mirosha to buy things. He always bought exactly the wrong thing. But I tried to arrange it so that I always went with him on his trips.

On one of his trips to Kiev, one of Balitsky's deputies began to invite us to his mansion. It was not far from the museum of sea monsters. We went there every day. Mironov became addicted to those meetings. Three men sat together—Balitsky's deputy, Mirosha, and another high official—and recklessly played cards. Moreover, they played for big sums of money. Balitsky didn't take part, and he didn't even know what they were doing. They played in the study. We wives sat in the dining room and, for lack of anything better to do, put a nail in the coffin of all of our acquaintances.

Later in the evening Mirosha calls out, "Aga, give me some money!" That means that he was losing. I gave it to him, what else could I do? I was furious, I could say goodbye to all the shopping I wanted to do. When we left, I reproached him.

"Look how much you lose!"

And he bursts out laughing. "Don't worry, you'll get all that money back."

And, amazingly, I did. Not a day passed that Mironov didn't bring money home—a lot.

I understood everything when once when I accompanied Mirosha to Moscow. They put us up in a two-room suite in the Hotel Metropole. Three men gathered to play cards in the evening. That same deputy of Balitsky, Mirosha, and one of his colleagues. I came into the room silently and stood behind the chair; I can see that Mirosha has a very strong hand. But he shrugs his shoulders as if he were upset and says, "Well, looks like your cards take the pot."

Then he noticed me and said with annoyance: "What are you doing here? Get out." I obeyed, wondering why he chased me out. And suddenly it was all clear. He didn't want me to understand that he was deliberately losing. But why?

Was he currying favor?

He and another bigwig in Kiev lost to Balitsky's assistant. They lose, and soon afterward the winner invites them into his study to work and gives them money in an envelope. Under Stalin those envelopes were handed out to all the higher-ups as if to say, here is something for doing this or that. It was money from some special funds which the recipient donor could not spend on himself. But he could take money out if he justified it as payment to another colleague for some task. The money he won at cards was a way of his reward from the losers.

But then something happened. One time Mironov received an envelope with five thousand rubles. For some reason we immediately took the money to the deputy's mansion. Mirosha says to me, "Hide this. Don't tell anyone that I asked you to do it and under no circumstances tell anyone that you have it."

I wrapped the money up in paper and when we got to the deputy's mansion I went to the toilet and put the envelope in some heavy tights under a long dress. They began to play cards. Suddenly Mirosha comes out of the study.

"Darling wife, give me some money"

I reply sadly (after all, I am an actress, I'm always playing a role with the other wives), "I have none."

"What do you mean? I gave you some money."

" Oh dear, I left it at home," showing him my empty purse.

The deputy's wife says, "I'll lend you some."

"Never mind," and Mirosha went back into the study.

Why he did he do that, why didn't he didn't want to lose money on that occasion? He never told me.

Mikhail Davydovich Korol, Mirosha's respected older cousin, was always distressed with the way Mirosha lived. He was appalled at the card-playing, at the easy money and lavish life.

"How can you live like that," he would say to Mirosha. "What kind of environment are you in? You have fallen under the influence of that life. Nothing good can come of it."

But Mirosha just laughed, dismissed it. After all, he was lucky, spoiled by his life. He had everything—good looks, intelligence, ability, success. He succeeded in everything. Everything had been given him. He was advancing without obstacles. Just at that time he got a sign of distinction. Yagoda—at that time commissar of internal affairs—gave Mirosha four special patches on his uniform, signifying that he had the status of an army commander.

෪ ෨

Mirosha had two lives. One was with me. That's the one I will tell you about, because I knew nothing about his work life. He brutally shut me out of it once and for all.

Coming home from work he cast off all his official cares as if he had taken off a coat of armor. He wanted to think about nothing but our happy domestic affairs. He was eight years older than I, but I didn't feel the difference in age; we were comrades and we never tired of frolicking and playing at our game of love. We loved to take long hikes. Or we went to the theater or traveled somewhere "on a spree," for example, to Tbilisi, Leningrad, Odessa.

Once, when we were still in Alma-Ata, a woman from Rostov showed up. She was a relative of a family with whom Ivan Aleksandrovich and I had been friends. Her son had been arrested. Knowing that Mirosha held a high position in the OGPU, she counted on his help. She called on me when Mirosha was not at home. I understood perfectly well that I couldn't invite her to stay with us, so I placed her with a miserable young man in a petty, demeaning job whom I had been helping. I would give him Mirosha's unwanted underwear and clothing and I gave him food and found him a place to live. Now, in return, I asked him to provide a place for the newcomer. He willingly agreed and was even grateful because she began to cook tasty food for him.

For a long time I couldn't bring myself to ask Mirosha to help her. I waited and chose a moment when he was especially jolly. You should have seen how all his joy instantly drained away. He answered me coldly and sharply; all such matters are investigated locally, and if this man was arrested in Saratov, they would decide his case there; he, Mironov, has nothing to do with it and is not prepared to intercede for him. Nor would he even if it were a question of my relatives or his own.

"Yes, yes!" I cried, offended. "I know, you said yourself that you would shoot me with your own hands if they ordered you."

He immediately softened.

"Agneska," he said tenderly, "Why would I shoot you? Because you are my darling little mischievous wife? Because with you everything is so good and so happy? I told you—if I had to shoot you, I would shoot myself as well. Come on now, let's make up. Only—never again for any reason ask me to do such a thing. Let's agree once and for all. My work doesn't concern you."

And so it was. I knew nothing of his affairs. I correct myself—almost nothing. Because from time to time snippets of his other life would intrude on mine.

One day in Dnepropetrovsk I came home and was surprised to find him home in the day. I ran to his study, looked in, and saw him sitting motionless. He had not even taken off his overcoat. His expression was blank, his thoughts far away.

"What's wrong?" agitatedly.

He answered tersely, "Kirov has been killed." This was December 1, 1934.

"Who's Kirov?"

"Remember—I pointed him out to you at the station in Leningrad."

Although I had only once had a look at Kirov in Leningrad, I have excellent visual memory and I remembered. I remembered how Mirosha had somehow squeezed out a couple of free days and we decided to "revive the good old days" in Leningrad: from Moscow to Leningrad on the Red Arrow, there and return in one day. On the platform Mirosha had whispered, "Kirov, the secretary of the Leningrad party."

A man of middling height with an engaging face, Kirov had greeted us warmly, saying, "So, you've decided to visit our Leningrad."

"Killed? I was astonished. "Who killed him?"

"The assassin has been apprehended, Nikolaev is his name," and he added with a harsh grin, "They don't work very well, our Leningrad comrades, do they."

As if to say, that could never happen to him. He was relieved that it hadn't happened in his area. The comrades he was referring to were Filip Medvedev, chief of the directorate of the Leningrad NKVD and his assistant Ivan Zaporozhets. We knew them both well from the sanatorium in Sochi. Filip Medvedev—tall and portly. Zaporozhets was tall and well-built. He had distinguished himself in the Civil War and limped from a wounded leg. His wife Roza was a beauty. They had long wanted children and now I had heard a rumor that they had finally succeeded and she was in her fourth month. Every day she took long walks to strengthen herself for the birth—seven–eight kilometers and seven–eight kilometers back.

The comrades' negligence was obvious, and we all waited to see whether Medvedev and Zaporozhets would be punished for allowing such a thing to happen. Rumors, rumors—I snatched them from the wives of Mirosha's colleagues, husbands who were not as guarded as he. The women said that Nikolaev had killed Kirov out of jealousy. Kirov allegedly loved women, especially actresses—he was the head of the Mariinsky Theater (later the theater was named for him). The beautiful Latvian actress who had been Kirov's lover happened to be Nikolaev's wife.[8]

Once before Nikolaev had attempted suicide. If the day we got the news "they don't work very well, our Leningrad comrades" escaped Mirosha's lips, and he spoke with annoyance and perhaps with a bit of malicious pleasure, now he was puzzled. He could not imagine such negligence on the part of a Chekist.

Medvedev was relieved of his post and replaced by Agranov. Medvedev and the entire top level of the Leningrad NKVD were to be tried. All of us expected that they would be shot.

Stalin himself went to Leningrad to interrogate Nikolaev. It was said that a White Guard plot was discovered in Leningrad. And in Kiev as well. This was a group of Ukrainian intelligentsia—neoclassicists—writers, cultural figures, among them the poet Vlysko. I remember him because apparently he was deaf. They were allegedly nationalists preparing terrorist acts against the high echelons of Soviet power.

Right after Kirov's assassination the Central Committee issued an order to hasten the trial and shoot the group immediately, without accepting any petitions for mercy. A call went out for heightened vigilance.

Mirosha began to work from morning into the late night. Maybe because of the Kiev affair—there were more interrogations. I don't know whether Mirosha took part in it.

Medved and Zaporozhets went to trial in mid-winter. As I said, we all expected that they would be shot. But Medvedev got only three years, and the other got two. Surprising.

After I was rehabilitated, I went to see Shanina (her husband, A. M. Shanin was deputy to Yagoda—head of the NKVD from 1934 to 1936). She told me that Shanin had sent a radio receiver and phonograph records to Zaporozhets (in a Gulag) and that Bulanov (another of Yagoda's deputies) took care of Zaporozhets's family. She said that both of them were taken to the camps in special comfortable train cars. In Kolyma, the camp to which Zaporozhets was sent, he became some kind of an important boss. And Solovkov and Medvedev, who went to that camp as well, also became bosses.

We didn't know those details then, but we were astonished at their light sentences.

---

[8] Although Nikolaev's wife was of Latvian descent, she was not an actress. By all reports she was neither beautiful nor Kirov's lover.

Then the entire episode was silenced as if it had been cut out with a knife. Nadya Reznik told me in secret that her husband categorically forbade her ever to refer to it.

Now, after the XXII Party Congress (1961) we know that Kirov was assassinated on the order of the "The Great Genius" himself, that Yagoda and Zaporozhets really did act on secret orders. One writer explained it all to me. The XXII Party Congress gave a group of writers information about Kirov's assassination—many thick folders. They didn't get to read all of it, but they did learn something. For example, the keeper of Kirov's personal archive, Borisov, was very devoted to him and took his death very hard, and he was suspicious of the whole affair. Once, on his way to Smolny on Stalin's orders, he was shot, but it was explained as an automobile accident. Yet another investigator began to get suspicious. Stalin said of him, "What kind of an incompetent investigator is he that he doesn't see that Nikolaev was a member of a counterrevolutionary organization?" That investigator disappeared.

But the Congress said not a word about "the greatest leader of all time and all peoples." And those White Guardists picked up in Leningrad and shot in batches and our Ukrainian "nationalists"—they were all, of course, innocent. And Zarnitsky's parents, who were sent away somewhere from their home, now I think they were all shot.

Stalin quickly settled with the executioners as well. He always did that. First use them to kill and then eliminate them. Yagoda was head of the NKVD and brought Zaporozhets in; they didn't let Medvedev in on the secret.

Since Khrushchev's speech we know that, but then everything was just puzzling. And to know too much could be fatal.

Medvedev and Zaporozhets were shot in 1938. They were brought to Moscow. Not long ago I was told that Medvedev immediately agreed to sign everything that they threw at him—the assassination, connections with the Right and the Left and with foreign spies and other such rubbish. Further, I was told that this is what he said immediately: "It's clear that I will not get out of here alive. I know your ways. So, I will confess to whatever you like—under one condition: that you give me cognac and a new girl every day. Then when you come to shoot me, have a hearty drink yourself."

That is how the "evil conspiracy" was born.

I can say this now. But then, I repeat, we didn't know anything. Everything was puzzling.

ദ ൨

Remember, I have already spoken about Frinovsky and how he took Zarnitsky's job in Rostov. Frinovsky was part of the border patrol forces. He was never assigned to secret service work. Yagoda didn't like him.

But now Frinovsky commanded the border army of the entire Soviet Union. He and Mirosha started off together. Frinovsky, it seems, was among those whom Evdokimov brought with him to Rostov.

We met with him in the sanatoriums in the Caucasus. He was presumptuous and jowly. And his wife Nina was very vulgar—plain, pug-nosed, and heavily and tastelessly made up. Mirosha and I made fun of her. Mirosha told me about an incident involving her, howling with laughter.

"Once I was in a restaurant sitting across from her. It was hot and she was perspiring and suddenly I see that from her eyebrows and eyelashes there is a stream of black mixed with her rouge streaming down her face from her chin, drip-drip in a cup."

But when we went to Sochi in the autumn of 1936, Mirosha said to me, "Take a look at Nina. She used to look like a prostitute, but now she has become an interesting woman."

I didn't believe my eyes—what a change! It seems that she had come directly from Paris. There they "did her up" and found a style for her. They showed her how to do her hair, how to coordinate her cosmetics, her clothing. I remember that she was wearing a dress with blue checks, a blue ribbon in her hair. Everything looked good on her, she was barely recognizable. She was fully aware of it, too, and held herself proudly.

In September of 1936 Yezhov replaced Yagoda as head of the NKVD (Commissariat of Internal Affairs). As soon as we got the news, Nina was entirely alight. She didn't hide her hopes from me: "This is very good. Yezhov is our great friend."

They had had holidays together and the families had grown close. And in fact a few days later I read in the newspaper: Frinovsky has been appointed deputy to the NKVD. You can imagine how the sanatorium reacted! All the underlings began to court her.

She left the following day. We accompanied her to her car, where she was making her farewells to everyone. She wore a black hat, an elegant black suit with a close-fitting jacket, light colored gloves. She singled me and Mirosha out, hugged me and looked deeply into my eyes.

If Frinovsky moved up in the world then all of the border employees, comrades of his past, could hope to ascend as well.

This time we were not deceived. In December 1936 Mirosha got an order: immediately leave all your affairs in Dnepropetrovsk and go to Novosibirsk—to be the head of the administration of the NKVD of all of Western Siberia.

☙ ❧

We went to Siberia through Moscow. We received an invitation to the palace in the Kremlin. Stalin read the new constitution to us, The Chosen. He read softly. Like the other wives I had a guest's ticket to the balcony and I couldn't hear more than half. The press and our husbands sat below in the orchestra.

I saw Stalin up close several times in my life. He was not tall. His face was pock-marked and he had a strong Georgian accent. He read softly and slowly in order to sound weighty. Even when he spoke of the most banal things, it sounded imposing.

It was very stuffy in the balcony. After all, on such weighty occasions we had to look like "bluestockings," we had to wear heavy suits. We couldn't even wear light dresses. I couldn't stand it and I decided that no matter what, I would go to the buffet to at least get some air.

At the door I was immediately stopped by two men who led me to the foyer, asked for my ticket and my passport and stared back and forth between me and my passport for a long time. If I had had to go to the toilet, I wouldn't have been able to hold it back.

I bought tangerines, returned to my seat, and they stopped me again for a long time, again—"your passport!" And again they scrutinized my face, comparing it to the passport. And when I went into the hall one of them was still on my heels. What did they think? That I bought a bomb in the buffet to throw at "his greatness?"

I sat down. The women around me began to ask for some tangerines, give it, give it, we'll buy more for you at the intermission. I gave most of them away and strained to listen some more, making a serious, important face, trying to hear at least something. But I could hear almost nothing.

Finally he finished reading to applause and ovations. This lasted a long time, and when it died down I spoke to an acquaintance who was seating next to me. "What a good constitution," I said.

She looked at me haughtily, condescendingly. "It is not for us, with our chicken brains, to judge such things."

That is to say, it was not *for me* to judge, but that she probably could. As if to say, you of course cannot understand such lofty matters.

She was arrested soon after, ground into the dust, squelched. She and I had an acquaintance in common whom I told, "Remind her, please, about the Great Constitution, and tell her that we, with our chicken brains, cannot judge her."

I was told that when she heard that she was not angry she wept. I, of course, don't hold grudges.

CB BO

I took everyone with us to Novosibirsk. Of course, Maria Nikolaevna—I can't manage without her. She was a wonderful cook. In those days I couldn't cook at all. In general, I didn't bother with the domestic affairs, I lived the "society" life. Everything was brought to us already prepared. I didn't have to worry about anything, the underlings did everything.

And of course I brought my people: Mama, Lena and Borya, and Agulya.

Agulya—she was named after me—was the daughter of my younger brother Pavel, or Pukha as we called him. Pukha had married a very young girl and they had two daughters. The older one was Tanya and the younger—Agulya. His wife, a sluggard, left him with the two children.

Mirosha really wanted children. It was his unfulfilled dream. He had no children with his first wife, Gusta, but they were together during the Civil War. Gusta also pranced around on a horse in Budennyi's cavalry with Mirosha. And now he had no children with me. I don't know who was responsible for that.

So here were these two abandoned girls, because actually no one really wanted them. Pukha was already aiming to marry again. So we took Agulya when she was one and a half years old. We would have taken Tanya as well—she was two years older than Agulya—but she was already sentient and was very sensitive to family relations. When Agulya was three years old, however, we brought Tanya to Dnepropetrovsk. Tanya immediately told Agulya that we were not her relatives and Agulya ran to us in an uproar. Then we had to decide that Tanyechka should no longer live with us. We raised Agulya like our own daughter. She never for a minute doubted that we were her parents. She was spoiled, like any only child, lively, impudent, mischievous. Mirosha said, "Just like you."

Mirosha's family invented a legend to the effect that Mirosha and I reproached each other, that we each blamed the other for the fact that we had no children. The story went that I decided to prove to him that it was not my fault. I pretended to be pregnant, I went off some place and returned with Agulya. Alter (Mikhail Davydovich) clapped his hands in glee at that story: "You played a joke on a Chekist!" he crowed to me.

But it was completely untrue. Mirosha knew that Agulya was my niece, but he was as attached to her as he would have been to his own daughter. And Agulya adored him in return.

In Novosibirsk we were given the mansion of a former governor-general. Guards were posted at our gates to protect us. We had a huge garden with a stage on which visiting and local actors would perform. We had a separate little house for playing billiards. A film viewing room had been constructed for us inside the mansion. And I, as the first lady of the city, chose from a list the films that I wanted to see on any given day.

I had my own "court," surrounded by "ladies-in-waiting"—the wives of the top personnel. It was I who chose whom to invite and whom not to invite, and they competed for my good will. They could advise, but the choice of films was ultimately mine.

We would sit in the hall watching a film; the "sycophants" bring us fruit, cakes. Ah, maybe that's not the right word for them. It would be more precise to call them "attendants." They tried very hard to foresee all of our desires.

They hovered around us. These days they would be called "attendants" not "servants" as they were called in the past.

What cakes they brought us, inside there was ice-cream with hot spirits that you could eat without burning yourself. Imagine, in the half darkness you could see the blue light of the cakes.

True, I didn't eat these cakes very often because I was always watching my weight. More often I ate oranges.

My ladies-in-waiting, the sycophants, didn't dare make a peep against me. Only with Mirosha did I occasionally argue about which film to watch. He always asked for *Gypsy Campground* with Lyalya Chernaya. There was a scene showing two gypsies fighting with whips and killing each other. Mirosha asked for that film so many times that I got angry; Enough—watch your *Campground*, separate out the scenes with your Lyalya Chernaya and revel in them!

Of course I was jealous.

ଔ ଓ

Soon after we arrived we were invited to Eikhe's. Robert Indrikovich Eikhe, a Latvian Communist, had become first secretary of the Western Siberian borderland.

Now, imagine this. Winter, Siberia, a freezing forty degrees below zero centigrade, all around us forest. Spruces, pines, larches. We are in the middle of nowhere, the taiga, and suddenly a clearing in the frost and snow, a gate and behind it, glittering with lights from top to bottom—a palace!

We mount the stairs to be greeted by a doorman who bows respectfully and opens the door. From the frost we have tumbled right into tropical warmth. The sycophants—excuse me—the attendants help us to take off our coats, and it is warm, warm like summer. We are in a huge vestibule lit up by candles. Before us—a staircase covered with a soft carpet and to the right and to the left, fresh blooming lilies in vases on each stair. I had never seen such luxury, the likes of which we didn't have even in our governor's mansion.

We walk into the hall. The walls are covered with reddish brown silk, the drapes, the table. In a word, a fairy tale. The pen cannot describe what we saw.

Eikhe greets us—tall, lean, stern. It was said of him that he was honorable and cultured, but not dignified. He extends his hand to Mirosha, but only throws a glance at me. I was beautifully and tastefully dressed. Barely glancing at me, he greets me negligently. I immediately felt scorned. To this very day I can't forget it. A table was set in the hall as it might have been in the tsar's palace. There are several women, all of them "bluestockings," dressed somberly and without a hint of make-up. Eikhe presents us to his wife, Yelena Yevseevna, who is wearing a severe but well designed English suit. I already knew that she was a well educated woman with two academic degrees. And here I am in a lavender dress shot with gold, bare neck and shoulders (I always believed that a woman should not hide her body and should display it within respectable bounds). I was wearing high-heeled shoes and cosmetics. My goodness, what a contrast! In all their eyes, of course, I was empty-headed and trivial trash. At that moment I understood why Eikhe had looked at me with such contempt.

At the table he tried to be polite, extending to me the menu for the first course, asking what I would like to choose. I didn't know myself, I was so scattered. I admitted that I didn't know. And he spoke to me as to a child, indulgently, even tenderly:

"Let me suggest. Order the fricassee of veal."

I ordered it. This is what it turned out to be: the transparent gristle of the calf pressed into the shape of a pancake, with the testicles rolled in breadcrumbs and fried.

"So, what do you think? Tasty."

"Very!"

The conversation was about this and that. How do you like Siberia? What do you think of our winter? It's very dry here so the frost is easier to bear. All the things that are usually said about Siberia.

Then the men adjourned to an adjacent room to play billiards. Mirosha—broad and solid; Eikhe—tall, dry, lean.

I would happily have joined them to play billiards. But I understood that it would not be acceptable. None of the women joined them. We sat in a circle, all the "bluestockings" and I, the brilliant canary. They all converse, excluding me except for murderous glances. Perhaps they were all scholars, like Yelena Yevseevna; they all held positions in the party, they were definitely *party types*.

I was silent because I could not participate in their conversation. But I listened. And, you know, their conversation was not so different from ours. We look each other over, who is wearing what; who has gone abroad, what to sew, and then—about this one and that one; who has been appointed to what post, who rose and who fell and why, who replaced him. I don't remember that kaleidoscope of names, but I remember that the conversation was like a game of chance: this one won, this one lost, this one is relieved of his job, this one doesn't deserve his post.

Finally, thank God, they brought us a list of films. Yelena Yevseevna chose and we all went to the viewing room.

When we got home Mirosha asked "So how was it?" He understood that I was uncomfortable there.

"How was it? How was it? They don't consider me a person."

Mirosha answers in an ironic tone, "I'm always telling you to dress more modestly."

But he himself could not stand the "bluestockings."

"I love you because you are so womanly," he said.

"And what else am I supposed to be?"

"I don't like them in caps and boots, and also smoking. Phooey! When you do up your hair, when you wear something new and short—I like it."

଴ ଺

Mirosha immersed himself in work. He would come home very tired and, I observed, very nervous. Formerly he had been able to conceal the torments he endured at work, but now they began to eat away at him. That little crevice through which I could glimpse his other life grew wider, revealing now this, now that.

When we came to Novosibirsk, A. I. Uspensky was appointed Mirosha's deputy. Mirosha couldn't bear him. He said that Uspensky was not a person but scum, an unprincipled, fickle careerist. Uspensky's work irritated and revolted Mirosha. The "Kemerovo trial" of saboteurs in the Kuzbas had taken place in 1936, not long before we came to Novosibirsk. A group of engineers in charge of a massive mining and industrial complex in the Kuzbas (short for the Kuznetsky coal basin in the south of Western Siberia) was accused of widespread sabotage.[9] Uspensky boasted that he had organized the trial after allegedly uncovering an underground printing press. He claimed that it was he who forced the engineers to confess.[10]

Mirosha, as I've already told you, normally slept like the dead. No sooner did his head touch the pillow than he was snoring. No one but I could sleep in the same room. He snores, and I sleep. Joking aside, I was so accustomed to it that I slept even better to the sound of his snoring. Suddenly, he goes to bed and doesn't snore. In the unaccustomed silence I can't sleep either. I understand that something is wrong.

"Mirosha, has something happened?"

What a miracle! Abandoning his usual restraint, he confides in me.

One of the engineers sentenced for sabotage in the Kemerovo trial asked to meet with Mironov. Alone in a room with Mirosha, the engineer told him in a tremulous voice, "I know what awaits me. I only want to say that I am guilty of nothing. We repeatedly wrote reports criticizing the inadequate safety measures in the mines, but no one paid attention to our reports. And when the explosions occurred, they sentenced us for sabotage." Further, he

---

[9] Although the 1936 catastrophe in the mines of the Kuzbas was neither the first nor the worst in that region, Stalin used the incident to divert attention from the inadequacies of this industrial complex with an open trial of the alleged treachery of Trotskyite terrorists.

[10] In the autumn of 1938, as Beria was replacing Yezhov as the head of the NKVD, Uspensky saw the handwriting on the wall and faked a suicide. He left a note to the effect that his corpse could be found in the river Dnieper. He was caught in 1940, arrested, and shot.

described the workers' appalling living and working conditions and how helpless the engineers were to improve them.

His voice and words lingered in Mirosha's ears. Mirosha lay awake all night. That's when he said to me that Uspenskii was not a person but scum.

"Why can't you write a report about him, so that he can be removed, sent someplace else?" I asked.

"How can I report him, when he is related to Yezhov?" he objected.

Soon afterwards another batch of prisoners from Kemerovo arrived, among them Shatov. Shatov was our good acquaintance from Alma-Ata days who later went to the Kuzbas to work as an engineer.[11] He, too, asked to meet with Mirosha. When they met, Mirosha told me, Shatov pretended that they didn't know each other. Mirosha did not tell me what they talked about, but he was very upset. Again, he couldn't sleep. He smoked, he thought, he ignored my questions.

Now I often ask myself—was Mirosha an executioner? Of course I want to think that he was not. Everything I've just told you proves that he wasn't. I remember still other facts that I'll tell you about later. But for now I will simply explain how I see it.

He willingly joined the Red Army, he fought against the bandits in the Caucasus in the name of Soviet power—the Soviet power that opened the door for him and gave us access to everything we had. He was devoted to Soviet power until the end. He was ambitious and audaciously pursued his career. When the terrifying trials of extermination began—wave after wave—he couldn't extricate himself from the machine, he was forced to crank it and to do as he was told. But the scales fell from his eyes. He saw it for what it was. That's what I think. That's what I want to think.

I compare him to Eikhe. In those days I didn't like Eikhe. I didn't understand then, but recently I learned that at the Plenum in February and March of 1937, Eikhe wasn't afraid to speak out against the repression. So when they arrested him they accused him of not exposing enough saboteurs and enemies of the people in Western Siberia.

And so it was for Mirosha. That's exactly how it was. After all, they were in charge of everything. I will give you an illustration, because I understand it all now. It took place before the incident with Shatov.

One day I was feeling lonely for Mirosha, and I decided to visit him at work. The reception room is full of people, big shots in epaulets, carrying briefcases. I don't recognize them. Are they visitors? I walk by them with my nose in the air. Mirosha is at his desk—broad, solid, serious—concentrating

---

[11] Vladimir Sergeevich Shatov (1897–1943) was a gifted engineer, responsible for the construction of several important railway lines. In 1936 he was in charge of building a railroad through central Kazakhstan, mainly with prisoners' labor. Accused by the authorities of slowing down the tempo of construction, Shatov was arrested. He was either shot soon after or died in a camp in 1943.

on the papers before him, his brow furrowed. He sees me and says with annoyance, "Can't you see that I'm busy, Aga? You'll have to wait."

I go into the neighboring room from which I can hear everything, but he says, "No, not there. Go to the secretary."

What's going on? He's sending me away? Is he expecting another woman?

"No," I say capriciously, "I want to stay here."

Mirosha presses a button to summon the secretary, who politely invites me to leave with him. I hold my own: no, I won't go.

Then Mironov leaps up in a huff and stalks out of the room, taking the secretary with him. As if I were being whipped, I dart out into the street past all those big shots with briefcases. The guards shout out to me, "Documents! documents!" But I break away.

Very well, Mirosha, I think to myself, now you can wait.

I don't go home. I sit in a park until night, imagining him coming home and asking, "Where's Aga?" They answer, "We don't know, she has been gone since morning."

Let him worry.

Around midnight, chilled to the bone, I go home. Mirosha is in bed, still awake. Without a word I lie down with my back to him. He says soothingly, trying to be conciliatory, that it was all nothing. "Oh, you! How you eluded the guards." I remain sulky, silent. He lets off, adding bitterly, "Ah, Agneska, Agneska!" He jumps out of bed and swallows some phenobarbital. Obviously, he can't sleep. I conclude that it's because of me. He loves me in spite of everything.

But it wasn't that at all. The next evening as we prepared to watch a film, my "ladies-in-waiting" told me what had happened as if it were a secret locked up behind seven locks. It turns out that all the region's bosses had been called to a closed conference.[12] A secret order had been issued to arrest Pyotr Gavrilovich Rud, that very Rud about whom Evgenia Ginzburg writes—remember? Mirosha had worked with him in the Caucasus. Subsequently this Rud became head of the NKVD of the Northern Caucasus and then of Kazan. He was being arrested for not having fished out enemies of the people—Trotskyists and the like. He had made too few arrests.

Aha, few arrests means that you are not doing battle. Are you covering up, shielding? The order was read out to all the bosses as an exhortation. Instructions of the NKVD.

Everyone understood perfectly: if you want to survive—not to speak of advancing—invent! Or take the consequences.

---

[12] See Appendix 1, letter sent by Mironov to the chiefs of all the NKVD heads in Western Siberia ordering the launch of an enormous act of repression involving thousands of "enemies of the people."

○3 ४०

Two days later Mirosha came home for lunch with Ivan Yefremovich, his assistant. They had become good friends. Sitting at the table Mirosha says to him, "Listen, Ivan Yefremovich. Even if we have to share Rud's fate, we will not fill quotas. Anyway, all the others fake their statistics!"

As a matter of fact, a bit earlier Eikhe had asked Mirosha to check out some former Trotskyists. Uspensky wanted to arrest them, but Mirosha wouldn't allow it. Mirosha was well acquainted with one of them. Once we met him on the street.

"You harbor Trotskyist views?" Mirosha asked.

"I stopped believing that stuff long ago," he answered.

"Just so you understand," said Mirosha, playfully shaking a finger at him, as if it were all a joke. But neither of them laughed.

Perhaps Eikhe was passing down the order to arrest Trotskyists knowing full well that Mirosha would not arrest them. Perhaps.

They were all arrested later.

○3 ४०

Mirosha and I had yet another misunderstanding. Suddenly he was called urgently to Moscow. Normally I went with him, and he was pleased to have me. But this time he said to me, "Stay home. My railway car is being renovated and won't be ready until tomorrow at the earliest. So I have to take a plane." With that he abruptly left for the airport.

I took myself off to the manager of the train station.

"Will Mironov's railway car be ready tomorrow?"

"Tomorrow? Yes, it will."

"I want to go to Moscow."

When my "ladies-in-waiting" learned that I was going, they crowded around me, twittering, "Take me. And me. And me." And why not? If they went on their own they'd have to pay for their own tickets. With me, it was all gratuitous. I, of course, agreed.

At home the servants prepared food for the journey. It was February, cold and damp. But the train car was well heated and cozy. We hardly knew it was winter. On the very first day we started playing poker and never stopped. We never even saw the road. The train conductor sat with us for the entire trip. He was young, scarcely more than a boy, and he happily played poker with us until he lost his last kopek. As we approached Moscow we glanced at each other and without uttering a word agreed that we must let him win something back. So we began to lose on purpose. As his luck turned, or so he thought, his head swelled with a false sense of his importance. How his eyes glistened!

Suddenly Moscow loomed before us. We hadn't even noticed it. Our belongings were strewn all over the place, and we had to hastily collect everything.

Mirosha was waiting for me on the platform. Novosibirsk had informed him that I was arriving. Stony-faced and unsmiling, he softly asked,

"Why have you come?" And, jerking his head towards the women, "And why have you brought *them?*"

I had no answer.

We went to the Hotel Moscow to an elegant suite with a living room and bedroom. There was a bowl of grapes and huge, juicy pears on the table. "Sergei Naumovich requests that I obtain fresh fruit for you. Is this satisfactory?" the concierge asked.

Aha, I thought. That means that Mirosha has been expecting me.

We enter the bedroom. Mirosha says softly, "Ordzhonikidze is dead. Tell no one. They say he killed himself. The official version is that he had a heart attack."[13] He sighs. "Now do you realize what an awkward moment you have chosen to follow me? And with *them*, as if you were coming to a festival. I suppose you played cards the entire trip. Why? Why? I *told* you to stay home. What am I supposed to say if I'm questioned?"

I made a mournful, tragic face. "You will say," I sighed, "that I came to join you in mourning the death of a great leader."

Mirosha couldn't hold back. He burst out laughing.

Truly, at that time I didn't give a damn about this or that Ordzhonikidze. I was totally indifferent to all those Leaders, those big shots. I couldn't tell one from another.

I made Mirosha laugh, I amused him. I could always do that. Within a half hour he was saying to me, "What would I do without you? You naughty, mischievous thing. You are a "ray of light in the kingdom of darkness." He was quoting the title of Ostrovsky's play, but it was absolutely accurate. I was also naive and ignorant. But it suited Mirosha very well.

I understood nothing. There was one arrest after another. All of Yagoda's cronies were arrested. They arrested Shanin, Bulanov, and Agranov. Shanin had been Yagoda's first assistant. I knew his wife Valya Shanina very well. She died not long ago. Years later we met again after we had been reha-

---

[13] Georgy Konstantinovich Ordzhonikidze was, like Stalin, a Georgian. His revolutionary activity began in the 1905 revolution. Shortly afterward he threw his lot in with the Bolsheviks and was instrumental in securing Armenia and Georgia and other places in the Caucasus for the Bolshevik cause. In 1930 he became commissar of Soviet heavy industry and organized several grandiose construction projects. Although he and Stalin were close, Ordzhonikidze was critical of the repressions and several times intervened to save the lives of comrades or to mitigate their sentences. He died in 1937. The cause of his death has never been satisfactorily established: suicide or murder on Stalin's orders?

bilitated, and she recounted to me how her husband had been arrested. Shortly before his arrest I spent a dreary evening with them. They lived in anxious expectation.

Valya was an active party worker. When she returned home from work on the day of the arrest, the housekeeper told her that her husband was asleep. He was recovering from an ulcer, which in those days was treated with phenobarbital. Valya lay down beside him. Suddenly the room was swarming with men in NKVD uniforms who descended on Shanin's bed and grabbed his arms in case he was armed. He awoke and tried to wriggle free. "You are under arrest!" Shanin asked them to call in the housekeeper. They consulted among themselves and acquiesced. He asked her to collect some warm things and some underwear. They took him away.

Valya dressed herself and went into the other room, where she found Frinovsky. He insisted that he had not been party to the arrest. He had simply accompanied his men. He kissed her hand, asking, "How are you?" Was he mocking her? Not at all. He was simply being gallant.

Then they sent her to Astrakhan on a party assignment. She took only a small suitcase. Her premonition had not betrayed her; two weeks later she was arrested in Astrakhan. When they came to take her, she went to the window. They grabbed her. "Don't worry," she told them. "I'm not about to jump."

They say that Chertok and some others succeeded in shooting themselves.[14] Later I found out that in that year more than 3,000 of Yagoda's people perished. And what can one say about Trotskyists and all the other left-right "deviationists"?

After Valya was rehabilitated she got a personal pension of 120 rubles—for her service to the party. Shanin was not rehabilitated.

When we returned to Novosibirsk from Moscow, some kind of commission came to see us. It was headed by a man with the same surname as Mirosha. This other Mironov was the head of the economic department of the NKVD that supervised all engineering projects. He was one of Yagoda's men. In his time he had interrogated Kamenev.[15] Stalin had been irritated that this Mironov had not extracted a confession from Kamenev. Still, he had advanced famously, this Mironov. Just one thing; now all the Yagoda men had been eliminated by Yezhov.

---

[14] Leonid Chertok was one of the NKVD's most feared interrogators. His brother-in-law described him as a "sadist and hangman." In 1937, as Yezhov made a clean sweep of Yagoda's staff, Chertok threw himself out of his apartment window.

[15] Lev Borisovich Kamenev (1883–1936). Kamenev, a Bolshevik revolutionary, was one of the original Bolshevik leaders in the 1917 revolution. He was head of state of the infant Soviet Union in 1917 and acting premier in 1923–24. Breaking with Stalin in 1925, his status in and out of the Party vacillated according to the exigencies of Stalin's rise to power. He was in the first group of Old Bolsheviks that Stalin put to death in 1936.

He arrived with a whole retinue of charming officers, wonderful dancers who kissed all the ladies' hands. Mirosha arranged a reception for them. It was winter, but we had fresh hothouse produce from a special Novosibirsk greenhouse. To a man they threw themselves on the vegetables and the fruits.

Mironov the Guest had the seat of honor. He caught sight of our daughter Agulya (she was four years old), and he attached himself to her. He couldn't tear himself away. He took her on his lap, stroked her head, whispered in her ear. She was charmed. It seemed very strange to me. He didn't court the women, nor did he pay attention to the men. He ate and drank and turned to the child for some tenderness.

Later I said to Mirosha, "This Mironov was sad."

Mirosha became very agitated and asked, as if he were challenging me, "What are you dreaming up? Why in the world should he be sad? We received him with great respect."

A week later our guest Mironov and his entire retinue were arrested. Moscow had sent them to us on purpose, to arrest them outside the public eye. They often did that.

And now I wonder... Is it possible that Mirosha was ordered to arrest them? First to invite them, bring them into the family, and then—bang!—arrest them and secretly deliver them to Moscow? Was this Mirosha's hand?

I don't know...

ଔ ଓ

Winter in Novosibirsk. I loved the Siberian winter, especially as spring approached and the sun appeared again. After all, Mama was Siberian. True, I grew up in the south, but when the frost was dry and the snow crunched beneath your feet, it was delightful and invigorating.

I decided to amuse myself by learning to ski. Our chauffeur drove me to a nearby ski base. The head instructor outfitted me with skis and boots, and I learned quickly. Before long I was covering great distances. I loved it! The snow sparkled, and one could see the blue ski track between the shaggy branches of the fir trees weighed down by snow almost to the ground.

The instructor, observing that I skied long distances, said, "I see that you have really taken to skiing, but I must warn you that as the spring approaches the snow begins to melt, and one can fall into hidden caves. That's happened to a few skiers here. We couldn't find them for a long time and they perished."

I paid no attention to him, so he began to ski with me. Now I understand that they were terrified that something might happen to me. They were afraid of Mirosha.

And Mirosha—Mirosha was also afraid.

For a long time I didn't understand how tense, how anxious and apprehensive he was. But once... He had a huge billiard room at work. From time to time I would go to his office, and if he had a free hour we would play a game or two. Once as we were happily playing, just as he was about to take his turn he suddenly stood stock still, gripping the cue in his hands. He turned pale. I followed his gaze. From the enormous window of the billiard room we could see three soldiers in service caps with red bands.

"Mirosha," I whispered. "What's wrong with you?" Suddenly I understood. "Mirosha, it's only the changing of the guard."

And, in fact, two mounted soldiers appeared to replace them at the sentry box. It was only that for some reason they had momentarily entered the court yard.

I have already described how warmly Eikhe received us at his princely dacha in the forest. We went there often. He had yet another dacha, just as luxurious but smaller and cozier.

Once Mirosha and I went, just the two of us. Only Eikhe and his wife were there. I don't count the servants. His wife was in bright pink lounging pajamas. At home I wore blue lounging pajamas. It was all very unpretentious and homey. True, Eikhe's attitude toward me had not changed. To me he behaved like a haughty grandee. He was probably asking himself, "What kind of a person is she anyway? All she cares about is her rags. Nothing like my wife Yelena Yevseevna who has two degrees and does lofty Party work." He was so proud of Yelena Yevseevna. Perhaps now I would see him differently, for now he is spoken of as an extremely honorable, principled man who put himself in grave danger because he was never afraid of speaking out against the repression or against the "great genius" Stalin. But I knew nothing of this. I could only see that he seemed to despise me.

They gave us a luxurious room on the second floor. It was cold, but we had great bear skins to put over the covers. One sleeps so well when the air is fresh and cold but one is well covered. I awoke at dawn. Still groggy, I sensed that Mirosha was not asleep either. I was right. He was awake.

"What's the matter?"

He whispered, "You know, I think that my secretary is spying on me."

"Osipov? What nonsense!"

"He sticks to me…"

"Oh, Mirosha, again? Just like with the changing guard!"

I tried to sooth him with caresses, but I was uneasy, infected by that pervasive psychosis—fear! I didn't show how I was feeling, but I too was haunted by the thought that they were sneaking up on Mirosha.

The men went off in the morning after breakfast. Yelena Yevseevna approached me, so interesting and so self-confident in her pink pajamas. She behaved as if she were my mother. Of course she was not only older than I, but more clever. I had only finished the gymnasium.

"You're not happy, my dear."

I burst into tears. Startled, she sat down beside me and looked into my eyes.

"What is it?" She clearly wanted to soothe and comfort me.

"I quarreled with Mironov."

"That's not like you two." She looked at me shrewdly, but with kindness. She was puzzled.

You may wonder why I didn't confess the truth to her. You can't imagine what those times were like. To confess to her would have aroused her suspicions. All you had to do was give an inch to make everyone suspicious. Everyone was suspicious of everyone else.

I pulled myself together and suggested that we go skiing. And, after all, I am cheerful, even frivolous, by nature. My bad mood just dissipated by itself.

Ah, Yelena Yevseevna, Yelena Yevseevna, how I would like to meet you now! I would tell you everything. There is no longer anything to hide. Perhaps now we would understand each other.

How could I have known then that the Eikhes were afraid as well? This was after that Plenum where he spoke out so candidly. Only now, when I recall the circumstances, do I understand how afraid they were.

03 80

Mirosha was informed that he had a new assignment. Where, why, he didn't say, but it was clear that it was a promotion. A special train was coming for us.

And what about Eikhe? Suddenly I perceived a different Eikhe from the one who had received us so ceremoniously in his country palace or even more intimately and affectionately at his ski chalet. I saw an ingratiating, servile man stripped of his pride. He became extremely attentive and courteous to me. At table he sat beside me and talked his head off about politics, about China, about Chiang Kai-shek. No shadow of contempt or arrogance passed his face when I confessed that all of those Chinese-Japanese names made my head swim. It was like signing a statement about my ignorance. He quickly changed the subject and began to ask my opinion of a film that he knew I had seen. He so wanted to find a common language with me, to make some contact. Hoping I would tell Mirosha that he repeated endlessly how much he lamented our impending departure, how we had become such dear friends, how he and Mirosha had worked so well together. Of course, Mirosha's sudden advance meant that he had some kind of power. As he advanced, he could offer protection. He could become a support, or so Eikhe hoped, in a world that seemed to be crumbling around us.

Was Eikhe a toady? How can I blame him when it was truly a matter of his and his wife's survival? He already felt as if he were hanging over a precipice by a slender thread. He was soon to be appointed People's Commissar of Agriculture for a short time. All the more shattering his ultimate fall.

Mirosha was ordered to be ready in three days. Take nothing unwieldy, he was told, only suitcases. We were to travel part of the way by car and the road would be difficult. Therefore, I couldn't take Mama with us. She was too frail.

"You're abandoning me?" she asked bitterly.

"Mama, you won't survive the trip. God knows where they're sending us."

What I didn't say was that I feared they might arrest us as they had that other Mironov. Anything could happen. But I tried to comfort Mama.

"You'll go with Lena to Rostov. I gave her five thousand rubles to exchange her apartment for a larger one where you can have your own room."

Three days to pack—and what a mountain of things we had. I had purchased everything. From the manager of the dining room I had bought a crystal service for two thousand rubles. And so many jars of jam! Lena took everything she could and there was still heaps left over. We distributed food, sweets, all sorts to the guard, the cleaners, the sycophants.

A train came for us three days later. It was full of soldiers, many in civilian clothes.

Frinovsky commanded the train. But how he had changed. If Eikhe had become hesitant and fawning, Frinovsky had become just the opposite. He radiated self-confidence, self-satisfaction. And why not? He was now second only to Yezhov, and in the entire country only Stalin was higher than Yezhov.

When he saw Mirosha he smiled and patronizingly slapped him on the back as if to say, "now you are my protégé and that's not a bad thing!" He barely glanced at Eikhe and Yelena Yevseevna, who had come to see us off at the station. Eikhe repeated to me how sorry he was that we were leaving. Between friendly effusions he managed to whisper, "Put in a good word for me if the occasion arises." Frinovsky so monopolized Mirosha that Eikhe could not even say goodbye properly.

☙ ❧

On the train I learned of our destination. Mongolia! There Mirosha was to replace B. Kh. Tairov, who had been arrested for spying in Japan.

Oh, how our anxiety just slipped off our shoulders. Once again success had crowned Mirosha, and what success! To slip out of the vise of terror, not just any old way, but to rise even higher. He had a responsible political assignment as ambassador to Mongolia in a tense moment of international politics.[16] Was that not success? Was that not a sign of respect for him, faith in him when all around us they were seizing one after another?

---

[16] Mongolia had long been a pawn in relations between China, Japan, and Russia. In 1919 China abolished Mongolia's independence. Under Chinese occupation the Mongolian People's Party was founded and looked to Soviet Russia for help. Between 1925 and 1928 Mongolia was securely in the Soviet orbit. Japanese incursions into Manchuria gave Moscow an excuse to station troops in Mongolia. At the same time, the Great

No sooner had the breath of advancement grazed Mirosha than he noticeably cheered up and became his old self with the old self-confidence and proud bearing. Once again he was recklessly decisive. His eyes sparkled with the flame of achievement. He seemed to be reliving his youth when he had fought against counterrevolutionaries in Rostov.

Throughout the journey to Mongolia Mirosha was constantly with Frinovsky, both of them former frontier soldiers. They poured over maps, consulted, planned. Here—Outer Mongolia, there—Inner Mongolia, then—Manchuria, occupied by the Japanese. They drew lines from Manchuria to Lake Baikal, they dissected the Far East. The Japanese already had a foothold in the Far East. After Tukhachevsky and other high-ranking military had been shot in 1937, the Japanese initiated a skirmish on the Amur river and occupied the Big Island.

Frinovsky and Mirosha spent long hours studying maps. As for me, I instantly forgot my fears and began to breathe easily, joyfully. But I, too, studied with enthusiasm. The higher-ups gave to us the Rules of Behavior for Soviet Plenipotentiaries Abroad. How to dress for receptions: evening dress, shirt fronts, cuff links made of mother-of-pearl instead of imitation pearl. The foreign diplomats wore diamonds, but we, of course, couldn't. Too expensive. Imitation pearls were tasteless and vulgar, evoking scorn and smirks. Mother-of-pearl, now that is elegant and modest.

We made a stop in Irkutsk, Siberia where the local head of the NKVD invited us to spend the night at his home. We had excellent meals. Agulya played with the children, I chatted with his wife, the men went off somewhere. I went to bed alone, leaving the lamp burning for Mirosha. I was beginning to doze off when I heard him enter the room. He didn't turn off the light. I glanced at his face. He was upset. And again, I was seized by terror. A new order? Do they want us to return? Will they arrest us? Anything was possible in those feverish times.

Mirosha sat at the edge of the bed and covered his face with his hands.

"Mirosha! What's happened?"

"You can't imagine."

"What? What?" I cried, beside myself with fear.

He recounted how he and Frinovsky went to the office of the local head of the NKVD. They were interrogated by a man who did not identify himself. Frinovsky was interrogated and would not confess. Without warning the interrogator seized Frinovsky's ear, threw him to the floor, and began to beat and kick him. Mirosha was in a state of shock. When they were released, Frinovsky was flushed and breathing hard. He could scarcely pull himself together. Observing Mirosha's astonishment, Frinovsky threw him a bitter smile.

Purge spilled over into Mongolia. Agnessa correctly understood that this was a tense moment in international relations.

"What's wrong with you? Don't you understand yet? Stalin's confidential orders—if you don't confess, then expect to be beaten, beaten, beaten."

So, was Mirosha was an executioner? Of course, I don't want to believe it. His reaction to that incident—that speaks in his favor. It means that until that moment he did not approve of torture. Isn't that what it means?

I mentioned that Tairov, the dignitary who was Mirosha's predecessor, had been arrested. Once, when the train made a stop, Agulya and I took a little stroll. We were both wearing white fox cloaks and wonderful little hats. The landscape was barren, like a desert. We could see only one little house. From the void I heard a soul-wrenching howl, an inhuman cry of anguish. Then, utter silence.

"Agulya, did you hear that? Where did it come from?"

Agulya fantasized that perhaps it was a plane and that someone had yelled from the plane.

Back on the train, I asked Mirosha. "It was probably Tairov," he answered. His face was like stone.

◊ ◊

The tracks ended in Ulan-Ude. We covered the remaining six hundred kilometers by car. Mirosha, Maria Nikolaevna, Agulya, and I in a closed car, the others in an open car. We seemed to be following in the wake of war. General Konev's corps had preceded us: branches, fallen trees, a road chewed up by tanks. Rain, snow, wind. Even in the closed car we froze. You can imagine how those in the open cars felt.

We came to a place on the steppe with only a few little houses. We were still a day's journey from Ulan-Bator, the capital of the Mongolian People's Republic. Mirosha said that he and Frinovsky would now take a plane.

"Moscow is going to call us and we have to report that we've arrived in Ulan-Bator. And you will spend the night here. The women are all weary. They can't go further just now."

"No," I protested, "we can go on. We'll come with you."

I called the entourage together—several men and women who had been sent with us and some women servants. "Shall we carry on?" I asked. With one voice they answered, "Let's go."

"The women are ready to go," I told Mironov.

The men were already snoring, sprawled all over the little house. It was the men, not the women, who "can't go further." They were tired and wanted to sleep, but they used the women as an excuse.

"Well, let them stay behind," I say to Mironov. "Agulya and I will accompany you."

"Listen, don't you understand, the plane is made of plywood."

The pilot was more optimistic. We'll get there," he said merrily. "For sure."

When I asked him about the plywood, he said there was a bit of it, but mainly the plane was sturdy.

But Mirosha wouldn't budge, and even I was secretly frightened. It was just in a fit of obstinacy that I had insisted. To this day I am afraid of flying and, in fact, I've never flown. I am convinced that as soon as I sit on a plane, it is sure to crash. We got to Ulan-Bator, the capital of Mongolia, the next day just before evening. Again we slept all in one room in a small house. Agulya and I slept on a sofa, the others wherever they could find a spot. The men slept side-by-side on the floor on their overcoats.

I awoke in the morning thinking that now we would be in a real city. Ulan-Bator would have houses, transport, comforts! I was soon disabused of my illusions about the "frontier capital" to which Mirosha had been appointed "ambassador." Steppe, wind, a few European-style houses, the rest— yurts! I was in despair. Of course, there were a few of our military men, but aside from them—no one.

Frinovsky and Mirosha went off somewhere to have important conversations with Moscow. Returning at last, Mirosha said to me, "For the moment we won't be living in dignitaries' quarters. Tairov's wife will leave only in three or four days."

He took us to a vacant apartment. I don't know who lived there before, but at least it was furnished. It was just opposite the ambassador's house, where Tairov's wife was having her belongings loaded in a truck. She passed me several times, giving orders. I had an urge to approach her and whisper, "Your husband has been arrested."

Then we went to look at Tairov's dacha. She appeared there as well to remove her things. She had a child with her. Had she greeted me, I would have whispered to her. But she pretended that she didn't see me, as if I were a piece of furniture. I wasn't offended. I understood that she didn't want to know me because I was supplanting her. In fact, I hardly cared. I still didn't understand. I had not yet experienced my own circle of hell.

The Tairovs' servant immediately transferred her allegiance to me and she told me that her former mistress was going to stay with a sister in Novosibirsk before going to Moscow.

In the evening Frinovsky and Mirosha reminisced about the old days in the Northern Caucasus and elsewhere. Mirosha's eyes glistened. They were both drunk with the power that had been given them here. They would be in control of everything. I overheard Frinovsky say of Tairov's wife, "Well as soon as Madame turns up in Moscow, we will have a little conversation with her." I knew what that meant! If I were a nasty person, I would have instantly told them, "But she's not going to Moscow. She's going to Novosibirsk." But I thought, oh no, to hell with you, and I said nothing.

Now Mironov cannot be rehabilitated. They say that in Mongolia he carried out Yezhov's orders. How could he have refused? Yezhov was the People's Commissariat's vigilant eyes, the most powerful man after Stalin. And even Yezhov could take no decisions about international affairs without Stalin's orders. Of course, General Konev's corps was sent to Mongolia on Stalin's orders.

Before we came, the head of the Mongolian government was Amor Agdanbugin. I met him once. He came to see us with his wife. Amor, with his greasy face and squinty eyes, smiled like Buddha. Mirosha told me that he was suspected of allegiance to Japan. Then he disappeared. I don't know, I just don't know where he went and whether Mirosha had anything to do with his disappearance. On the train Mirosha had shed his army uniform and changed to civilian clothing. Frinovsky organized everything.

No, I don't know where Amor went. After he disappeared his staff was invited to Moscow. On the train they were fed jam. Not one of them reached Moscow alive. It's not hard to guess what was in that jam.[17]

We replaced Amor with Choibalsan, our protégé.[18] He had studied at the military academy in Russia. It's not that we trusted him, but we had him in our hands. Our soldiers had occupied Mongolia.

ᛰ ᛱ

Now I will describe Mongolia as it was at that time. Syphilis was rampant, and the birth rate was very low. Children were valued above everything. A girl who had already borne a child was the most desirable wife. For that reason, girls played around at will before marriage, and the more the better. If she bore a child and it survived, she was a good bet. I remember a girl we knew who was incessantly changing lovers. Her parents were delighted. Once I asked them, "Don't you think you should marry her off soon?" "Why?" they asked, surprised. "Let her have a good time, maybe she'll have a child!"

One of Choibalsan's ministers explained why his wife didn't come to receptions. This minister had just returned from somewhere. In his absence his

---

[17] Amor Agdanbugin was actually prime minister of the Mongolian Republic and not always prepared to do Stalin's bidding. He was replaced by Choibalsan and then taken to Moscow. Agnessa has confused a rumor about another Mongolian dignitary who was alleged to have been poisoned on his way to Moscow. Amor lived until 1941, when he was arrested and shot.

[18] Khorloogiin Choibalsan (1895–1952) was the Communist leader of the Mongolian People's Republic from the 1930s until his death. Brought to power with Soviet backing, over time he occupied every important state and party position—simultaneously. He was a strong ally of Stalin and, like him, mercilessly eliminated his rivals, both secular and religious. On his watch the Tibetan Buddhist monasteries were eliminated and roughly 5 percent of the population was annihilated. He also followed Stalin's lead in creating a cult of personality around himself. For the most part a Soviet puppet, Choibalsan nonetheless dreamed of creating a pan-Mongolian state. That was something Stalin would never have allowed.

wife had a romance with a soldier. She often went to the soldier's yurt, where he took her so often that he exhausted her. She became pregnant with this soldier, but to her husband's dismay, she had a miscarriage. And now she was ill and couldn't come to our receptions.

There was already a theater in Ulan-Bator. The Mongolian actors presented Lope de Vega's *Fuentes Ovejuna*. Do you remember the plot of the play? The suzerain is preparing to take his "first night's rights." And when, on the stage, the heroine tried to defend her honor, the entire Mongolian audience burst out laughing. They found it hilarious that she would turn down a suitor. What's all the fuss about? She should rejoice!

We became friendly with General Konev's family. I spent an evening there once without Mirosha. It got late and I was reluctant to return alone to the Soviet enclave. A Mongolian minister and two of his men offered to drive me home. I made the excuse that I was waiting for my own car to fetch me. I surreptitiously took Konev's wife aside and explained why I couldn't possibly go with them, that a woman alone with strange men would invite gossip. She laughed. "Not at all! They don't care a bit about who a woman is with. They would even consider it praiseworthy."

Choibalsan, as head of the government, had a European house where he held receptions. But he and his wife and children really lived in two yurts in the courtyard. At one reception, I recall, sausage was served. To keep my figure, I never ate fatty foods, and I pulled all the bits of fat out of my portion. Suddenly I became aware that all the Mongolian women were doing the same. Good heavens, I thought. They are imitating me. But their concept of beauty was peculiar. Choibalsan's wife wore what looked to me like a floor-length dressing gown. I tactfully took her aside and told her that a dress would be more appropriate for a reception. She threw back the sleeves of her robe to show me how thin her arms were. I told her that thin arms were good, pretty.

At that time I wore my hair very short in the latest style, and I wore a long cornflower blue dress. Choibalsan's wife had a gorgeous braid into which real pearls were woven. At the next reception, I see that she has cut her hair exactly like mine and that she is wearing a blue evening dress! True, not of crepe-georgette like mine, but of silk. And all the other ladies were in blue dresses as well. In a flash I understood that it was not that they were blindly imitating me. They simply interpreted whatever I said as an order.

In the summer most of the Mongols left town to live on the steppe like nomads. Including Choibalsan. We visited him in his summer encampment. He sits in his yurt, one arm bare to the elbow, and on it pieces of fatty cooked lamb in a row. He deftly pops them one by one into his mouth. The ground is covered with luxuriant rugs. His wife, dressed in a robe, runs in from another yurt. I am amazed. She is all but a queen, and she dresses that way at home. Can it be that she does housework? She sees us and runs away to change her clothes.

Some of the aristocratic Mongolian women wear a hairdo that lasts for months. They smear their hair with some kind of paste, shaping it into two twisted horns. It is a very haughty look. But the young women are charming, lithe like young goats, wearing long trousers, many black braids, and little embroidered skull caps. They perfume the air.

The Choibalsans had no children of their own, but several adopted ones. At one point Choibalsan's wife disappeared. He explained that she was hostile to the Soviet Union, so he had kicked her out. I think that was nonsense. That little wild nomad who obediently imitated me? No. It was that Choibalsan tired of her. He just got rid of her to take another wife.

We were always afraid of infection. When we went into society and were served cooked lamb, we peeled the skin and ate only the parts that no one had touched with their hands. An acquaintance of ours brought a silk robe back to Russia, but before she wore it she disinfected it with an iron. In general it was forbidden to take back Mongolian robes. She asked me to wear it out so that the customs would let it pass. But Mirosha protested, saying, "How do we know which syphilitic woman wore it?"

And the hygiene! Anyone who has an urge to relieve himself simply squats by our fence. To be sure, covered by his robe. He sees me pass by? He greets me amiably. We tried to introduce some culture. We drove them away from the fence and ordered them to build a toilet. But one can't dig their land. They consider the land to be God's body.

But the absolute worst was what is called the Valley of the Dead. The Mongols are Buddhists. Buddha forbade them to dig the land. They are animal herders so they don't need to till the soil for food. Fish and dogs are holy animals to them. They can eat only sheep and cows. They do not bury their dead. They wrap the corpse in a shroud and take it to the Valley of the Dead. The sun and the wind dry the body.

I went there once with Mirosha and Frinovsky. It is a huge field strewn with skulls and bones. Fearsome wild dogs live on the periphery with rags dangling from their bodies. When a corpse is brought for disposal, they call these dogs—who are well accustomed to the procedure—and hang strips of cloth on them. The dogs with many rags are those that have eaten many corpses.

I was told the following story. Once a Mongol girl fell ill during a smallpox epidemic. When people die of infectious diseases, the doctors order that all their belongings be burned, including the yurt. So, the girl's relatives, fearing that the doctor would force them to burn all their possessions, didn't wait for her to die, but dressed her in a shroud and took her to the Valley of the Dead. The corpse-eating dogs didn't attack her immediately. She came to and began to wail. Just at that moment a car with Russians passed by and, hearing cries, stopped, saw that she was alive, and took her to the city hospital.

When she recovered, her Russian benefactors went to her family, recounted the story, and asked whether they would take her back. Her kinsmen said, "Yes, yes, of course." But the girl refused to go back to her family. "They will kill me," she said. "If I have returned from the Valley of the Dead, that means that I am an evil spirit." She begged the Russians not to tell anyone in the town. She stayed with the hospital, studied, and became a nurse.

The Russians ordered that the dead be buried in the ground. They even dug deep ditches in the valley. The Mongols simply ignored the order. They just began to throw their corpses into the Valley at night.

The terrible impression that the Valley made on me was aggravated by the story Frinovsky told on our way back. The wind was blowing furiously and my heart was heavy. Frinovsky wanted to distract me. And he spoke freely in front of the chauffeur, who was in any case his man. Besides, we were in an open car and Frinovsky's words were hurled behind us by the powerful wind.

The story was about Ye. G. Yevdokimov, who had been Mirosha's boss in the Northern Caucasus. Yagoda didn't care for Yevdokimov. They quarreled furiously, and Yagoda kicked him out of the NKVD. Naturally, Yevdokimov hated Yagoda in return.

Later, when Yagoda was losing favor and he was interrogated, he refused to give the required testimony. Stalin, learning of Yagoda's recalcitrance, said, sucking on his pipe and smiling wryly, "Give him to Yevdokimov."

At that time Yevdokimov no longer worked for the NKVD. Stalin made him a member of the Central Committee and First Secretary of the Rostov regional party apparatus. Normally he did not do interrogations. When he was called upon to interrogate Yagoda, he drank a glass of vodka, rolled up his sleeves, and sat at the table with his arms akimbo, a hulk of a man with fists like hams. Yagoda was brought into the room, his hands tied behind his back and his trousers falling down (the buttons, naturally, had been removed). When Yagoda saw Yevdokimov at the table, he recoiled. He understood what was in store for him. Yevdokimov said to him, "So, you international spy, you don't confess?" And he began to beat Yagoda on the head.

Stalin was satisfied and amused when he heard. As a gesture of good will he summoned Frinovsky. "Well," he asks, "how are things?"

Frinovsky summons his courage and says. "Everything is going well, Iosif Vissarionovich. But don't you think we're shedding too much blood?"

Stalin smirks, approaches Frinovsky, and pokes his shoulder with two fingers. "Never mind," he answers. "The Party will take all the responsibility."

And it was that Frinovsky who tried to court me at one time. Now he completely ignored me. He and Mironov were too busy with politics.

❦

Although Ulan-Bator was nothing more than a big nomadic camp with a bunch of yurts, the pathetic little shops were bursting with merchandise.

English and American fabrics, knitted sweaters—what didn't they sell! There was free trade there. Our shoes, for example, you could buy at half the price of the stores in Russia.

And the chocolate! We ate ourselves sick in the first days. When the women came to visit me they said, "Please, no chocolate. We can't look at it."

As the wife of the ambassador I was entitled to two hundred tugriks of Mongolian money for each reception that I organized. I would say to Mirosha of an evening, "Mirosha, tell the secretary to give me money for a dress."

"But you already have money."

"Haven't you read the instructions? I need a new dress for each reception."

What fabulous materials we had! And I found a talented seamstress. For the October holiday she sewed me a blue and white dress with puffy sleeves and a stand-up collar "à la Marie Stuart." No one had a dress like that. I can't forget it.

I often sent packages to my family in Rostov through the diplomatic courier who went to Moscow. I would pack a box with fabric, chocolate, and money at the very bottom. Once I embedded a watch for my little nephew Borya in a bar of chocolate with a note saying "Borya, don't give anyone the chocolate bar until you have inspected it." I sewed the package into the brightly colored material that Mongolian men wore as a sash. The diplomatic courier who took it to Moscow tore off the material and sent the plain box by ordinary mail.

After the first package I received the following letter from my sister Lena. "We hadn't had news from you for so long. We were upset, we didn't know what to think." I understood what she meant, for I had told her that perhaps we were being sent to Mongolia to be arrested. "Then, such a package from you! It arrived late at night. We spent all night unpacking it, one marvelous thing after another. Borya squeezed the chocolate bar and found the gold watch, and we found the money at the bottom."

I don't remember any more how many thousands of rubles I sent them.

On all of our previous assignments we had taken Mama with us. She blessed our house, she was our good angel. Our Mongolian assignment almost ended in tragedy because she wasn't with us. Agulya fell ill with a raging form of scarlet fever. It was my fault. I refused to have her vaccinated in Novosibirsk.

Mirosha's extraordinary mission to Mongolia was coming to an end. Moscow summoned him, but we couldn't go with him. Agulya was near death. Mirosha couldn't refuse to go, and I remained alone with my dying child.

View from the Outside: Agulya

In Mongolia I went to a school for Russian children. It was a disgusting place. The food was inedible, but they forced me to sit at the table until I finished everything. Maybe that's how my illness began. I had scarlet fever followed by serious complications. You can still see the scars on my hand. They are not smallpox scars, no. They are the traces of the injections that saved me. I had lost the use of my arms and legs. I seemed to be paralyzed. Mama sat with me two days and two nights holding a blue lamp over my arms and legs. Only at the end of the second night some movement returned. I could wiggle my finger.

◦ ✤ ◦

That first terrible night that Agulya lay dying I sat at her bed with the lamps and prayed to God, "If she lives, if she recovers, I..." And I made a vow. Until then I had ignored my husband's family. To my own family I sent parcel after parcel. To his people—nothing. He had a brother in Rostov, a ninny and a failure. But he had a wife and children whom I vowed to help.

General Konev summoned all the army doctors and a pediatric professor who flew in from Novosibirsk. He saved Agulya. I will always be grateful to Ivan Stepanovich.

As soon as Agulya began to improve I sent a parcel to Mirosha's brother in Rostov. Later his wife Nadya told me that when the parcel arrived, all the neighbors gathered. When they saw what the parcel contained they said to Nadya, "When Agnessa comes you must kiss the ground under her for such a parcel."

I will tell you about Mirosha's brother later, but now I will tell you more about Agulya's illness. She needed an X-ray. I categorically refused to let her be taken from the house to the clinic. The head of the clinic calmed me. "OK, never mind. We will bring the X-ray machine to your house."

And so it was. They brought a huge machine to the house. The radiologist stood at the door, rooted to the ground, mute with embarrassment before such a *grande dame*.

His surname was familiar to me. As he stood in the doorway it seemed to me that he bore a family resemblance to a Maikop family, so I inquired whether he was from Maikop. Yes, he was. I asked him if he remembered the Agripopolo family.

He grew even more flustered. "I remember the family."

"Do you remember that there were two sisters and a brother?"

"Ah. Are you Lena or Agnessa?"

"Agnessa."

He stayed a while after he took the X-ray. I remembered all the details of his family. His family were wealthy merchants, they had a store. I remembered him as a snotty little boy of ten. Once my girl friends and I, a few years older than he, almost young ladies, were playing some kind of game of fantasy. We decided we needed someone to play a bloodhound. Catching sight of the little boy enviously watching us play, we asked him if he'd like to play with us. "Yes!" "We need a bloodhound to catch dangerous criminals." He immediately dropped to his knees and began to bark furiously.

Of course, that's not why he was flustered now, but because I knew that his father had owned a store and that his brother had been a scoundrel. All Maikop knew that.

That evening I invited him and his wife to supper. I dolled myself up in my finest. I couldn't resist shining before them, the Maikopians. And the supper was worthy of royalty. But it was a mistake. They were already overcome with embarrassment. And then I got myself in deeper by asking about his scoundrel of a brother. The doctor tensed up, as if he had swallowed a stick.

"No," he answered, "I never had such a brother. You are mistaken."

Thank heavens I didn't remind him of the store. Now I understand that he was not exactly ecstatic with our meeting. He was on pins and needles all evening.

Mirosha called frequently from Moscow to ask how Agulya and I were doing and to tell us how he was. But he divulged no details, only subtly hinting that when we got to Moscow we would understand everything. As soon as Agulya was well enough to travel, we hastened to Moscow.

View from the Outside: Agulya

> *I remember crossing some border. Mama, Maria Nikolaevna, and I traveled in closed autos to Ulan-Ude. In Ulan-Ude a special railway car awaited us that was then attached to the train. Mama brought so much stuff from Mongolia that the entire "salon" was filled floor to ceiling.*

ಐ ರಿ

We arrived at the Yaroslavl Station in Moscow. Agulya saw Mirosha from the window and, jumping up and down, yelled "Papa, Papa." When he entered the train car she threw her arms around his neck. She was pale, almost transparent, after her illness.

Mirosha had remarkable chestnut colored eyes—large and expressive. I had learned to read Mirosha from his eyes. At a glance I saw that he was happy, and not only because of our reunion. I itched to know what was happening, but he said not a word. He only smiled mysteriously. I noticed that he was not wearing his NKVD uniform, but a beautiful imported overcoat.

There was a lot of bustle over our luggage, how to unload it, how to carry it. But that was the affair of our "underlings." An enormous elegant car awaited us, and we set off through the Moscow streets. After Ulan-Bator, it was if we had fallen into a boiling cauldron. We pass Myasnitskaya Street (then called Kirov Street), Dzerzhinskii Square, Sverdlov Square. I'm expecting us to turn into a hotel. But we carry on—Okhotny Row, past the university, the Manezh. I don't understand. The Great Stone Bridge... where are we going?

Finally we enter the courtyard of the Government compound, the House on the Embankment.[19] An elevator to the seventh floor to a marvelous six-room apartment. What furnishings! Fresh flowers, fresh fruit. I look at Mirosha, he laughs happily at my surprise, embraces me and whispers in my ear, "Are you surprised? Don't be. I am now the Vice-Commissar of the Far East. Look!"

He shows me the Lenin medal on his chest. And his eyes sparkle. How well I know that sparkle of success.

And so the terrible roller coaster once again lifted Mirosha higher.

That very day we were invited to the Bolshoi Theater for a special celebration. You've probably never seen Yezhov close up. Well, I have. Small, puny, one side of his face crisscrossed with scars. A non-entity. They say his wife was a decent woman. The writer Ilya Ehrenburg told that the great writer Isaac Babel, who had gone to school with her, once visited her just to try to understand the mysterious power of that pygmy. He went, tempting fate, before he himself was caught up in the web.

In fact, Yezhov's power was hollow, although he believed it was real and was so puffed up with it that all the members of the Central Committee feared him. For example, Molotov's secretary would call him to arrange a meeting and Yezhov would say arrogantly, "Why the hell are *you* calling? Let him call me himself."[20]

And Molotov would come, bowing and scraping.

On the stage that evening, I recall, was Mikoyan, small and brisk, in a military jacket and boots. They all dressed like Stalin. Kaganovich even wore his mustache to imitate Stalin.[21] Mikoyan scurried onto the stage and began to

---

[19] In 1931 the government built an apartment house to provide luxurious accommodations for the Soviet political, intellectual, and artistic elite. At the time it was the largest apartment building in Europe. Every apartment was fully and elegantly furnished and had amenities, like all-day hot running water, that were not generally available to the ordinary Moscow inhabitant. The writer Yuri Trifonov wrote a successful novel called *The House on the Embankment* about life in the government apartment building. It has been known that way ever since and I refer to it that way as well.

[20] Vyacheslav Mikhailovich Molotov (1890–1986) was an Old Bolshevik, a Soviet politician and diplomat. He became a protégé of Stalin in the 1920s, and from then until he was dismissed by Khrushchev (1957) he was major figure in the Soviet government and the Communist Party. From 1939 to 1949, and then again from 1953 to 1956 he was minister of foreign affairs. He retired in 1961 after several years of obscurity.

[21] Anastas Ivanovich Mikoyan (1895–1978) survived intact through the Stalin years, remaining active in the high echelons of Soviet power until 1965. He sometimes took "softer" positions in the political machinations of the Stalin period, at the same time managing to avoid breaking with Stalin. Although he had no formal connection with

praise Yezhov as "the People's Commissar made of steel," "Stalin's talented pupil," "the Soviet people's beloved who vigilantly preserves our security," "the man from whom all the Chekists should learn," and so forth and so on. When Mikoyan finished, everyone stood up. Applause, ovations, ecstatic howls, as if the audience was seized by some kind of madness. That's how it was in those days.

But I was instantly swept away by another current: how to find a seamstress, to prepare a wardrobe. After all, this was not your Mongolia. This was not Choibalsan in his dressing gown. There were receptions in Litvinov's mansion for the ambassadors of all countries. I was not about to fall on my face in the mud.[22]

I frantically called all my acquaintances and finally found a seamstress. For a change, Mirosha didn't nag me about dressing more modestly. Here in Moscow he allowed me to "spread my wings."

Once I saw a White Russian émigré newspaper with a photograph of Litvinov and his wife abroad: she was covered with diamonds. The journalists wrote with irony, "For this the revolution was necessary?"

But Litvinov's wife was right. She had to hold her head high to avoid the scorn of the West.[23]

Finally Mirosha and I were invited to a reception at Litvinov's mansion. I wore a brocade evening dress that was pinched at the waist and had a train. My neck and shoulders were bare. Little shoes with gold buckles, my hair piled high. Maria Nikolaevna, another servant, and Mama dressed me, rapturously oohing and aahing. Mama said, "Well, you will be better than everyone."

---

the Soviet secret services and held only state and party positions, he was not above initiating mass arrests of innocent people.

Lazar Moseevich Kaganovich (1893–1991). One of Stalin's most faithful allies, Kaganovich was also one of the most merciless Bolsheviks in matters of repression. He held some of the most important party posts in Stalin's lifetime. In 1957 he was relieved of all of his posts. He appealed personally to Khrushchev, begging to be spared the fate of his own victims. In 1961 he was thrown out of the Communist Party, retaining the rank of a pensioner with special privileges.

[22] Maksim Litvinov (1876–1951). Litvinov was drawn to revolutionary activity in his early 20s. He lived in England for some years and married an English woman. In 1921 he was made minister of foreign affairs, a post he held until 1941, with one brief hiatus. Litvinov was a gifted diplomat, well liked and respected by Franklin Delano Roosevelt and other foreign leaders. United States recognition of the USSR and Russia's acceptance into the League of Nations were his work. Always an outsider to the internal machinations of state and Party, he was dismissed from his position in 1946 and died a natural death in 1951.

[23] M. M. Yakovenko's footnote: Ivy Litvinova never wore diamonds. She dressed very modestly.

I lift the train and walk with my nose high. Mirosha says to Mama, "Look at how she carries herself. Where did she get those habits? You might think that she was born a duchess."

Mama answers, "She has been preening in front of a mirror since her childhood. She would make a train out of rags, turn this way and that way, practicing how to carry it."

"Nothing of the kind, Mirosha," I protest. "I was born to it. I *am* a duchess. Don't tell me you didn't know."

Mirosha is delighted. He calls me his little White Guardist.

We arrive at the reception. The rooms are brilliantly lit. What ladies! What finery! The young women are all in décolleté, like me. Everywhere you look—necklaces, rings, gold. Even the older women are beautiful. One woman of fifty wears a red dress and a red rose in her hair. There are two red spots on her cheeks. Rouge was fashionable.

The wife of the American ambassador was very interesting in a black dress with a transparent top, her hair parted in the middle. Her husband was also in black, simple and elegant. Others were in brilliant livery.

Litvinov's wife was not living with him at that moment. A young woman, his protégé, presided at the reception. She was lovely with reddish hair and a green dress. We approached Litvinov. I caught his glance. He approved of me.

And then a Japanese man appeared, an evil looking person who couldn't take his eyes off me. He stood very close to me and deliberately—it was obvious—stepped on my train. Not for nothing had I practiced in childhood. I deftly pushed him away with my elbow and skillfully extracted my train, drowning him in a contemptuous look. He slackened and flashed an insincere, toothy smile.

Mama had said, "You will be better than everyone." It's not for me to judge, of course. I only know that everyone noticed me. And Mirosha as well. He was so handsome in his tails with his gorgeous head of wavy hair (already flecked with silver). Later I heard that many people at the reception had asked, "What country are that new ambassador and his wife from?" Mirosha and I were imposing.

Arrests were made. Not a night passed in our Government compound that someone wasn't carried off. At night the Black Marias circled endlessly. But we had no longer suffered from that fear that had seized us so acutely in Novosibirsk. It isn't that it disappeared completely, but it was much milder. Perhaps because Frinovskii and Yezhov were firmly in power and their staff was still immune from arrest.

Indeed, we lived very well. Mirosha was happy with his new responsibilities. From time to time he would tell me about some curious episode at work in his relations with the "Japs" and the "Chinks." He was always in a good mood and spent a lot of time with the family. Our house was always filled with children, and he would dream up amusements for them, clowning, joking, spoiling them mercilessly.

For example, once he announced, "Today is International Woman's Day. I'll take care of the festivities and the women will relax." He began to set the table, deliberately doing everything wrong. Little Agulya danced around him in delight, choking with laughter. "No, Papa, not like that. Not like that, Papa."

Another time when Mirosha had to wear all his medals (he had many, even a Mongolian medal from Choibalsan), he laid them out for us to admire. He was so proud of them, and he joked with self-satisfaction, "Now, look here. You and Agulya are now secure forever. They will accumulate for you."

That happy, peaceful interlude was a breathing space.

Although some unpleasant things happened as well. Once there was a call from the militia: "Comrade Mironov? We have your brother here." It was that very brother whose family I had vowed to help with parcels. He was like Mirosha's shadow, a cursed shadow. Wherever Mirosha went, he followed. He would drink himself into a stupor, come to us, weep, beat his chest, and swear never to do it again if Mirosha would only fix him up with work. With a heavy heart Mirosha found him a place on his staff. But his brother completely compromised Mirosha, getting so drunk that he no longer seemed human.

Or he played such pranks. For example, when there was a famine in the Ukraine we spent our holidays in Berdyansk at that special sanatorium that supplied us with marvelous dinners and had freezers full of ice cream. I had brought my entire family there to feed them. Nadya, the wife of Mirosha's brother, had married that boozer only because he was Mirosha's brother. She was small and unattractive with a button of a nose, like an Uzbek. So, once she calls us while we're in Berdyansk to ask when my sister Lena was planning to leave. She and her family wanted to come. Lena leaves, they arrive. They eat, they drink, Mirosha's brother gets roaring drunk. On the day of their departure, he sobers up and calls the director of the sanatorium.

"If you please, prepare a *pud* and a half (fifty-four pounds) of meat for our departure."

"Who's calling?"

"Mironov," he answers, imitating Mirosha's voice. The director, believing it was really Mirosha, brought the meat in sealed jars.

I didn't want tell Mirosha at the time. I wanted to avoid a quarrel, but when I told him later he exclaimed indignantly, "That son-of-a-bitch!"

Physically Mirosha's brother resembled him. He was also handsome with a charming, winning face. Nadya indulged him in every way. When he got drunk, she locked him in their apartment so that he couldn't leave. He frequently drank himself almost to death.

So, at a time when they were arresting people for no reason at all, Mirosha's brother got drunk somewhere away from home and engaged in some kind of anti-Soviet conversations. Someone immediately informed on him. He was arrested, thank God not by the secret police but by the militia. He put on airs, shouting, "How dare you arrest me? Do you know who my brother is? He'll grind you into dust!"

Mirosha boiled with rage, but managed to take himself in hand and went to fetch his brother. What that did to his nerves, I can't say. But the affair was patched up.

I, however, remained furious. I called Nadya. "Are you aware of what your husband is up to? Why didn't you lock him in the house when he was drunk?"

She retorts, "Worry about your own husband!"

"That's exactly what I'm doing. You, I see, don't think about yours." And I hung up the phone.

And that was the woman who had bowed to the ground in gratitude for my parcels.

And then there were Karutsky with his Abrashka. A. V. Karutsky was Mirosha's chief in Alma-Ata until Yagoda sent him to be head of the NKVD in Moscow.[24] Abrashka followed him. And again, as in Alma-Ata, that Abrashka got into the habit of visiting me during the day when Mirosha wasn't home. He loved to tell me gossip, for example, that Stalin had married Kaganovich's younger sister Rosa.[25] He sometimes brought me gifts.

I didn't hide his visits from Mirosha. Suddenly Mirosha became terribly jealous of that ugly little dwarf. Mirosha insisted that some women have perverted taste. They like freaks. We had a terrible fight about it.

Karutsky worked in the People's Commissariat as an operative. He too often drank himself into a stupor. After a drunken evening with friends, he shot himself. I think that he knew that one day they would come for him—if not today then tomorrow. He couldn't bear the anxiety. And I, I lived with my eyes screwed shut. We had it very good, and it would always be so. We had landed on a safe, lucky island. As everyone around us was falling, we were rising.

Just at that time, Mikhail Davydovich Korol returned from abroad. He was Mirosha's cousin. The family called him Alter, which means "the elder" in Yiddish. He was, in fact, the eldest of his brothers and sisters, and he married Mirosha's sister Fenya. She was a beauty, like Judith in the Bible. They had two daughters. Maya, the youngest, was also a beauty, the spitting image of her mother. When Alter returned, she was sixteen. The older sister, Brusha, was eighteen. She was not beautiful, but her face shone with such sweetness

---

[24] As the purges of the NKVD gathered momentum, A. V. Karutsky committed suicide on May 13, 1938.

[25] Rosa Kaganovich probably never existed. But somehow legends about her and her alleged relationship with Stalin began to circulate after the death of his second wife, Allilueva.

and goodness that it was impossible not to love her. She had an amazingly serene character and a subtle, warm sense of humor. It's hard to describe her. You had to know her. Both were lovely girls, but thoroughly impractical without the slightest sense of how to keep house. Fenya was an economist for the Department of State Planning. She wasn't interested in material things and she brought up her daughters to scorn finery. It was beneath them, bourgeois. They were both principled "bluestockings," very sweet and very kind.

For several years Mikhail Davydovich had worked abroad on a secret mission. Before he was based in the United States he lived for a time in Europe and then in China and Japan to cover his tracks. He entered the United States through Canada posing as a Jewish businessman and settled in New York. His mission was to establish a firm whose earnings he would use to finance the American Communist Party and the Communist press. To be precise, he was not sent to *spy*, but to conduct propaganda and to agitate for the overthrow of the *status quo*.

Five men were sent on this mission. Once abroad they divided into two groups, three in one group and two in the other—Mikhail Davydovich and Mark Pavlovich Shneiderman.

In 1938 they were all called back to Moscow. On his way back Mikhail Davydovich stopped in Paris where a friend in the embassy said to him, "You're going home? Do you know what's going on there?" He told Mikhail Davydovich about the arrests. "Try to stay here at least a year," he advised him. Mikhail Davydovich believed him, but he was afraid that his family would suffer if he remained abroad and feared that in any case they would catch him wherever he was.

He returned and immediately tumbled into the horror of the arrests. The "Troika," his three colleagues who were separated from him and Mark, were arrested the minute they returned. His partner Mark was also arrested, even before Mikhail Davydovich arrived. Mikhail Davydovich remained at liberty, but they took his Party card from him and left him without work. He hated being without work. Mirosha loved Mikhail Davydovich, but now he avoided him. I saw him once, without Mirosha.

Alter and his family lived at their *dacha* in Kraskovo. Our government *dacha* was in nearby Tomilino. I love to take walks and often visited them. In the warm summer, I walk in a little crepe de chine sundress, my neck and shoulders bare. Passing through the village, I throw a little bolero over my shoulders.

Fenya was always affectionate and welcoming. She was a person of extraordinary character. I well remember that when Mirosha "kidnapped" me and we stopped in Moscow on our way to Alma-Ata, none of Mirosha's family wanted to know me. They were extremely upset that Mirosha had abandoned his wife, Gusta, whom they had all known from childhood. Even Mikhail Davydovich said sharply, "You can't build happiness on someone else's misfortune." Fenya alone had accepted me. She came to the Hotel Metropole to meet me, wearing a black velvet dress with a white pique collar, perfectly coifed, beautiful, young, radiant. I was enchanted. We took to each other and kept up our friendship until she died. At Kraskovo she greeted me like a good friend.

One would never call Mikhail Davydovich good-looking. Mirosha was solid, broad, strong; Mikhail Davydovich was, frankly, stout. His belly preceded him. Mirosha had thick, wavy hair. I never saw Mikhail Davydovich's hair. He was bald at an early age. Mirosha had beautiful eyelashes, arched and fan-like. Mikhail Davydovich, well, his eyes were not so much beautiful as intelligent, expressive, thoughtful. He was interesting, erudite, and had a sense of humor. He had seen a lot of the world. He returned from his travels completely Americanized in his habits and deportment. Sometimes he had to grope for Russian words. All those years in America, playing his role, he had not spoken a word of Russian.

He had so many interesting stories to tell. For example, he was taught English by our Russian teachers from text books. When he came to America, it turned out that no one understood a word he said. On his first day he left his hotel, lost his way, and asked for directions. People just looked at him and shrugged their shoulders. Finally he turned to a shoeshine boy, who also didn't understand him. But he was Jewish. He guessed that Mikhail Davydovich was also Jewish, and they spoke in Yiddish. The shoeshine boy advised him to speak in Yiddish henceforth because there would always be someone who understood him.

Mikhail Davydovich bought a gramophone and some language records. Day after day he sat in his hotel room repeating texts. It was a cheap hotel with thin walls. His neighbors could hear every word. They listened day after day until they concluded that he was mentally ill and called a psychiatrist. Mikhail Davydovich told the psychiatrist that he was a German Jew trying to perfect his English pronunciation. Once he mastered the language he established a business.

Now he found it oppressive to sit home without anything to do. Fenya worked and brought home the wages. Their housekeeper Maria Aleksandrovna was Mordvinian, coarse but utterly devoted to them. She worshiped Fenya. When Mikhail Davydovich returned and began to sit around the house she decided he was a parasite, living off her beloved mistress. Her resentment silently accumulated until one day it burst out.

It was at dinner. Maria Aleksandrovna had prepared a meat dish. She served meat to everyone at the table—me, Fenya, the two girls—except Mikhail Davydovich. She gave him only some vegetables. He said jokingly, "What's this? No meat for me?" He thought she had just made a mistake.

Maria Aleksandrovna said sharply, "He who does not work, does not eat."

He blushed, rose, and left the room.

Fenya, normally the soul of kindness, turned to Maria Aleksandrovna and barked, "From tomorrow you will no longer work for us." And she followed Mikhail Davydovich out of the room.

Later Maria Aleksandrovna apologized and wept. Fenya relented.

I've already mentioned that Mirosha avoided meeting with Alter. But finally they met by chance at the home of a relative. This time he did not avoid Alter's eyes. They sat apart from the rest of us and carried on a long, intimate conversation. Mirosha asked Alter endless questions about his life. And then Alter began to question Mirosha.

Alter always had firm opinions. He looked directly into the depth of things without any hypocritical lenses.

I don't remember exactly what Mirosha recounted. I remember only that suddenly Alter said to him, looking him straight in the eye, "You are up to your elbows in blood. How can you stand yourself? You have only one option — to kill yourself."

"I am Stalin's cur," Mirosha grimaced. "I have no choice."

And so it was. Even if he had wanted to, Mirosha could not have extricated himself from the machine, he was forced to keep working it. True, here in Moscow one had the illusion that he had broken out of *that* machine.

And I? As for me, I was carefree. I liked our "diplomatic" life very much. And besides, Mirosha hinted to me that he might be appointed to a consulate, not in Mongolia, but in a more important place. Maksim Maksimovich Litvinov was very well disposed to him.

Mirosha heard about Mark Shneiderman, the one who had been arrested immediately after he returned from abroad. And Mikhail Davydovich came running to us. This was most unusual: aware that Mirosha avoided meeting him, Mikhail Davydovich usually did not make overtures.

But now — he said to Mirosha, "You know, Mark has been freed."

It was as if the air around him grew brighter. No comment from Mirosha.

We immediately pulled together — Mirosha abandoned his vow not to speak to Mikhail Davydovich — and we went to the Korol apartment. Mikhail Davydovich telephoned Shneiderman and his wife Vera Vasilevna — and we spent a happy evening of celebration.

Many years later Mikhail Davydovich revealed something to me.

"Do you know that it was Mirosha who engineered Shneiderman's release?"

I think that's true. At that time, Mirosha said to me, "They called me to the Lubyanka and they grilled me about Shneiderman."

"And?"

"They asked me to tell them what Shneiderman was like."

Now I think that Mirosha wasn't telling me the whole truth. It is not that he was summoned, but that he went to the Lubyanka on his own, using his high-level contacts.

And I also think that's why Alter was not arrested along with many others who had been abroad. I think that here, too, Mirosha used his influence.

Of course, maybe it also served Mirosha's interests. It would not have been good to have a relative who had been arrested. Once Shneiderman was arrested, could Mikhail Davydovich be far behind? So Mirosha used all his influence to defend them against arrest.

Mikhail Davydovich was very well read. He had seen much, he knew a lot, he was thoughtful, and he loved to philosophize. I remember one evening when Mirosha came home after some kind of a conference and spoke about a talk that Nadezhda Krupskaya, Lenin's widow, had given on the subject of pedagogy. Mirosha spoke scornfully of her, expressing the widespread opinion that one goes to hear her speak only because she was Lenin's wife.

Mikhail Davydovich hotly defended her. He understood her humiliating position. He understood that she dared not make a peep, otherwise she would not have survived. (The "greatest genius" could manipulate history to suit his purposes.) It was rumored that he had threatened Krupskaya: if she didn't keep a low profile it might be that they would give Inessa Armand or Fotieva the honor of being Lenin's widow.[26] And Mikhail Davydovich began to point out to Mirosha that a great many of Lenin's Marxist positions and policies were now surreptitiously thrown to the winds.

Alter had great respect for Lenin, but, you know at that moment it was risky to openly express such an opinion. It might be taken as a reproach of Stalin.

They had such conversations, but of course they never went beyond the front door.

ෆ ෮

Frinovskii invited us to his dacha to celebrate his wife Nina's birthday. Choibalsan was invited too because he happened to be in Moscow. It seems that they wanted to make an agreement with him that had been discussed in the People's Commissariat on Foreign Affairs. Mirosha had participated in that meeting in his capacity as deputy of the Ministry of the Far East.

Mirosha returned from the meeting very upset, he smoked, he pondered. Something had happened at that meeting. When I put Agulya to sleep he began to tell me about it. At first it seemed to me that everything was fine. Stalin had personally addressed Mirosha several times, asking for his opinion as an expert on Mongolia who had lived there. Given his ambitions, Mirosha could not be indifferent to that. But something strange and oppressive was going

---

[26] Inessa Armand, a French Communist who spent many years in Russia, was reputed to have had a romance with Lenin. Lydia Fotieva (1881–1975) was drawn to the revolutionary movement as an adolescent. She worked for the Bolsheviks in many capacities, most notably as Lenin's secretary (1918–24).

on. Stalin also addressed everyone present—Mirosha, Choibalsan, Molotov. But not Litvinov.

Litvinov, minister of foreign affairs, sat there listening, yet Stalin said not a word to him, as if he didn't exist. Stalin didn't once look at him. His gaze passed over him as if he were an empty spot, even when questions arose that Litvinov above all was best qualified to answer. Stalin was demonstratively shaming him. Litvinov was pale, but calm. He had incomparable restraint.

Mirosha told me that if Stalin was so openly scorning him, Litvinov probably didn't have long. And if Litvinov were to be removed from his position, perhaps there would be other changes in the Commissariat. I could see what Mirosha was thinking: "And in that case, will I keep my position? Will I fall? Or—maybe, just maybe... I will rise higher?"

He was drunk with success and at the same time very alarmed.

Soon after that we went to Frinovsky's dacha. He had recently returned from the Far East. He had gone with Lev Mekhlis, a high-ranking figure in the armed forces, to "clean up." Especially the Far East. They went with a whole trainload of special soldiers. And they were not only "cleaning up" the army. Frinovsky liquidated all the heads of the Far East section of the Ministry of Foreign Affairs. I remember how Mirosha said, "It's a good thing I'm not there. Otherwise Frinovsky would have cooked my goose, too." And then he added: "Only one thing saved me."

"Saved?" I was astonished.

"Lyushkov skipped to Japan."

I couldn't believe my ears. "Saved me?" Was this Mirosha with his devotion to the Party actually talking like this?

Frinovsky's dacha was formerly a nobleman's house. It had columns. The lower terrace was open and there were baskets of real flowers between the columns and chaise longues were scattered among them. There was a glassed-in veranda in back of the terrace where later we were served a sumptuous meal.

We came earlier than the other guests. Nina was still fussing with the preparations. Frinovsky received us. He was unrecognizable: he had become a gracious nobleman. With a negligent gesture he suggested that we sit in the chaises longues.

They immediately began to discuss how Choibalsan had been received by the Commissariat of Foreign Affairs. Frinovsky asked for all the details: Why was this done? How did Stalin comport himself? What did he say? How did he behave to Choibalsan?

"What about Litvinov?" Frinovsky asked Mirosha. "Don't tell me you don't know that Stalin is not fond of him?"

And he smirked, "He would have been arrested long ago if it weren't for Mister Capitalists. For the moment he cannot be arrested."

I understood that he was talking about Litvinov's popularity abroad. In other words, it was the only thing that protected Litvinov. But even more menacing was "for the moment."

Then the conversation turned to affairs of the Far East. Frinovsky told Mirosha how Lyushkov had fled. Frinovsky had personally investigated that affair. This is how the conversation went.

Genrikh Samuilovich Lyushkov was the head of the NKVD in the Far Eastern Territory. He controlled intelligence and the military. When rumors began to circulate that Frinovsky was planning to destroy the Special Far Eastern armed services, Lyushkov decided not to await his arrest. Frinovsky didn't like Lyushkov, he saw him as a competitor. Although now they were both friends of Yezhov, Lyushkov had been one of Yagoda's men. He was spared the fate of Yagoda's entourage only because he had routed the Japanese.

One could hear predatory annoyance in Frinovsky's story—oh, he was not caught! He slipped away—the rat. Here are the details of Lyushkov's flight.

Lyushkov told the Chekists who worked for him that he had to meet personally with our agents in Japan. Late at night he took a car, a chauffeur, and two Chekists and drove to the very border. His employees didn't ask him anything—after all, he was the boss, he must know what he was doing. Lyushkov told them to wait for him. And he left on foot by himself through the plains and the bushes into the no man's land. They waited for him one hour, two hours, three hours. Nothing. Dawn broke. They were very worried, they deliberated, they went on a search. They searched for a long time and suddenly found him—sleeping under some bushes. "We thought you had been killed!" He replied, "It didn't go well. I waited and waited for him and didn't even notice that I was falling asleep." It was clear that Lyushkov simply got lost in the dark and was pretending to sleep.

The next day he said to his aides again, "I had actually chosen two days for the meeting. He didn't come yesterday, maybe he'll come today. I'll take some medicine to stay awake."

And off he went again. Again they waited and waited for him, again they went to look for him. But this time they didn't find him. By daytime there were already transmissions on foreign radio that a powerful member of the NKVD, former aide to the head of the political section of the secret police—Lyushkov—Lyushkov had crossed the Manchurian borderland and asked for political asylum in Japan.

Sensation! Press conference! An English correspondent scornfully asked Lyushkov, "What led you to betray your country?"

Lyushkov answered: "Stalin likes to assassinate."

Of course, now I can talk about this freely. Frinovsky could not, and I would not have said it then, either.

Lyushkov's wife was immediately arrested.

At that moment Frinovsky's wife Nina entered the room. There was still a whiff of Paris about her, but her natural vulgarity was already showing through. She was made up like a prostitute.

She took me to see their garden which was like a fairy tale.

"And look, there is Mikoyan's dacha, and there…"

"And where is Stalin's dacha?"

She immediately retreated.

"I don't know."

"Who has Stalin married."

"I don't know.

She pursed her lips and launched into a story of how she had reproached Mikoyan's son, taking the side of a girl who was pregnant by him. They were both pupils in the same class. He had a car and they drove around in it together. And there she is—pregnant. Nina reproaches him and he laughs. He says it's not his child.

"Mikoyan's children are very spoiled." Saying this, Nina was signifying that her children were not spoiled.

Frinovsky had two sons, one seventeen years old and, Nina's favorite, a little boy of three. Nina took me to the younger son's room to show him off. Before entering his room she asked me to wash my hands and put on a clean robe. The room was kept sterile so that the little boy would not catch anything infectious.

Nina's sister later told me that once when she came to visit she hung her coat in that sterile room. Nina flew at her, "How dare you?" She all but said "Get out of here." The sister was insulted and left in a hurry.

Many years later Nina told me she had just received a letter from prison from that very child who had been kept in a sterile room. He wasn't long in that room—he was yanked out and thrown into the cruel world. He ended up in an orphanage, ran away, joined a gang, and became a professional thief.

We didn't stay in that sterile room for long. Choibalsan arrived, dressed in a European style suit. He saw me, grinned and bowed.

When Mirosha was denied rehabilitation, they added to his crimes that in Mongolia Choibalsan had a cult of personality. He did—but what did that have to do with Mirosha?

After a lavish meal we adjourned in the film-viewing room where there was a billiard table. Frinovsky's elder son, Oleg, was there playing billiards with two young men who looked Armenian. They were Mikoyan's sons. I don't know if his son the seducer was one of them. Mikoyan had many children.

All at once I heard a whisper of delight. "Vasya, Vasya has come."

I looked around. All the faces wore a servile expression. Who could evoke such delight, such awe? I see a pale, redheaded young man in a khaki uniform, his face full of pimples. Breeches, shiny shoes with spurs. He was obviously shy. Everyone is yelling "Vasya, Vasya," and he is so confused that he doesn't know where to look.

Frinovsky introduced him to Choibalsan in an unnatural voice, almost singing with pleasure. "This is Vasya, Iosif Vissarionovich's [Stalin's] son!"

Aha. Everything became clear. Frinovsky now lost all interest in us.

"Tomorrow we are going to disband some stables and show the horses to Vasily Iosifovich. He can chose one or two that appeal to him."

Vasya blushed with pleasure.

Very soon Frinovsky was transferred from the NKVD to the army, or rather, the navy—the Naval War fleet. Mirosha was envious.

But one thing was peculiar and it troubled Mirosha—why was the announcement in the newspaper so small, so modest, as if it were by-the-way. Why wasn't it announced in big letters in a full-page announcement with a portrait, as was usually done in such cases? Stalin was not stingy in passing out fame and glory to his favorites.

○3 ○○

How awful those times were. We went to hear that general speak—I've forgotten his name. He read from his memoirs about the meeting of the Central Committee soon after the generals were shot. He told how Voroshilov stood on the platform and beat his chest and forehead with his fists, repenting, repeating over and over, "I am a fool, I am an old fool! I didn't perceive the traitors, the betrayers." And as he spoke, every few minutes the commandant of the Kremlin brought in one group after another—to be arrested.[27]

True, Mirosha and I were in Mongolia at that time, but 1938 wasn't any better. Remember, it began with the trials of Bukharin, Rykov, Yagoda. Zaporozhets, Medvedev, and "the doctor-poisoners" were sentenced.[28] They were all sentenced. At the meetings one heard only "We demand the death sentence! We demand that the traitors be shot!" They say that Lenin's sister Anna Ilinichna had been in love with Bukharin all her life. She died a month and a half after he was shot. She could not bear it.

---

[27] In June 1937 Stalin launched an unexpected attack on the high command of the armed services. Nine of the highest ranking officers, including some of Russia's best military minds, were accused of treason and immediately executed. General Klimentii Voroshilov (1881–1969), a major military and political figure, was not among them. In fact, he was complicit in the plan to eliminate this stratum of military leaders. Voroshilov was a prominent military figure in the civil war. He was very close to Stalin.

[28] In March 1938 four doctors were accused of poisoning four people, two of them members of the secret service elite, and two of them a writer (Maxim Gorky) and his son. The affair was convoluted and murky and remains so to this day. The four doctors all died (or were killed) within the year.

Mirosha told me that Frinovsky and Zakovsky engineered the trials of Bukharin and others. At the beginning of 1938 Frinovsky enjoyed great respect.[29] In the summer he and Mekhlis went to the Far East, as I already said. The Japanese, learning of the defeat of the Special Far Eastern Army, immediately invaded our territory in the area of Lake Hassan, but Blyukher organized a successful defense. No sooner were the Japanese defeated than Blyukher was called to Moscow and arrested.

Mirosha and Blyukher were old acquaintances.[30] Blyukher had a strong face, a wide jaw, a wiry mustache, grey hair. Once we went to the theater with him and his third wife, a young Komsomol member, daughter of the well-known machinist Krivonos.[31] She was pretty and pink and serious. Although Mironov and Blyukher used the familiar "you" with each other, Blyukher did not introduce her to us. Perhaps she was simply his lover?

That was several years earlier. Now Blyukher was arrested, but never given a trial. It was said that he was horribly tortured during the interrogations; they tore out his eye and Yezhov shot him in his own office. When Blyukher entered it was said that Yezhov shouted maliciously, "What, you couldn't make off to Japan in your brother's plane? Ah, you with your spy's mug, you Japanese spy!"

Blyukher answered him, "And who are you? Where in the hell did you come from?"

Yezhov was full of himself. He imagined that he had the right to decide the fate of everyone and everything. It seemed to us that he had risen even higher than Stalin. They said he shot Blyukher to death point-blank.

Two or three years earlier an article had appeared about the Bolsheviks of the Transcaucasus, celebrating Stalin's merits. It was signed with a name as yet little known in Moscow: Lavrenty Beria.[32] We, however, knew it! From

---

[29] Leonid Mikhailovich Zakovsky (1894–1938). Zakovsky began his career in the Soviet secret services in 1918. He was known to be utterly ruthless. He organized and orchestrated many aspects of Stalin's terror, not least of which was the organization of the gulag system..

[30] Vasily Konstantinovich Blyukher (1889–1938) was a popular and successful military commander. He escaped Stalin's attack on the Soviet high command, probably because he had been a successful leader in the Far East. But he was arrested in 1938, perhaps because of the defection of Lyushkov, the NKVD chief in the Far East. He refused to confess to the charge of espionage even under torture and died either from the torture or execution.

[31] Pyotr Fyodorovich Krivonos (1910–80) was a talented machinist who invented a way to double the speed of freight trains. He received the award of Hero of Labor.

[32] Lavrenty Beria (1899–1953). Beria replaced Yezhov as head of the NKVD in 1938. He remained in high office until after Stalin's death. Although on his watch the gulag population declined, he made a clean sweep of the NKVD and was responsible for the arrests and execution of many. During World War II he was appointed Minister of

then on the name appeared more and more frequently. Mirosha said that Stalin had called Beria from the Caucasus and had made him Yezhov's deputy.

Something peculiar was happening. Yezhov sits in his office and all the employees begin to avoid him like the plague. They are like rats on a sinking ship. No one brings him reports, everything goes to his deputy—Beria. Yezhov still holds his post, he is still formally at the head and sits in the NKVD office, but everything has already slipped away from him.

Then he was appointed to the People's Commissariat of River Transport. He couldn't understand how he had become a nonentity, how he had lost his power. He couldn't reconcile himself to this and he lost his mind, behaving like a madman. In the People's Commissariat of River Transport people began to avoid him again, to shun him. Finally, he was kicked out of that post as well and ultimately shot.

There had always been arrests in the People's Commissariat of Foreign Affairs, but not like now. While Frinovsky was in the NKVD, Mirosha felt protected. But Frinovsky had become Commissar of the Navy. All the Yezhov supporters were removed, like Yagoda's supporters before them. One arrest after another. Today Mirosha works with an employee, tomorrow the employee is gone. Arrested!

And the ambassadors! How many of them were snatched away? Mirosha began to repeat obsessively, "I don't understand, I don't understand."

Not a night passed that the Black Maria didn't come to our apartment house. They would arrest someone, carry him off, and put a new tenant into the apartment. Then in a little while they would come for the new tenant, arrest him, carry him off, put the next one into the apartment. The third layer had already been carried off. The servants were terrified and ran to the kitchen to our Maria Nikolaevna. "It is too dangerous to work in this house, we can't work here anymore. What if they begin taking the servants?" One servant simply went into hysterics. She was so convinced of the danger that she wanted to take her pay and flee. I told Mirosha and he went to the kitchen to try to reason with her.

"Why do you listen to gossip?" he asked. "No one will bother us. Go and work calmly."

But he was not so calm either. Fear—not the fear that he had experienced in Novosibirsk, but a fear ten times worse was poisoning our life.

Once, returning home, Mironov entered the elevator with Shvernik and suddenly an unfamiliar man in a white cloak jumped in. Mironov and Shvernik froze.[33] How they suffered as the elevator rose. Which of them would that

---

Defense and as such was extremely powerful and greatly feared. When Stalin died, he lost his invulnerability and was condemned to death in 1953.

[33] Nikolai Mikhailovich Shvernik (1888–1970). Shvernik held many state and party posts throughout his working life, including chairmanship of the Supreme Soviet of

man—clearly an employee of the NKVD—present with an order for arrest? Mirosha on the seventh floor or Shvernik on the eighth floor? The man got off on the sixth floor, and only then did they joke about how they were still alive. But they did not smile at each other. They joked only with their eyes. In that situation one did not smile.

My brother Pavel worked in Sukhumi on the Black Sea in the Gas Works. The director was Beria's brother, Kvartskheliya. Pukha wrote us that the brother was coming to Moscow. "My boss will come to see you while he's in Moscow. Meet him, receive him nicely. He is coming to get a prosthesis for his amputated leg."

I immediately sent off a telegram: "I am waiting for him!"

Time passes—no one shows up. Every day when Mirosha comes home he asks, "Has he come?"

I answer, "No, he has not come."

We lose hope. Oh, how we counted on that brother. It would signify Beria's good will. It would mean confidence.

After a week had passed Mirosha said to me, "You know, I think he will never come."

And I understand, I understand what that means. Still, I hope. Perhaps he was detained, fell ill, decided not to come to Moscow at all. I question my brother, "Why hasn't your boss come?"

And Pavel lets the axe fall. "But he has already been to Moscow and returned."

Still, there is hope. Pavel writes that his boss told him that "I stayed at Lavrenty's (Beria), he sent a car for me and we went to a restaurant to find girls, so I had no time to visit Mironov." Could that be true? Was he having so much fun with his brother that he simply had no time to come to us?

Mirosha was inconsolable. He said to me, "If they arrest me, I'll shoot myself."

One night he suddenly jumped out of bed, ran to the entry hall and with a stick bolted the door of the service elevator that led directly into the apartment. Then he put a chain on the door. But it didn't end there. Utterly beside himself, he grabbed the dresser and shoved it up against the elevator door.

"Mirosha," I whispered. "What has gotten into you?"

"I don't want it. I don't want them to come from there and take us by surprise!" he yelled.

I understood: he wanted a knock or the scraping of the dresser or the snap of the stick to wake him so they could not burst in on him as he slept, as had happened to Shanin.

"I must know, I must know when they come!"

---

the USSR. He was a solid bureaucrat, uninvolved in the many party intrigues and acquiescing to all changes of policy.

Again I understood. He must know so that he could shoot himself. "What are you saying, Mirosha?"

He began to sob hysterically, crying out in despair, "They are taking the wives as well. The wives!"

I had never seen Mirosha weep. I couldn't believe what I was hearing and seeing. The moment had come when I must be stronger than he to comfort and calm him. I embraced him and consoled him... well even if you are arrested that may not be the end, you could still be justified, released, after all you are guilty of nothing and there can still be a life for you. But if you can't stand it and you shoot yourself, then there is no return, that's forever, that will be the end. I gave him valerian drops and we talked and he finally fell asleep.

That night we devised a code. If he were to be arrested and allowed to write me and things were going well, he would end the letter with "I kiss you tenderly." If he wrote only "I kiss you," that would signify that things were so-so. But if he were to write "regards to everyone"—bad. Although I tried to reassure Mirosha to a certain degree, he expected the worst. Now this, now the other member of the Commissariat was arrested, fired. Every day new people turned up, only to be quickly replaced. It was like a kaleidoscope. Mirosha was expecting his turn.

And then, just before the New Year he phoned me and I hear his jolly voice, mischievously asking, "Have you already prepared your outfit for New Year's Eve?"

I don't understand a thing. He had never been interested in such things. He thought everything I chose was just wonderful. But to take an interest beforehand? Never.

"Yes," I answer. "An evening dress for the reception at the Commissariat."

"Ah, but we're not going there" joyfully, like a little boy jumping from one foot to the other. "We are invited to spend New Year's Eve at the Kremlin."

And that's it. I had to sit down. I almost burst into tears. Such a load fell from my shoulders! How gay and light everything felt, all the fears suddenly disappeared, they seemed so trivial, so funny. He continues, "Only two of us from the Commissariat have been invited: Maxim Maximovich (Litvinov) and I."

Aha, I think, recalling the meeting with Choibalsan. That means that Stalin is thanking Mirosha, he values him. Can it really be a success, another advance, a victory?

In any case, we cheered up. After all, wasn't it clear that he was not in disgrace, it had only seemed so? But Beria's one-legged brother hadn't stopped by because he didn't care about us at all. He needed girls, restaurants...

Mirosha was happy: "It means that they trust me."

Oh, what a fearful roller coaster. Your heart is constricted with fear and suddenly you are at the top, you can breathe, live, think about trivialities, about this and that as well as about serious things. That's the best—when your spirit is calm, you live well. And then suddenly a new swing throws you down; you don't know what to think. They say that Stalin loved that—to ride that roller coaster. But maybe that had nothing to do with Mirosha. Stalin was the problem here.

I had to quickly assemble a new outfit. To greet the New Year in the Commissariat I had a black evening dress sewn, black with train and a rose at the waist. But one doesn't go that way to the Kremlin. There you find the *party* ladies, there you have to be a "blue stocking" in a severe dress. God forbid that you display your shoulders or show a bit of your bare neck.

And here it is, December 31, 1938. The night that becomes January 1, 1939. Late at night we go to the Kremlin.

The large open hall of the Kremlin palace, I will describe it—where the tables were placed, where the New Year's tree stood, and who sat where.

An enormous Christmas tree, consisting of three trees fastened together, stood between two halls. Stalin sat at a wide table in the middle of the room. Opposite him sat Zhemchuzhina, Molotov's wife, and some other *party* ladies, all of them dressed in blue suits with a scarf. Only the gradations in the color of the scarves were different. The servants brought food—one brought caviar, another brought sturgeon, the third brought shashlik and something else. The dishes were amazing, varied, although the piquant cuisine of the Caucasus predominated. The tables were laden with wine.

Stalin loved these nocturnal feasts and he ate and drank like a man from the Caucasus—fatty lamb, sour wine. He did not listen to the doctors who dared to say that these habits were harmful to a man of his age.

Mirosha and I sat side by side at a table not far from Stalin. Careful attention was paid to each person's degree of subordination to Stalin. If we were given that place it meant that we were in his favor. We were sitting among people who were very close to him, those whom he had anointed at that particular moment. We all kept our eyes in his direction. As I said, the ladies were sitting opposite him. Molotov's wife, Zhemchuzhina, loved to create a retinue of obsequious men around herself. She normally behaved sassy and brassy. Abrashka told me that she was so sure of her and her husband's solid, invulnerable position that whenever she met an acquaintance, she would ask cynically, "Haven't you been arrested yet?" That was her way of joking.

But of course in front of Stalin she didn't behave that way. She sat more modestly than modest, and of course she was dressed accordingly.

But here is something that happened even before we went to dinner. The entrance was behind the fir tree. To get to Stalin's table, you had to pass close to us. Everyone had just sat down when Beria appeared at the door: small, fat, bald, his face gray and sickly and pasty, his gold pince-nez flashing. I caught sight of him and lightly touched Mirosha. Beria had reached the fir tree and was passing us when he saw Mirosha before him. That so struck me—or better to say my heart sank. Our eyes met but Beria's face remained impassive. He passed us by indifferently.

Still, that was a fateful moment. Mirosha had been a comrade of Abulyan, whom Beria had killed. He could not have been unaware.

Of course, I can comfort myself—if you can call it comfort—that Beria, in removing all of Yezhov's people and installing his own, Beria, perhaps, scanning the entire list of the important people in the Commissariat, might have known about Mirosha even without that incident. Mirosha—that one who once worked in the Caucasus.

Still, when I look back at that sudden face to face meeting, I ascribe to it everything that happened. Because the subsequent events happened very soon and very quickly. But at that moment I didn't obsess about that nasty impression. That Mirosha was the only one from the Commissariat invited to a nighttime feast in the Kremlin (besides Litvinov)—that overcame any anxiety. After that New Year's invitation all of our alarm and dread evaporated and we had six fully relaxed, calm, and beautiful days.

ଔ ଚ

January 6 was a free day for Mirosha. The work week was still six days a week.

We spent the entire day with the children—Agulya and Borya—and I think that Leva, Mirosha's nephew, was still with us. We went to the Park of Culture and rode on the carousel, the Ferris wheel, and the "devil's slide," and skated on the rink. Mirosha amused the children, behaved silly like them, just like a little boy. To make them laugh he would deliberately fall on the ice, although he was a very good ice skater ... and to Agulya's delight he slid down the hills on a little sled and fell over on his side just like the children.

Then, just the three of us, Mirosha, Agulya, and I, went to visit with our friends the Kolesnikovs, planning to go all together to the circus.

In the morning of that day, as I was making the bed (I didn't permit the maid to make the bed because she could never do it to my liking—she did it just any old way), I discovered Mirosha's Mauser under his pillow. Oh, I thought, that means he hasn't yet let go of his anxiety. And what if he were really to shoot himself! I hid the gun in a drawer where I kept my underwear.

Kolesnikov worked with Mirosha in the Commissariat. Mirosha always had friendly relationships with his co-workers.

Mirosha loved to dress up and that day he said to me "I think I want to wear my military uniform to go to the Kolesnikovs'." That was a jacket with medals and square buttons. Like any man, Mirosha looked very good in a uniform. He was accustomed to wearing one and missed it when he wasn't. He wore civilian clothes to the Commissariat.

The Kolesnikovs lived at the Pokrovsky Gates on the seventh floor of a large building that had no elevators.

We were having a jolly time. The telephone rang. It was a call for Mirosha. He takes the phone, he listens. I see confusion on his face.

"But that was already decided," he says.

It's clear that there was insistence on the other end. Mirosha, looking very perplexed, says, "Alright, I'm coming."

He slowly puts the phone down, stands by the telephone, looks at it. He's thinking.

"Mirosha, what is it?"

"I'm called urgently to the Commissariat because of fishing agreements with Japan, something unpleasant has happened. I don't understand, everything was settled."

And he whispers to me, "Maybe an arrest."

Until the New Year I had had to deal with his pathological fear, I was accustomed to it. And now I gaily brushed it aside.

"Don't worry, Mirosha. Just come back quickly, we'll wait for you. Try not to be late to the circus."

He dressed, he was obviously anxious. He asked Kolesnikov for the use of his car, saying that he would return in it. I accompanied him to the stairs.

"You'll call me as soon as you get to the Commissariat?"

He promised.

That day there was a frost. But even when it was freezing Mirosha never wore a muffler. I had with me a very good wool scarf from abroad.

"It's so cold," I said, "and you're coughing. Take my scarf."

He agreed. In ordinary times he would never had agreed, but this time he just took it. He looked at the scarf with tenderness, stroked it, and put it around his neck. Now, looking back, I understand it. It was mine and perhaps it would remain with him.

He was silent for a moment. Then he looked into my eyes, hugged me and kissed me very hard, gently pulled away from me. He didn't look back as he began to descend. I stood watching as he appeared on one landing, then another, lower and lower. He never once looked back. The door to the outside slammed shut. Everything was quiet.

You know, I never smoke, but this time thinking about this... I smoke a cigarette with an anti-nicotine filter. Well, of course, I was upset, remembering difficult things, but it is better to talk to someone about it than to carry a stone in your heart.

I returned to the apartment. It was happy there, the children were playing, but all my thoughts were with Mirosha. Some time passed—the telephone rang. I rejoiced, it must be Mirosha calling from the Commissariat. I grabbed the receiver and heard an unfamiliar voice.

"I am calling for Mironov."

"He's not here."

"Well, where is he?"
"He went to the Commissariat."
"Long ago?"
"About twenty minutes ago."

I stay close to the telephone. I wait. Mirosha will call and tell me in a happy voice that he's coming back right now to take everyone to the circus. And sure enough, the telephone rings.

Again, an unfamiliar voice, asking the same questions. When did Mirosha leave?

I answer, "By now, it must be about forty minutes ago."

I went back to the company to the conversation, but a call from Mirosha doesn't come. Suddenly there's a knock at the door. The housemaid opens it. A man comes into the room wearing white felt boots with leather soles (the kind that the NKVD men wore at that time). He very politely excused himself.

"Please excuse me for the interruption. I'm looking for comrade Mironov. Is he here?"

"And who exactly are you?" Kolesnikov asks.

"From the People's Commissariat of Foreign Affairs."

"Mironov isn't here. He left for the Commissariat."

"When?"

"Two hours ago."

"Excuse me for troubling you…"

He was being excessively polite. And then he left.

Kolesnikov asks me, "Agnessa Ivanovna, do you know that man?"

"No."

"I know everyone who works at the Commissariat. He is not from there. He's from the NKVD."

I felt a cold shiver. And then, again, the telephone.

"Agnessa Ivanovna, is that you?"

In an instant I was myself—it must be Mirosha!

But it was Maria Nikolaevna. "Please, Agnessa Ivanovna, quickly. Come home quickly."

"Why? What's happened?"

"Your mother is ill…"

But I already understood. "That's not true, Maria Nikolaevna. Tell me the truth. Are there strangers in the apartment?"

Silence. I hear how she whispers to someone: "Tell her? Can I tell her?" Apparently she got permission.

She said only one word.

"Yes."

"I'll be right there."

Kolesnikov was terribly upset: "Oh, this is terrible, I'm so upset, I can't stand it (not clear to me—exactly what couldn't he bear?). I'm so upset, I…"

"Calm yourself," I said. "You're upset and I'm not? I'm going home."

I called for Mirosha's car on the telephone. The car came quickly. Agulya didn't understand what was going on. She jumped around, frolicking, joking around. She purposely put the wrong arm in her jacket sleeve...

"We're going to the circus, right? Papa's waiting for us, right?"

We went downstairs. The chauffeur was also in a good mood, as if nothing were happening. (He still didn't know anything.) As we approached the government building, he asks:

"So, tomorrow shall I come for Sergei Naumovich at 9 o'clock?"

I'm evasive: "He'll call you himself."

But he answered eagerly, "I'll come at 9 o'clock." Everyone loved Mirosha.

We entered the apartment. It was full of them. With their fascist mugs. One of them, I remember, had a bulging lower jaw, a papirosa[34] insolently dangling from his lower lip, leering. They were waiting.

But I... I never lost my dignity. I calmly took off my coat, sat on a chair and removed my boots. Agulya silently stared at the strangers. I said to her, "Take your coat off, we're home."

"And what about the circus?"

"Now we have a circus at home."

"But I want to go to the circus," she wails.

Mama meets me on her crutches, her face drained of blood, her lips trembling.

"Aga, who are these people. Why are they here?"

"Don't worry, you can go to sleep. Maria Nikolaevna, please put Agulya to bed and help Mama." Mama was on the verge of sobbing.

They waited patiently. By law, as a formality, they could only do a search in my presence. I sat down on a chair and leaned on my elbow, not looking at them. They burrowed around in the first room, turning everything upside down and went to the second room. I followed them.

Suddenly that specimen in white felt boots with leather soles who was allegedly from the Commissariat turns up. But where is his politeness, his gentlemanly behavior? He screams at me coarsely, "Where is your husband? You have lied to me about everything. You've hidden him. Where have you hidden him?"

I calmly answer, "I assure you, he went to the Commissariat."

Aha, I think. That means that he hasn't fallen into your clutches—that's the best news so far.

But White Boots continues to yell: "What kind of car did he go in?"

"I haven't the slightest idea."

---

[34] A Russian cigarette. The papirosa is made of flimsy paper rolled over very harsh tobacco and has a cardboard mouthpiece. The papirosa is still available today.

He throws himself at the telephone and calls Kolesnikov, using that polite voice, unctuous as syrup, as treacle.

"Excuse me, tell me please, where is your car?"

Apparently Kolesnikov answered that he didn't know.

White Boots then calls the garage. It seems that Kolesnikov's car is already there. And still no Mirosha. I rejoice, I am so happy. He has not been caught, he isn't caught. He is free!

White Boots shouts, "Do you have relatives?"

"Yes."

"Give over their telephone numbers."

I opened my purse and found my address book. He roughly tore it from me. And never returned it. He began by calling Mirosha's brother. Mirosha, of course, was not there.

He raged like that until 2 o'clock in the morning. At 2 a.m. I heard a long conversation, conducted in calm voices, with the secret police. Then I understood that Mirosha had appeared. His freedom had come to an end.

They were all hoodlums except for one. He was the only one who spoke with me as if I were a person. He was young, his face was not swinish like the others. In the kitchen he dictated an address to me.

"You can go there to ask about your husband. There they will explain everything."

"Tomorrow?"

"Tomorrow is still early. Better in a few days."

"Can I send him a message?"

"They'll tell you there."

ଓଃ ଛ୦

After the search they sealed off five rooms in our apartment, leaving us only one. We all piled on top of each other: Mama, our devoted Maria Nikolaevna, Agulya, Borya (only for a little while, for I then sent him back to my sister), and I.

Three weeks after Mirosha's arrest we were suddenly called from the Lubyanka. I had run around all day to everyone I could think of, to my friends, acquaintances. I even called Abrashka to meet me at the public park to talk, maybe to find out something from him—after all, he insinuated himself into everything. I didn't look for work yet. A decent amount of money was deposited in my name in the bank. Mirosha had thought of that earlier.

After a whole day of dashing around I came home. Mama: "Someone's been calling you all day long."

"Who?"

"They didn't say."

The call came at midnight. A very young, polite male voice: "Agnessa Ivanovna? Hello. Forgive me for calling so late. We called you several times during the day. I am speaking from the People's Commissariat of Internal Affairs. Can you come here right now? Only, don't forget your passport."

I said directly, "Are you going to arrest me?"

"Are you afraid? Well, if you're afraid, then don't come. But it would be in your interests to come. If you decide to come, come to the reception. Number 24, Kuznetsky Bridge. Do you know it? There you'll find out everything."

He knew perfectly well that I would come. I was so afraid, but I had to know, I had to know what had happened to Mirosha.

I dressed warmly in whatever was at hand: woolen tights, a woolen shirt, a squirrel coat. I gave Mama and Maria Nikolaevna detailed instructions about what to do if I didn't come back.

All the service personnel loved us: the concierge, the doorman, the cleaning women. We always gave them tips. And there they were, the concierge and the doorman, surprised to see me going somewhere so late. I told them that I had been called by the NKVD. "I'll go with you," said the doorman. "I'm not working now"

And the concierge said, "I won't go home, I'll wait so that I can open the door for you."

The doorman accompanied me to the Lenin Library metro stop. I rode to the Dzerzhinsky metro stop, and walked to Kuznetsky Bridge. At the receiving window everyone already knew who I was, wrote me a pass and appointed someone to accompany me to the main building of the NKVD.

We ride up the elevator. A long corridor, rugs, silence. We go into an office. A very attractive young man, blonde, sits at the table and very politely sits me down. To the person who accompanied me he politely says, "Thank you, Ivan Alekseevich, you can go back to your work."

What can his work be, I wonder: preparing for my arrest?

The young man at the desk had not told me his name. But the man who had accompanied me said to him, " Yes sir, Pavel Yakovlevich!" and left.

I am emboldened. "Who are you?" I ask the man behind the desk.

"I am Mironov's handler. I have something for you," laying a piece of paper in front of me.

Mirosha's handwriting. "My dearest wife and friend. I have only now understood the degree of my love for you. I never believed I could feel such intense love. Everything will turn out alright, don't be afraid. Everything will soon be sorted out and I will come home to you. I kiss you tenderly. Mirosha."

Although I recognized his handwriting at first I didn't believe the letter was from him, until I saw *"I kiss you tenderly."* That was the code we had devised to convey that everything was alright. If he wrote "I kiss you tenderly," that meant that everything was fine.

"And now," said Pavel Yakovlevich (his surname was Meshik and he was Beria's assistant), "write an answer."

I wrote about all of our mutual acquaintances and about the fact that I wanted to leave Moscow.

"No," said Pavel Yakovlevich. "You are allowed to write only about yourself and your family. And you may not write that you want to leave."

He scrunched up my note and threw it in the waste basket. So I rewrote the note, very short, that everything was fine and ended with "I kiss you tenderly." He took it and said he would pass it on.

"And now," turning ever so politely to me, "tell me if you have any complaints."

I said that most of our apartment had been given to others and that we had not been able to take our belongings.

"Well, we'll fix that." He pressed a button and stood up.

I stood up, too. Someone entered the office.

"Accompany her," said Meshik.

I said goodbye and walked out with my escort. But now the corridor seemed dark and ominous to me, I couldn't see the elevator at the end of the hallway. I was suddenly stricken with fear.

"Where are you taking me?"

The escort looked back at me and I saw the face of a simple, kind Russian man.

"Don't be afraid..." he said softly.

I saw the elevator. We rode down and he walked me to the exit where I returned the pass signed by Meshik. The door opened and I found myself free in the empty nocturnal Dzerzhinsky Square. I took a long deep breath.

But what had happened with Mirosha? Why, leaving the Kolesnikovs at six o'clock did he appear at the Commissariat only at two o'clock in the morning? Where did he go? What did he go through those last hours of freedom?

I learned from the Kolesnikovs' chauffeur that Mirosha had not gone straight to the Commissariat, he went home. Mirosha asked the chauffeur to stop at the gate. He got out of the car and thanked the chauffeur, who never saw him again.

I pondered, what did he do? The letter that Meshik gave me to read did explain something.

He went home first to get the gun that he had prepared under his pillow. He already understood, in spite of all my assurances, that this strange call could mean only one thing—arrest. He had been thinking for a long time that he would not give himself up. But walking across the courtyard his experienced eyes told him that there was a plainclothes man in the entry way, so he walked into the still noisy streets of Moscow in the evening. He didn't go to anyone else. If he had, someone would have told me. What was he thinking? To walk in some other direction? To run? To save himself? But would that have been salvation? Wouldn't they search for him? And what kind of salvation would that be. And me? And Agulya? Find a way to kill himself without his Mauser?

There are many ways to cut one's life short. For him that would have been easier than to go through what awaited him. He didn't believe that they would release him. Such a long list of friends and acquaintances who had been shot passed before his eyes, bosses and underlings: Balitskii who, it was said, yelled horribly when he was about to be shot; Blyukher who was shot by Yezhov; Uborevich who was executed immediately after he was sentenced.

Kill himself? If he did, they would say: aha, you shot yourself, or threw yourself from a ladder, under a bus—that means that you were guilty, you were an enemy, you knew something about yourself. When Gamarnik was shot they cursed him as an "enemy of the people," and they made quick work of his family. How would they be with me and Agulya if he killed himself?

So, to save his family he accepted physical and moral torment, and that's what he meant in his letter when he wrote, "Only now I understand the depths of my love for you."

What did he suffer that night before he gave himself into their clutches?

I thought and thought about that, about that sentence, about his love for me. Did he sacrifice himself for my sake? I don't want to say that he didn't love me. He loved me as only one can love another person—passionately, fiercely, he loved! But as a reason to decide against suicide—it was a reason, but not the only one. He was immersed in his love, and it probably even seemed to him that he did not kill himself for that reason. But in fact he loved life too much and simply could not destroy it by annihilating himself. He was healthy and strong—to kill himself?

And my words helped when I dissuaded him from suicide and showed him that even if he were arrested, he could hope to prove his innocence, to get justice, after all he had been so successful all his life. Did he hope he could win that last game? Chances were small, but there were still chances.

He did not annihilate himself.

And I truly believed that there was a chance. For a whole year Meshik summoned me and gave me Mirosha's letters to read, letters he consistently ended with "I kiss you tenderly." And I answered with short vivacious letters. Sometimes it seems to me—after all Mirosha was so charming, he could bring even Beria's supporters to his side. Why was Meshik so kind to me, why did they let us stay in the House on the Embankment so long, and why did they make no attempt to arrest me, as they did the wives of other "enemies of the people?"

Or were they playing a sly game with him? They needed some kind of evidence from him and they used me as a bargaining chip. And they were using me and my freedom as a reward for his "evidence." Maybe he didn't believe that I was free, so they showed him my letters. They gave him my letters and promised not to touch me if he would meet them half-way.

What do I know? What can I possibly know? To this very day they have not showed me his dossier. What is written there? If only I knew. But, no, I am left with guesses, only guesses.

I've been told that were trying to get a diplomat called Gnedin to help cook up evidence against Litvinov and that maybe Mirosha got dragged into that.

Only one thing is clear: I lived for a relatively long time in the House on the Embankment, and the government did not arrest me, not that year, nor the next year, nor the next. I was not arrested because of Mirosha. My arrest in 1942 had nothing to do with him.

CO ED

On January 31, 1939 Mikhail Davydovich appeared and gave me an envelope. It was a ticket to the Bolshoi Theater to a memorial on an anniversary of Lenin's death. Just think. If we were really "enemies of the people," I could walk into the event with a bomb.

I say to Mikhail Davydovich, "But Mironov has been arrested."

"Arrested? So, that's that."

He did not take the elevator. He went on foot, repeating to himself "so, that's that." He was probably thinking that it was a situation he'd rather not touch.

As I've said, five rooms of our apartment were taken away from us and sealed up. Men from the NKVD began to visit us, one after another. They would ring the doorbell, enter, remove the seal that closed the five rooms to us, stay there for a while, come out, paste the seal up again. They would take something out. For a long time we couldn't figure it out. Finally, when one of them came, I said: "My things are in there."

"Things?" he repeated, and then casually said, "Well, take them."

I quickly began to grab my dresses from the closet—evening dresses, woolen dresses, silk dresses. I grabbed and grabbed, I took one fur coat (I had several more) and at that point the NKVD man said, "Enough!" Another time a policeman came with a package, he opened it showed us a collection of silver spoons, forks, knives.

"Are these yours?"

"Yes, they are."

"Write a receipt for them."

"I'll give you a receipt," I said. "But I can't accept them, because they were requisitioned."

"OK, just sign," giving me a paper. As I signed I read what was written: so-and-so was detained with a set of silverware. Later we regretted that we had not kept it.

And during the search, these bandits seemed to have the right to leave with full pockets of our valuable things—little boxes, pens, souvenirs.

Finally Maria Nikolaevna said, "Agnessa Ivanovna, look at that pathetic seal. It's nothing more than a twisted string. Pull it off, go into the rooms and then put it back." She was right and that's exactly what we did. We went into the rooms on tiptoe so that the inhabitants of the apartment below us wouldn't hear and began to retrieve our things.

This is how. We took the crystal and packed it under some ordinary dishes. We took some lovely tablecloths out of a trunk and packed them in with old sheets. We took new dresses and in their place hung up old dresses. The same with fabrics, and so on.

It turned out that it was not only we who did that. I was once sitting next to a woman in the clinic, waiting for my turn with the doctor. We chatted. She had experienced the same torment and hell as I. And she told me that they also managed to get their possessions. But in a different way. They overturned an entire requisitioned wardrobe, pulled off the back of it, and took everything in it.

In other words, we stole our own belongings.

When they put us out of the House on the Embankment, they gave us a room nearby, across the Moscow river on Kosovo Pereulok. It was in an old house with frescos painted by Vrublev on the façade. They moved others into our former apartment—who were also soon arrested.

Some good people taught me how to submit a request for the return of my mother's confiscated possessions. I was called on the telephone.

"Is it you who submitted a request?"

"It is."

"Come to this office."

It was not far, just across the bridge in the basement of the House on the Embankment. An escort was waiting for me. There was a concierge at the door, one of those who we knew. The escort showed him a paper that granted permission go to the storehouse. He asked me to describe my mother's possessions. I said a bearskin, a certain crystal, a fur coat, and so forth.

"I can point them out to you myself," I said.

He was terrified. "No, no, just wait here, I'll bring them to you."

He disappeared into the storehouse. The concierge began to tell me that the basement was stuffed with things. They had to turn things away. But people were coming for things all the time. They came with a release document and took things out, more and more, and still there were things up to the windows. Some thieves broke the grill and also took, took, took.

So we chatted until the escort returned, empty handed. No crystal, no bearskin, no fur coat. "Did your mother live separately from you?" he asked curtly.

"No."

"You lived together, like one family?"

"Together."

"Together?"

"Well, then, you can't have anything. These are Mironov's things and they have been confiscated. By law we cannot return anything to you."

"How can that be?"

"That's the way it is," and he left.

The concierge even threw his cap on the floor in anger.

"Ekh, can you imagine such illegal impudence!"

And, in fact, if that man were telling the truth, then they would have immediately turned down my request, they would not have taken me to the basement, where there were the riches of "a hundred and one nights." He was just using the permission that belonged to me for his own profit, whatever that may have been.

The concierge and the guard pitied us. They were sympathetic to us and they said, "Whatever is going on, to arrest such good people!"

When we had to move out of the apartment, they helped us carry things in a car. We were already in the new apartment, when I suddenly remembered, "Oh dear, I left a sideboard behind!" And it was such a pretty one, and expensive." The concierge said, "I'll bring it to you." And so he did, that night on his back.

CB 80

I never stopped hoping. Meshik called me regularly to let us exchange letters, and he gave me his phone number and permission to call him. Judging by the tone of Mirosha's letters it seemed to me that his case was moving in a good direction.

Mikhail Davydovich also believed in Mirosha's "lucky star." He said to me, "I can't believe that Mirosha can't extricate himself."

A whole year passed like this. A treaty was signed with the Fascists and the Soviet Union invaded western Ukraine, western Belarus, and the Baltic countries. Then there was the war with Finland.

Suddenly Meshik called me and gave me a letter from Mirosha:

"My dear wife and friend! I advise you to leave Moscow..." followed by a few more words, ending with "Regards to everyone. Mirosha."

"Regards to everyone." Not "I kiss you tenderly. Not even "I kiss you."

I burst into tears.

"Why are you crying?"

I pulled myself together. "Look, he says that we should leave Moscow."

"You don't want to leave?"

"I won't leave until I know what his fate is."

"Well, then don't go. I think that Mironov is probably still discussing things."

I waited a few days before I called Meshik again. His tone was completely different. He said coldly, "I am no longer Mironov's handler."

"How am I supposed to find out about him?"

"Call Lefortovo." And he hung up the telephone.

I called him again. An unfamiliar voice answered: "Pavel Yakovlevich isn't here. He doesn't work here anymore. Who is calling?"

"I am Mironov's wife. I need to know what's happening to him."

"Mironov isn't here anymore either. Call Lefortovo."

Other women, in a position like mine, told me what to do. They said: "Don't ask anything. Just go there, bring money, and give it over. If they take it, it means that your husband is there. And the women said not to give all the money at once. Divide it into two, meaning that I could go twice in a month to find out about him. They would take seventy-five rubles. The money was different in those days. That sum meant less than it means today. They advised me to bring seventy-five rubles the first time I go and in the middle of the month to bring five rubles.

So that's what I did. The first time, they took the money, meaning that Mirosha was in fact in Lefortovo. I began to go twice a month, giving money each time.

Lefortovo! Not long ago I was visiting Moisei Iosifovich Model and I asked Polyak[35] to talk about the conditions in Lefortovo. This is what Polyak said about himself; that he was lucky to have been arrested in 1936. If he had been arrested later, he would not have been sitting in this room. He was in Lefortovo from 1936 to the beginning of 1937. In solitary. The doors of the solitary cells were arranged around the periphery of an oval that opened to a terrace surrounded by grating to prevent anyone from jumping. In each cell there was a bed, a sink, a toilet. Food was brought on a tray. It wasn't bad. You were not allowed to sleep facing the wall. You would scarcely turn over in your sleep, when a guard would see you through a little window and yell out, "Face the door."

This was so you wouldn't kill yourself. You could have smothered yourself with the sheets. You could have attached them to the foot of the bed, made a loop around your neck of them, and choked yourself.

I was surprised. "You mean they actually had sheets there?"

That means that the conditions were good. But as Evgenia Ginsburg wrote in *Into the Whirlwind*—the dirtier, the worse the conditions, the coarser the guards, the more crowded the cells—the less dangerous. If the prison was lighter, more orderly, more comfortable for the prisoner—the closer the prisoner was to death.

---

[35] Polyak, "The Pole," was Kazimir Kazimirovich Petrusevich, a former gulag inmate, active in circles of rehabilitated former prisoners. His father, Kazimir Adamovich Petrusevich, a lawyer and active early Social Democrat from Belarus, emigrated to Poland in 1919, after a long period of exile. "Polyak," his son, at some point after his own arrest and years in the Gulag, became an eminent biologist, member of the Polish Academy of Sciences.

On a certain day I went to Lefortovo with my bribe. I went to press the button, but the sentry booth was closed. I was already irritated and started to leave. Suddenly a young officer came out of the booth holding a lock. I say to him, "Oh, I must have come too late."

He looked me over, hesitated for a moment, unlocked the booth and opened the little window.

"The surname?"

"Mironov."

He looked over his list.

"He's not here."

"What do you mean?"

He looked at me and I understood from his eyes that he pitied me (he already knew, he knew the truth). I understood this from his eyes. He said: "He's not here anymore. Go to the Kuznetsky Bridge, you'll find out there."

He did not have the right to tell me anything more.

At that time the following occurred. Agulya and I slept soundly through the night, and I slept especially soundly towards morning. This night that I'm telling about, I awoke abruptly as if someone had hit me. I look at the clock — it's six o'clock in the morning. I felt like there was terrible heaviness lying on my heart. I wrote the date: "February 22, 1940."

I told Mikhail Davydovich about it. In that period of my life I often turned to him.

"Alter, I just know that it's all over."

"Why do you say that, Agnessa? We will all be together again around this table, and you and Mirosha will reminisce about how you wrote down that date."

It didn't happen that way.

At Kuznetsky Bridge everyone was told how to find out about sentences. We were to come just downhill from Dzerzhinsky Square to the statue dedicated to the first printed book in Russian. There was some kind of a reception office there. I was already working, so I couldn't come until close to 4 p.m. There were hundreds of women there. A line, a crowd. I stood in line and waited until midnight before I got into the office. They received several people at once in the office.

This is what it was like: a man, no longer young, stood in the middle of the office. He wore the uniform of a military judge, looking crazy from lack of sleep, his hair plastered to his forehead by perspiration. It was stuffy, crowded. He looks at his list, mumbling in monotone.

"Mironov... Sergei Naumovich. In accord with article such and such, mumble-mumble, his sentence is ten years without the right to correspondence."

It was the same for everyone there: "Ten years without the right to correspondence."

That was another way of saying—shot! We didn't know it then, but there were rumors, rumors.

We heard and left. No one wept, no one sobbed, no one said a word. Silence.

At that time our war with Finland was going badly, and, as always when there were failures, our "Great Genius" would fall into a rage, and out of pure malice he would order that everyone, everyone, everyone be shot. That's why there were so many women there. It was a massive undertaking.

I want to bring up Polyak again. It was not for nothing that I questioned him in such detail. I recalled that he had told us that in Lefortovo interrogations were conducted upstairs where there were rugs and luxury, but there was also a place downstairs. Whoever was taken downstairs never returned.

Downstairs there was a powerful ventilator and one could shriek anything before being shot: "Hail to the revolution!" "Hail Iosif Vissarionovich Stalin." "I would die for the revolution!" It didn't matter, no one could hear you, not your voice and not the sound of the shot. I can imagine what it was like.

ଓ ଓ

After my rehabilitation in 1958, I needed a document verifying Mirosha's death. I was told to go to the regional ZAGS. The young girl at the reception asks, "What is this about? Has someone been born into the family?

"No," I said, "I need a death certificate."

She gave me a form to fill out. These were the questions: surname, name, patronymic, date of birth, date of death, cause of death.

"But," I said, "I don't know when and why he died."

She was astonished. "How could you not know?"

Another employee, somewhat older, quiet, said pointedly, "Katya, this one..." And he pulled a list.

"Ah." Katya guessed. She looks down the list and finds what she's looking for. I see that she writes the date of death. She writes it down, and I already know that she is writing "February 22, 1940." Where it asks for the cause of death, she leaves it blank.

Then she asks for fifty kopeks.

The older employee takes the document from her and writes at the top "no charge."

"Oh, I see. They're paying me fifty kopeks for my murdered husband. He didn't die, he was shot."

Speechless, they averted their eyes.

Oh, Mirosha, Mirosha. I often dream now. I dream about Rostov and the days of our secret meetings. I dream about how we quarreled and made up. We forgave each other everything and passionately threw ourselves at each other. But our meetings somehow slip away from me. In my dreams I am in

Rostov, I know that he is somewhere in Rostov, but for some reason I don't meet him. Or, I have already decided to run away with him and we're at the railway station. The train is approaching, but Mirosha disappears. I enter the train car. He is not there.

And after racing after shadows I wake up with a shattered soul.

Mirosha's nephew Lev is so like him. The shape of his head, his forehead, and his hair that grows tousled like Mirosha's. Sometimes I glance at Lev's head and it seems to me that there is Mirosha.

After Mirosha

My true husband was Mirosha. Not Zarnitsky and not even Mikhail Davydovich, although I bow to his intellect and talent.

But Mirosha was no more. When I heard "ten years without right of correspondence" I understood—this was the end. All sorts of rumors circulated, information from behind the stone walls. Abrashka surfaced again. But my feeling that Mirosha was no longer alive was verified. And I understood that Mirosha would *never* come back.

But I can't live alone, a widow. I love life too much.

Ivan Aleksandrovich had written me twice making overtures to me. He wrote that he was married, but if I agreed to return he would divorce his wife, because he had never stopped loving me and he still loved me.

I answered, "How can I come to you, how can I abandon my husband while he is in prison?"

I didn't write to Ivan Aleksandrovich after Mirosha was no more. I had already been spending more and more time with Mikhail Davydovich.

View from the Outside: Maya, Mikhail Davydovich's Daughter

Papa's father and Mirosha's father were brothers. Therefore, Papa and Mirosha were first cousins. Papa married Mirosha's sister. Both families were from the Shuliavka district of Kiev. Mirosha's fortunes improved when Grandmother Khaya bought a dairy story on the Kreshchatka and they moved out of the Shuliavka district. Papa's family remained in Shuliavka. Papa was the eldest son in a large family. He dreamed of studying but was never able to pursue his studies because he had to begin working at an early age.

He never stopped dreaming, and he actually went through a gymnasium curriculum on his own; self-taught, correspondence courses, a voracious reader.

When he was only a child he served as an apprentice in a store. He would stand in front of the store, whole days at a time, yelling at the top of his lungs, "Wool, muslin, calico, sateen, stockings." Then he was apprenticed to a metal engraving business and began to bring home a paycheck—pennies.

In 1910 Tolstoy died. Papa was so struck that he borrowed money to go to the funeral in Yasnaya Polyana.

Grandmother wailed in horror: "No, just think how much a ticket costs. I can't even imagine how long one has to work for that kind of money. He needs to go to the funeral of some kind of a count? So what if he's a writer, what if he's even God himself! But I ask you—what for? What does a poor Jewish boy have to do with a Russian count?"

Thanks to his erudition and intellectual development Papa had many acquaintances among Russian and Ukrainian intelligentsia families. Once, the girls in one of these families were trying to guess who Papa was: Armenian? Greek? Bulgarian? One of them suggested that he might be a Jew. The other one immediately cried out, "Oh, how disgusting."

After that Papa always presented himself to his acquaintances like this: "So that in the future you won't be disappointed, I want you to know that I am a Jew. If that doesn't suit you, then we cannot sustain our acquaintance." Papa had a great sense of his own dignity.

Even though he had completed his external studies for gymnasium, he was not able to take the examinations. It was 1912, and he was taken into the army. And soon after the First World War began. This is how he remembers the soldier's life.

Mikhail Davydovich's Diary:[1]

Winter 1914–15. I march with a company on sad Polish land. I am a soldier. In front of me I see sweaty necks and strong legs marching in formation. I am part of a huge many-legged creature. Above, a wet grey sky, wet and grey underfoot. I don't feel the fatigue and the cold. What do the war and the Germans mean to me? What does the grim soldier's story mean to me? I have a more profound grief that means more to me and my personal suffering. More than once I saw how the Don Cossacks hung, slashed, beat my co-religionists. I heard their cries and wails, I heard and saw the Cossacks' bestial hate for them.

I, a soldier in the Russian army, was transported into the world of my forebears who stood meekly before their God, asking him about the meaning of life.

But my Russian comrades sing foolish songs. They live only for today, because tomorrow they may be corpses. Today you have to eat, sleep and—if possible—get drunk, and—the pinnacle of bliss—a woman.

Stop, wench, stop, stop
And with us a song, do sing.

---

[1] Mikhail Davydovich's younger daughter, Maya, is quoting from his diaries and letters. Originally, they were to be published in the journal *Sovremennik*, but the journal fell on hard economic times. Thus, in 1999, Maya Korol compiled and self-published Mikhail Davydovich's diaries and letters, adding her own reminiscences to a book called *Odyssey of an Intelligence Agent: Poland, USA, China, GULAG*. In 2011, it was given to me by Agulya.

I don't sit in judgment of my poor friends. I love that simple charm and naiveté and honesty. Those qualities make more sense in life than any rhetoric. But, on the threshold of death, I could not share their joy in life.

Maya:

Then Father was badly wounded. After he recovered he was sent back to the Front. He was awarded the Medal of St. George for bravery.

In 1915 he joined the Jewish Workers' Party. "I joined that party" he writes in his autobiography, "because of the beastly anti-Semitism that I met with on the Front."

He was still on the Front when the February Revolution occurred and he served under Denikin. After the October Revolution he made his way to Kiev and headed the underground Jewish Workers' Party. Under the Reds he was the head of the city defenses and then he commanded the first Communist brigade in Kiev. Finally he was the secretary of the right bank Jewish Workers' Party.

I have taken all of this from his autobiography. I don't actually know much about this period in his life, only that he threw himself into the Revolution and gave his all for the ideals of the Revolution. They seemed to him to be the ideals of truth, justice, of everything better and brighter. The kinds of things he had dreamed of all of his life.

It is just as Agnessa says of Mirosha. Mirosha was just like Mikhail Davydovich. The Jews suffered from anti-Semitism, from pogroms, and contempt. The Revolution had put an end to anti-Semitism. It was their revolution.

My father began to work for the Ukrainian reconnaissance and information authority. In 1920 he was sent illegally to Poland where he organized a "red underground." A bold man, he loved risk. He worked in the Underground for seven months. Then he fell into the hands of the Polish military-field court that sentenced him to hanging. But our embassy intervened and Papa went to jail and then to a concentration camp. The Underground helped him to escape.

He returned in 1922 and organized a conference of the Jewish Revolutionary Party where he convinced everyone to dissolve the party and join the Communist Party. In 1923 he joined the editorial board of Red Star. Then he was editor of the army publication Crocodile. He wrote many things: serials, articles, brochures, and books.

In 1930 he was the head of the directorate of cinematography and the executive director of the journal Cinema.

From 1934 to 1938 he was in the intelligence service of the Workers' and Peasants' Red Army—Special Assignments.

Brusha and I did not think our Papa was handsome. He was not very tall, he was inclined to be overweight, sometimes he was simply pot-bellied. He had very expressive eyes, peaked eyebrows, a large nose, thin lips. I was often surprised that Mama, such a beauty, actually married him.

But all he had to do was begin to talk. He had beautiful diction, a lot of humor, and great erudition. You couldn't listen to him enough!

Papa loved books above everything on earth. He constantly bought books until there was no place to put them and then he built more shelves. When Brusha was ten years old, Papa gave her Don Quixote. Not to read it would have insulted Papa, so Brusha forced herself to read it. And he would ask her eagerly, "Is it interesting?"

"Interesting," Brusha would answer politely with a sanctimonious expression and Papa would be satisfied.

But more than once we disappointed him. Brusha got "very good" marks at school. Once when she was in the upper classes Papa asked her who Catherine the Second was. Brusha answered distinctly, like a textbook:
"Expresses the interests of the serf-owning class, a product of the monarchy."

Papa was horrified, clutched his head, and went to the school to confront the teacher.

"Why do you mark her 'very good'? She doesn't know anything."

Papa was passionate, irritable, explosive, very emotional, jealous. But his ideal was people who were calm and reserved. He was always striving to be like them, but, alas, he never succeeded.

He thought that jealousy was the worst possible emotion and passionately condemned Othello; if you can't live with it, than kill yourself. Why kill your beloved?

Papa had a strong sense of his worth. He was never ashamed to be a Jew. He was distressed that we had no interest in the history of our people and made no effort to understand that history, let alone learn the language. We hadn't the vaguest knowledge of it. Papa took us to the Jewish Theater where we didn't understand one word, although we were attracted to the acting of Mikhoels, a great Jewish actor. Before the war, when Papa's mother, father, and grandmother were still alive, he took us to Kiev.

Babushka said to me, "If you marry a goy, I won't give you a dowry.[2] I won't give you pillows or a feather quilt or blankets."

Papa revered his parents and regularly helped them with money. Each month when he was getting a "big" paycheck, the first thing Mama did was mail his parents a relatively large sum of money. The family revered Papa as the eldest. It was therefore natural for him to take the greatest responsibility for the parents. He did not reproach his brothers and sisters for helping less. As the elder, he was obliged to support the family, first and foremost, the old people.

---

[2] In Yiddish *goy* means a man who is not Jewish.

Papa was very sociable, always surround by relatives and friends. We frequently had guests who talked about the international situation, literature, art, theater, history. He was a good chess player, and he taught Brusha, who even achieved a ranking.

Papa was preparing to leave for the United States. For this reason we had coupons at the Foreign Trade Store (Torgsin) and were able to buy things for Papa and for ourselves. Before that he and a neighbor who both held the army rank of brigade commissar—high ranking-bums—had had one pair of uniform trousers for the both of them.

They began to teach Papa not only the English language, but American manners and Western dances—fox trot, tango.

Although they were getting us ready to leave, too, in the end Papa went without us. The real plan was to make his journey so complicated that by the time he got to the USA his original point of departure would be vague. First he went to China and from there to Japan where he almost perished. He was almost caught. They shot at him, but his airplane had already taken off.

He was traveling with Mark Shneiderman. From Japan they went through France and Germany. Then—Canada, and from there to New York in the guise of German Jewish businessmen. They made a lot of mistakes. For example, to economize they took just one room in a cheap hotel. That is something that a well-off businessman would never do. But they got lucky. It was just assumed that they were homosexuals.

Of course, I didn't understand anything. I didn't understand what was happening around me in 1936, 1937, 1938. Mama understood. She did a thorough sweep of his books, some of which had been published in the 1920s, like Trotsky and Bukharin, Radek, and others. Some had Papa's bookmark. Mama collected them, wrapped them and buried them in a closet, preparing to take them out to our dacha as soon as possible.

In those days I loved cocoa with milk. I brought a bunch of the books that Mama had hidden away and sold them to buy myself cocoa. I lapped it up.

Then Mama happened to look into the closet. She was stupefied: where are the books!

I confessed what I had done.

She was horrified.

"You little fool," she said. "Don't you think I would have given you money for cocoa? Do you understand that we could all be arrested?"

For several months she expected to be arrested, waited for that frightening knock at the door in the evening. But, it never happened.

Then in 1938 Papa came back. We met him at the station. It was a frosty winter day. Out of the train comes a well-dressed, stylish foreigner carrying a suitcase with an amazing zipper.

He found us and we all kissed and hugged. Papa began to speak; he had a strong accent and he sometimes had to grope for words or slip into English. He didn't say baggage, he said, "The freight is coming separately."

Oh, that "freight." It was packed in huge trunks, wardrobe trunks like real clothes closets. I remember well what Papa bought. But Mama had no interest in things and she was scornful of obsession with things. She reproached people who valued things for being "bourgeois," and she gave things away right and left. Papa tried to stop her. "What are you doing? You are raising two daughters!" But she gaily dismissed him. To care about things—that was the heritage of the cursed capitalist past. That is what she believed and that is how she raised us. We, alas, were more materialistic.

Papa told us about the wonders of the other world, about refrigerators with shelves that were found in every apartment, about how zippers had replaced buttons.

When Papa returned from America he could not find work and the Party even took away his Party card (they returned it three years later). He sat home, going out of his mind without work.

Mark Shneiderman was arrested. Papa expected to be arrested every day. We were very short of money. Papa passionately insisted that we should sell his clothes, because he couldn't take care of his family.

That was a hard time in our lives.

Mama fell ill with breast cancer. She had a successful operation and Papa said to her in the hospital, "My little bird, you just get well and I'll carry you in my arms." They had a close and tender relationship.

But the operation came too late. The cancer had already metastasized. Mama was terribly ill—her liver was enlarged and painful, she was nauseated.

I didn't understand how serious her condition was. Everything was hidden from me. But Brusha was older and she knew.

I was fifteen. Returning from a walk, I saw the emergency vehicle at our door. Worried, I asked, "Who are you looking for, what apartment?"

They said our apartment number. "A woman is dying there."

I darted up the stairs, saw my dying mother, and I cried out in terror.

I finished school and applied to medical school. Brusha and her boyfriend Borya helped me prepare for the examinations. They were already students.

The examinations. I and a classmate of mine did only middling well on the examinations, but I wasn't upset. But my girlfriend's mother had connections and made a call asking for someone....

I turned to Papa. "You have connections, call, ask them to accept me."

You should have seen his face at that moment. He pushed his chair away from the table, abruptly threw himself back, shot me an outraged look, and barked at me

"You want me to intercede for you? How could you think such a thing? You want me to demean myself because you didn't study hard enough? You had everything you needed to study well. You had everything."

And sternly, "If you don't pass the examinations, you will work in a factory. Many girls of your age have already been working for a long time. That's it. I will not lower myself."

I passed.

I remember something else. This happened just before the war in 1940. Papa translated the narrator's text for a documentary film about Professor Filatov, the ophthalmologist.[3] The film was made to be shown in the United State. Filatov was a deeply religious person. Before every operation he prayed for a good outcome. In the film Filatov operates and returns sight to a child. The child's mother thanks him. He answers, pointing his finger to the sky, "You should not thank me. You should thank Him."

The director ordered a fade-out at that point and inserted an enormous portrait of Stalin. As if Filatov were suggesting that Stalin was the one who should be thanked.

Papa objected. "You have to take that out. Americans will not understand what Stalin has to do with it."

The director smirked, "Oh, does that mean that you don't believe in Stalin?"

Maybe Papa was reminded of that when he was arrested.

Papa worked with enthusiasm, and now he was being paid. It was contract work and he began to earn well. He was a suitable match for the work. Mama was still alive, but everyone knew that it was hopeless and two of our good friends, Gusta (Mirosha's first wife) and Aunt Aga were very helpful in caring for her.

When Mama died, Aunt Aga swept away her competitors.

CB ВО

A relationship with a painful subtext was developing between me and Mikhail Davydovich. Mikhail Davydovich believed that our relationship was impossible. Mirosha's fate seemed to literally put me beyond his imagination.

Sometime after Mikhail Davydovich was arrested he was sent to the Spassk. But he wrote me long beautiful letters from the camp. Actually, he was in a clinic there to which "used up" prisoners were sent to die. Here is one of the letters he wrote.

> The first time I saw you—do you remember, in a hotel in Moscow?—you didn't make much of an impression. Yes, she's beautiful and nice, but not memorable. Then I met you in your home in Dnepropetrovsk. I danced with you. I liked you, but it was like the government's money. Not one kopek of it is mine. I could only look at the money.

---

[3] Dr. Vladimir Filatov (1875–1956). He introduced the tube flap grafting method, corneal transplantation, and preservation of grafts from cadaver eyes.

In 1938 you came to us in Kraskovo and I accompanied you to the electric train. We spoke for a long time. That time you attracted me not by your beautiful face and figure but by something else—you seemed very interesting and winning to me. I was reluctant to part with you. I went back to the dacha, and when I thought of you I was sad. You were forbidden, you were taboo. And every time I met you after that I was very kind to you, but I never lost sight of the taboo. In 1939 we met in the hospital, where my wife Fenya had had an operation. When we left I suggested that we walk home, and you so joyfully agreed. We chatted, I tried to be an interesting conversationalist, and somehow I managed it. I could see that you were pleased and considered me to be a good friend. But the taboo was still in place.

The first time the taboo was broken was when I put you on the tramway. I very lightly place put my hand on your waist. You felt it and turned to face me. Your eyes said—yes, you may.

I was confused. The taboo cannot be broken.

And only in the course of several months when we were like brother and sister, dear to each other but not essential, did I cautiously kiss your head, without transgressing the taboo. I sincerely wanted to reassure you, I kissed your face and it was wet with tears. I clearly felt your grief.

The next day I came to you and you greeted me warmly. You approached me and kissed me so naturally that I understood how close we were. That kiss was our marriage. You became my wife.

His love for me was beautiful. We became husband and wife.

Mirosha and I were merry comrades, playful like little children. My relationship with Mikhail Davydovich was entirely different. He was thirteen years older than I, but that really wasn't it. It was his authority and intelligence. He was like a beloved father, teacher, and I deeply respected and revered him for his knowledge, his talents, his wisdom.

But he loved me fiercely, like a young man loves.

He was jealous of the past. His attachment to Mirosha changed to unconscious distaste. Once I found his letter addressed to Mirosha, written in the event that Mirosha escaped and returned. In his heart he would not dare to hope for Mirosha's death, but his return would have been the death of Mikhail Davydovich. He wrote explaining why he married me. He wrote that I was helpless and unhappy and that among the Jews there was an ancient law that when a brother died, a living brother had to take on the care of the widow. As if to say that Mikhail Davydovich was obeying that custom. He was explaining, not justifying himself. The tone of the letter was dry and unfriendly. With all of his amazing qualities, Mikhail Davydovich could not overcome his male egotism. They are all like that, proprietorial. They say, "This is mine!" Mirosha was no longer his close cousin, but a competitor.

We became husband and wife without ever speaking of it. We continued to live separately, only frequently coming to one another. That is because my Agulya had not forgotten Mirosha, and his two daughters, still girls, might have seen our marriage as a betrayal of their mother. They might have been jealous. And they were.

View from the Outside: Maya

Agnessa told us that Papa loved Mirosha. But aside from a family feeling, Papa was often sharply critical of him. For example, for his card playing. Once when Uncle Mirosha invited the whole family to spend the summer in Dnepropetrovsk, Mama and I went but Papa stayed home.

Papa found Mirosha's circle offensive.

Uncle Mirosha was a talented man and he had military gifts. In less than a year in the tsar's army he rose from soldier to lieutenant. And in the Red Army he went up in the world. If he had remained in the army he probably would have become a marshal. And he might have been shot, just like Tukhachevsky. His life was probably longer by several years because he became a Chekist.

I remember him well. How handsome he was! I couldn't take my eyes off of him. I would sometimes say to him, "Uncle Mirosha, you are so handsome."

He would answer, "Take my good looks and give me your thirteen years."

Papa writes that he had been in love with Agnessa for a long time. But I remember when she came to our dacha in Kraskovo. Uncle Mirosha didn't come, but she came almost every day. They were staying not far from us in Tomilino and she could come on foot. She would come all dressed up, openly showing off her beautiful figure in tight brightly colored crepe de chine, showing off her décolleté. Under the fashionable long skirts of the time she wore very high heeled shoes. Very modest make-up. She would dash over, lively, vivacious, talkative. Mama always greeted her warmly. But Papa, I remember, called her a "lady," meaning lazy, and it seemed to us that he was not happy with those visits.

After Mama died, she and Papa spent a lot of time together, but I didn't think that was very important. I only noticed that Papa spoke differently about her. Now he would say, "What a hard worker she is. And so beautiful, just like Mama." He even thought they resembled each other.

But our neighbors began to whisper whenever they saw me: "Poor, poor orphans," shaking their heads. "And their mother's body is not yet cold in her grave."

"What do they mean?" I couldn't understand why they talked like that.

Or they would be more direct. "It will be very bad for you, with that stepmother."

"What stepmother?"

"What's the matter, can't you see? That aunt of yours that comes around all the time."

I could not understand what they were about. I couldn't put that together—Aunt Aga and Papa? What nonsense!

June 22. Noon. Molotov's agitated voice over the radio. War!

Papa went straight to army headquarters. He was more than fifty years old, but he insisted that his health was excellent, that he had experience from World War I, that he could be very useful on the front. They turned him down. He went back. They turned him down again. Probably because of the suspicion of anyone who had lived abroad.

Sometime in the first days of the war I opened a drawer of the desk. I was looking for some documents. And I saw the marriage license with his name and Agnessa Ivanovna Mironova's name. I couldn't believe my eyes. Brusha came by. I said, "Have you seen this?"

She smiled. "I've known for a long time." Brusha was just like Mama: good-hearted, tolerant, understanding, and forgiving.

Maybe Brusha was like that because she was preparing to marry Borya and everything was new in her life. She was drifting away from our family.

Papa had earlier put in his will that twenty thousand was for Agnessa, five thousand each for me and Brusha. And right into her hand he put a "gold loan," a state bond that could be cashed in with interest. All of his worldly goods. Maybe that influenced her choice of Papa. After all she was a woman who knew how to take care of herself.

Brusha and Borya got married. But Brusha couldn't bring herself to tell Papa. She would often stay over at the Berkenheims (Borya's family) and little by little she began taking her things there. But how to tell Papa? I advised her, "Don't tell him that you are already married, tell him that you and Borya want to get married. Or better yet, ask his permission."

"I can't lie."

After the explanation took place, Brusha told me how it went. When she told Papa, his expression was stony and he said coldly, "I don't think you need my opinion. I have nothing to do with this, I am not central to this issue."

I told you Papa was a very jealous person.

I don't know what else they said to each other. Only that they sat closeted in Papa's study for one and a half hours, and they both came out tearful and reconciled.

In those times nobody had weddings. The war was going on; the enemy was grabbing one city after another. No one was interested in a wedding.

But as soon as Agnessa found out about their marriage, she was on fire. A wedding, absolutely a wedding! At home everything was already done the way she wanted it.

The wedding took place in our big apartment. Although it was no longer so big. After Mama died one room was taken away from us and given to other tenants. We ended up living in a communal apartment!

But what a table Agnessa laid. The marvelous dishes, the napkins, the table cloth, the appetizers. Agnessa even managed to find fresh roses. She probably longed for a holiday, to take our minds off of what was happening and to shine as she had in Mirosha's time, to bring back that very air.

She presented the young couple with a camel-hair blanket that she brought back from Mongolia.

And she herself was dressed as she loved to; in a brilliant brocaded dress that displayed her arms, neck and shoulders. Borya's father—Boris Moiseevich Berkenheim—began to kiss her little fingers and then higher, higher up her lovely white arms. Noting the glances of the women, he pulled himself together. At home he said of Agnessa, "What a disgusting woman."

Ah, hadn't Papa talked like that about Agnessa to Mama?

Brusha was full of her life as a young wife. And I—for me my father's wedding was full of grief.

View from the Outside: Agulya

The wedding was like that for me, too.

We were moved out of the House on the Embankment to a building across the street—on the other side of the river on Kursovy Alley. It is quite a prominent building, made of red brick with a design made of a brick of another color. On one of the corners there is a bay window. That's where our apartment was. The bay window made it look bigger than it was.

I could not forget about Papa. We all dreamed that he would return. And when Mikhail Davydovich began to visit us so often, and even stay until the morning, I began to understand that something was going on. I was very hostile to him. He would often bring sweets for me—but I wouldn't take them. I wouldn't eat them. I would glower at him.

At the beginning of the summer of 1941 Mama and I went to Sukhumi on the Black Sea, to Uncle Pavel who lived and worked here. And suddenly— war! People ran around looking for food. We immediately tried to go to Moscow. But people fell all over each other to get to the trains and we could only get tickets for twenty days later.

In Moscow, the bombardment began. We children spent the night in bomb shelters. Often they took us there early in the evening. We stayed there until the all-clear. One morning when we went upstairs the courtyard was covered with broken glass. Everything was helter-skelter in our room as if things had moved about by themselves. The window opposite had no more glass, and the broken window frame swayed on its hinges. A bomb had fallen nearby and made a mess like a wave of air.

From a letter of Mikhail Davydovich to Agnessa:

Camp Spassk, April 22, 1955

My wonderful friend!
September 1941. An air attack. I led the children, Agulya and Maya, to the bomb shelter, and I remained in the apartment with my wife.

I loved my wife very much and was always happy to be alone with her. We had recently married, not more than a year and a half ago, and I loved her, not with a young fleeting love, but solidly and profoundly. Neither of us was young and we both knew life. I had long loved her, but it was a well–suppressed love, never expressed, kept under lock and key. Time pitilessly took beloved people from us and freed my conscience from its difficult servitude. I came to her like a physician and a teacher, and my liberated love attracted her to me. I became her husband, loving and protective. There was no greater joy for me than to hold my beloved in my arms, my Agnessa, to follow her tirelessly, to watch her. Aginka had the most abundant human character. An excellent housekeeper and at the same time a circus performer, a trapeze artist floating under the circus tent or in a cell with wild animals.

I can see her on a circus stage in a cage, wearing a short accordion-pleated skirt and spangled boots. Yes, she could be a lion tamer. Her large eyes are round. This gives her face a kind of cruelty, even rapacity. Her lips, pressed together, went along with that impression. But she had a kind and sensitive soul. Perhaps cruelty was a part of her character when she was pursuing a goal. But her main characteristic was independence. This is a woman who could never be a sweetheart, submitting to the role of the companion, merging her will with the will of another person, voluntarily submitting to a beloved person. And truly: her independence never wavered and even in love she remained restrained and retiring. If her restraint supported her independence, her timidity was a veil under which she jealously hid her body to protect independence. Well built with a Rubensesque figure, middling height, lively with a wonderfully pleasant voice, she was always impeccably and appropriately dressed. She always created an atmosphere of order and comfort that made life pleasant and attractive. I was constantly observing her, trying to read her—this interesting creature. Every day brings new puzzles.

Episodes of great distress revealed a lot to me about Agnessa and about me. Only separation and the passage of time help me to understand what we have gone through, I and my marvelous beloved friend.

The War: We stood embracing in the door to the balcony and anxiously looked at the square; people were rapidly deserting as the hum of unfriendly enemy airplanes grew louder. They hit our anti-aircraft guns. Detritus fell on the roofs. We knew what this meant. We heard the sound of falling bombs. We shivered and hugged one another, as if to protect ourselves from the danger that threatened us. The sound was somewhere close to us. Aginka hid her head on my chest. Her dear eyes were open wide, but they showed no fear. I kissed your eyes, embraced you. Your desire to assert life in the midst of thunder and death poured into me.

View from the Outside: Maya

On October 16 the Germans penetrated the front and Moscow was in a panic. Papa summoned me. "Hurry and pack up, take the most essential things and come with me to Mosfilm [Moscow Film]. We're going in trucks and they won't wait.

I was very sloppy. Mama never taught Brusha and me to be efficient. She thought: why should I torment them in their childhood?

So we were occupied only with our studies and with community service. Community service—that was very important then.

We were phenomenally impractical. I learned to dust only when I got married. The first chicken that I cooked was unplucked. So first I pulled out the feathers with a tweezers.

After Mama died our housekeeper Maria Aleksandrovna began to actively pilfer from us. Although she had done it while Mama was alive, she was very devoted to Mama. We had a trunk that was full of linens. We girls didn't know what was in it. Now, when I looked in it, it was empty.

I began to quickly grab whatever fell under my hands and stuffed it into my rucksack. Papa's white felt boots, his shaving razor, an old pair of astrakhan gloves, and a midseason coat for myself. I forgot about feet and remained in my slippers.

ଔ ଓ

It was the "escape from Moscow." I had fourteen trunks, full. Three held the most valuable things. We dragged them, huffing and puffing. The cars belonged to Moscow Film. They grumbled at us, "There's not a spot to sit on and you are loading us up with those things?" Mikhail Davydovich was embarrassed and he said to me, "Let's leave several suitcases for another car to take." In the end we had to do that. In one of the abandoned suitcases were my thick-soled shoes, but I was wearing warm indoor shoes. One of Mikhail

Davydovich's colleagues offered to leave some things with her aunt and we left other things with Mirosha's sister-in-law Nadya.

Off we went. There were traffic jams everywhere. People were on foot with bundles and children. I looked at them and thought, we at least are in a car. We have to be thankful for our luck, just look at how hard that must be for them. I was very sad for them. What do all my things mean! Just as I feared, when we arrived my suitcases were not in the second car.

View from the Outside: Maya

> *Agnessa could not bear the loss of her things and she reproached Papa for allowing them to be put in the second car. "I was a rich woman," she said to Papa, "and now I have nothing."*
>
> *But what could he have done? There was panic, irritation, hysterics and the Mosfilm people shouted that the car was full of our things and that there was not room for other people's things. They yelled, "Get them out of the car!"*
>
> *When we got to the steamship, Agnessa had not yet cooled off and talked incessantly about those things. (These were things that she had brought from Mongolia; in spite of the confiscation she had been able to hold on to them.) She was so annoyed.*
>
> *Gusta, Mironov's first wife, was on the boat. First, Agnessa conquered her to get Mironov and then Papa. It goes without saying that our Aunt Aga was not Gusta's favorite person. Agnessa complained even to her, exaggerating the story of what wonderful things she had lost.*
>
> *We were standing on the deck. Agnessa went below and I remained with Gusta. Papa and Mirosha were first cousins, so Gusta was also our aunt. She had never had children. She was alone. She said to me, "Mayechka, come with me to Kazan. You can continue to study there. You can see for yourself what she is [that is, Aunt Aga], what kind of a petty bourgeois. Such a war is going on and all she can talk about is her things."*
>
> *She convinced me. I went below to the third class—that's how we were traveling—and I told Papa that I was going with Aunt Gusta. He was calm.*
>
> *"As you wish, Maya. It's your business."*
>
> *But then he found a moment when we were alone, and he asked, "Why do you want to go with Gusta? Is it hard for you with Agnessa?"*
>
> *"No," I answered, "it isn't hard, but I will be able to study in Kazan." (I had already finished one year of medical school.)*
>
> *"But you can study in Kuibyshev, too."*[4]

---

[4] Kuibyshev is a small city about 500 miles east of Moscow. It was originally called Samara. The Soviets renamed it to honor Valerian Kuibyshev, a leading figure after the Revolution and Stalin's economic advisor. Since the fall of the Soviet Union, it is once again called Samara.

I understood then that it would be hard for him to part with me, and I went to Kuibyshev with them.

There they gave us one room, sixteen by eighteen meters, for several families. It had been an office in the Mosfilm studio. There were several desks in the room. Agulya and I slept on one. Our father and Aunt Aga slept on the floor with several other couples. The desk was narrow. I pushed Agulya in my sleep and she answered me with a pinch.

The Karavaevs slept right next to Papa and Agnessa. Not long ago their son had perished on the Front. His mother was in a state of depression. The head of the family, a womanizer, was small and wiry, like a monkey. At night, taking advantage of their proximity, he tried to flirt with Agnessa. She gave him a good pinch.

There was another "film type" who made advances on two fronts—to me and to Agnessa. But I was only seventeen years old, I was just a girl. So he decided that Agnessa would be more compliant. Oh my, did she give it to him, how she gave him an earful, it was something to hear!

Besides the Karavaevs, the Genins and the Sinyavskys lived with us. Every night Mr. Sinyavsky came home drunk and would sing "Let's go to that flaming Kakhovskaya" and on to "her blue eyes," at which point he would sob. The Kakhovksaya region was the site of a furious battle between the Reds and the Whites during the civil war: he probably had some kind of a girlfriend there. So that's how we lived. It all began peacefully. Nobody had anything.

○8 80

We had an immersion heater that we would lower into a pot to make soup. They say it is dangerous to cook with an immersion heater, that you can only boil water with it. I don't know about that, we cooked soup and nothing happened. There was only one pot for everyone. I bought it at the market. It was enameled. We took turns cooking.

View from the Outside: Maya

As soon as we were settled in Kuibyshev Papa went to the war office to insist that he be sent to the front, where his experience would be useful. They turned him down again. Papa took it very hard. He was anxious and began to talk about going back to Moscow.

I started to work as a helper to a film engineer in the documentary department of Moscow Films and in the viewing room. During the day they would show the news from the Front, at night the government people would watch these films and captured feature films. When our leaders came the viewing room was full of bodyguards and all the rooms were taken by military guards.

The man who had been the film engineer was replaced by a woman. They got rid of the man because he mixed up a segment of a film about Kirov; first he showed Kirov's funeral and then he showed Kirov making a speech. They not only fired him but they sentenced him on Article 58—treason—and sent him to a camp.

The woman who replaced him was scared to death. For example, once when we were fooling around with some film, a very interesting man joined us. My boss sent me to the basement to get some boxes of film. They were very heavy. I was completely convinced that the unexpected guest was there because of my indescribable beauty. I said to him as if I were doing him a favor, "Let's go, you can help me." He came and carried the boxes, and I with my calm soul considered it his job. I just couldn't understand why she looked awful and stared at me with terrible eyes. Only when he left, she screamed, "What have you done! That is the head of the entire security."

He could also have fallen under Article 58 because he disappeared for a minute with me.

But nothing happened.

Then there was this adventure. Once I was walking down the street. Winter, cold. And suddenly a door to a half-basement opened, someone came out, and I felt a blast of warmth. I got a look inside—food! This was a store open only to the chosen.

I told everyone in our room about it. Their idea was that I should dress up more elegantly, and they would all give me their ration cards to redeem food. Everyone began to search their things for the best clothes—one donated a hat, someone gave a chinchilla coat, someone else—elegant boots. I got dressed and left. I approach the door with an independent expression on my face. The porter took all my ration cards, looked them over, and said very respectfully, "Your cards are not yet validated. Please go to the next room, they will validate the cards for you." I look down at my wristwatch (gold—someone gave it to me) and said airily, "Oh my, you know, I am in a big hurry. Could you please validate them and tomorrow I will definitely go to the next room." And he did it.

But first I dashed into the jewelry store to have a look. And then I went to buy bread. I left the jewelry store and reached for the ration cards. Where were they? I remembered how some character in the jewelry store was fussing around the display, looking so intently that the display window fogged up. I was irritated because I couldn't see the jewelry clearly. And he was almost rubbing my shoulder. It's clear! He took the cards. Only a person who has been through a war can understand what that means.

But, wait, there was still a small hope. Maybe I left them at home? I went back home and frantically looked here, there, and everywhere. And Agulya—clever little devil. In those days she hated me, she was in competition with me. After all, until then she had been a single child in the Mironov household and was unbelievably spoiled. She immediately understood what was happening. She sat on a heap of rags and said to me with evil delight, "What, have you lost the cards? Can't find them? Well, that's good, I'm so happy." She was exuberant, gloating.

So I lost the cards, now what? At the loading zone you could buy commercial bread but you had to stand in line all night and half the next day. And they would only give out one big round loaf of heavy grey bread.

So I went and stood from the evening to the morning. They wrote a number on your hand with indelible pencil. It was so cold. The tenants of the building next to the loading zone would not let you warm yourself in the entryway. They locked up the entrance. I tried to shelter under the balcony where at least the wind was not so strong. Then some boys noticed me and began to throw things. They poured water on me and jumped around with joy when the water hit me. Then the whole balcony with the boys on it collapsed on me. Fortunately, no one was hurt.

In the night, almost early morning, Papa came. "Go home, warm up," and he took my place. Agnessa didn't come. I thought, if that had been Mama... Then Papa went to Moscow. It was all so bitter, it was so hard to live.

My only pleasure was writing to Brusha. To whom else could I turn, if not her? I wrote, I poured everything out.

But, of course I was careless and I left a letter I had written just wherever it happened to fall. Aunt Aga read it. I was expecting a storm, an outbreak. Not at all. I really liked her reaction. She said to me in a good-natured tone, but with irony: "I read your letter. You certainly horsewhip all of us. Well, just keep it up!"

And that was it. Not another word. She behaved as if it had never happened.

Of course, I was biased against her. But she was never the "wicked stepmother." She stood up for our family. I remember the time that Mrs. Sinyavskaya said with irritation that I simply did not know how to brush my hair properly. "What are you trying to do with your disheveled hair? Are you trying to make a crow's nest?"

It was something to see how Agnessa exploded.

"Are you talking about our Maya's disheveled hair?" She roared like an enraged mother tiger. "That she has a crow's nest on her head? And your Masha, with two hairs on her head, both of them thick. Our Maya has excellent hair, anyone would envy hair like that."

Agnessa always tried to praise my "talents." Once I was drawing something. She looked at my picture and fell into raptures.

"How well you draw, Mayechka. You must study drawing."

And since I denied it because I was harshly critical of my "gifts," it was she who found an art school that had been evacuated to Kuibyshev, bragged about me to them, and arranged for me to attend "on a trial basis" and encouraged me not to waste this opportunity.

Besides her kindness to me personally, she believed that a woman does not have to yield to a man's wishes in anything; a woman should use everything that has been given to her; a woman must not retreat into herself, she must be assertive.

She watched over me like an experienced woman protects an inexperienced woman, that is, a young woman. I had bad posture, I slouched. She would say to me, "Why do you carry yourself like that? You are very capable. You should carry yourself proudly, like a queen."

Our life with the neighbors grew more complicated. First, it was all about the water heater. But Agnessa with her natural energy and her practical nature sold something on the black market and bought a kerosene stove. That was to rid our family of the immersion heater business. But the neighbors began to ask permission to cook on our kerosene stove in our pot. (They still had not settled the question of exactly how to share one heater, and also there was so much pressure on the voltage that sometimes the lamps only gave off a little red light.)

Aunt Aga agreed and we began to share our stove with them. But the lines to buy kerosene were very long, and we got tired of it. So Agnessa told the neighbors that they could use the stove and the pot, but that we should all take turns standing in line to buy kerosene.

CS ʙO

They were too lazy to go for the kerosene. So, I refused to let them use it. Old lady Genin (an obnoxious old lady) began to beg, "Give it us, give it to us, tomorrow we'll go for the kerosene." So I gave in. But the next day there was no kerosene left and no one went for it. After that I wouldn't give it to her again.

View from the Outside: Maya

Then I was mobilized for the war effort!

The Sinyavsky's daughter Masha and I became good friends. In May 1942 we both received the call-up. Masha's father (the one who sobbed at night and called out "Kakhovka") was the secretary of the Party organization of the Kuibyshev branch of the Moscow Documentary Studio. He told Masha that he could get her out of the mobilization.

"Either Maya, too," Masha answered, "or neither of us. Otherwise I'll never be able to look her father in the eye."

Sinyavsky couldn't get two exemptions. We were sent to Saratov to a government school to train as Morse code specialists. Our relatives accompanied a group of mobilized young women to the quay. The mothers wept and wailed, embracing their daughters. Aunt Aga and Agulya accompanied us. Aunt Aga had prepared food for me, and the entire time Agulya whined "Mama! Let's go. Is Maya leaving soon?"

There were lots of officers on the boat in the cabins. It was very cold on the deck, and the officers began to invite the girls to their cabins. They all went—except for Masha and me. We preferred to freeze.

In the school—a sensation. The girls have come. The kids swarmed all over the balconies and just about spilled out of the windows. We went straight to the sanitary station. We undressed and got towels and soap from a small window. And who was sitting there but a pilot, young and dashing. The girls shrieked and pressed themselves against the walls and into the corners.

"What's the fuss, girls?" he said calmly. "We're at war. I came here on a break simply to replace my wife who's gone to eat. I'm just substituting for her."

We washed up and then they told us that all the new recruits had to have their mouths cleaned. After that we could get dressed. These were my first impressions of the school.

Papa had deposited money in the bank, 5,000 rubles for me and 5,000 for Brusha. He hoped we would keep if for a rainy day. Before the war began he checked the account regularly to see if we had spent it. Brusha didn't touch her money. But I couldn't restrain myself. Papa was upset by my frivolity, but he replaced the amount I spent. Then, when I was mobilized Agnessa proposed that she put my money in her name. "Mayechka, just for safekeeping." I did it. Agnessa gave me 400 rubles for the road. When we got to the school I found that I could take out a "golden loan." In a burst of patriotic enthusiasm, I bought one for the entire 400 rubles. When we finished the Morse code school we were to be placed in a job. We could have requested that we go together to the same pace. But Masha, out of pride (or principles) didn't make the request and neither did I. So they sent us to two different places. We didn't see each other for a long time, and when we met again...

CS SO

For a long time we wondered why I had been arrested. I found out at when I was rehabilitated.

After Agulya and I said goodbye to Mayechka, I was alone with Agulya. Our roommates—the Karavaevs and the Sinyavskys and especially old lady Genina—were fiercely jealous of me. What was there to envy? That I am not in despair? That I energetically find the means to survive? They, on the other hand, just dawdled. They had no idea how to do it, but I did and I acted on it. This exasperated them.

Although I lost a lot in the evacuation, I had managed to keep some things from Mongolia. Choibalsan had given me a piece of silk—blue with orange and yellow flowers. I tore it up into kerchief-sized pieces and hemmed them artistically, the way I know how. You could sell such kerchiefs for two hundred rubles. My roommates saw my kerchiefs and began to tear up whatever rags they had left and asked me to hem them. I did. But they couldn't get as much for them. They burned with even fiercer hate.

Oh yes, and there was still the business with the kerosene stove. Wasn't I right? Bring your own kerosene and you can use it, I told them, we can't stand in line for all of you. And I wrapped myself in my plaids. That enraged them, too. I had some wonderful wool plaids from Mongolia.

Although I was somehow getting along, the bad blood, the congestion, and some other things made it almost impossible to tolerate Kuibyshev. We had kicked the Germans out of Moscow, so I wrote Mikhail Davydovich to ask him to take us back to Moscow. At that time one had to have an invitation and an identification card.

Mikhail Davydovich went to the police to wring out of them identity cards for me and Agulya. At that very moment there were setbacks on the Front. Failure—our troops had retreated, so they began to maliciously "purge," "erase," grab and arrest. So when Mikhail Davydovich raised the question of an identity card for me, my name came to their attention. And also that I was the wife of Mironov "an important state criminal" (with a smirk), that was a thorn in their side. That's why they arrested me. Or so we thought until my rehabilitation.

By that time Agulya and I had a small room, and everyone else we had shared the film studio's room with had also been given other quarters. Two uniformed bandits showed up in our room. The neighbors—the Genins, the Sinyavskys, the Karavaevs—witnessed it.

I had a supply of food. I had squeezed out enough money from the sale of the kerchiefs to buy food on the black market, as they call it now. We didn't call it "black." On the contrary for many it was the only way to avoid dying of hunger. Everyone tried to keep some stuff in reserve. I'll say something else. Some sort of people came to Kuibyshev—directors, bosses, god knows what else—with suitcases of money they probably grabbed when there was panic in the government. They inflated prices. So prices rose from day to day. But that band of rich men, they lived off the black market, and were delighted to do it.

But I digress. They came to do a search. They searched my little cupboard. That's where I kept little jars of melted butter and several bottles of vodka (I got those on exchange, too). One of the bandits pointed out the vodka to the other. But he furrowed his brow and shook his head—no, no. They began to leave, but the first one winked at him. If it hadn't been for the presence of the neighbors in the room, they would have gone off with the butter and the vodka. But the neighbors stood and stared them down, gloating, as it seemed to me then.

My eleven-year-old Agulya was left all alone. She lived with those neighbors for a whole month, they had to feed her until Mikhail Davydovich came for her.

And that was the beginning of many dark years—prison, camp, years without rights—and then, rehabilitation.

> **Translator's Note:** Agnessa is now jumping to roughly 1960 to describe the following scene, her interview that would, she hoped, grant to her rehabilitation for having been wrongfully sent to the gulag.

It was on the Arbat, in that building where there is a plaque "War Tribunal." A general received me who, like me, hated "The Greatest Genius," and who had also suffered.

He looked at my documents. "I don't understand why they arrested you," he said.

"I don't understand either. Maybe because I was Mironov's wife?"

"Maybe, maybe..." he says absently, tentatively. He turns the pages of the documents. He looks. He finds nothing about Mironov. But suddenly he stumbles upon something, makes a vague sound, "Hmm... well... aha," and quickly looks up at me.

"Let's not rake up the past..." he says apologetically. "Here, just sign here that you have been rehabilitated. And he gives me my "case." My "case"!

At once I see the word "denunciation." "Anti-Soviet conversation" flashes by. I greedily look for the signatories: "Karavaev, Genina, Sinyavskaya." My neighbors in Kuibyshev!

I clutched the "case." I read, I read and I find these words: she said to this one and that one that "the electrical voltage is bad, that there is nothing to buy anywhere, the water pipes have frozen" and so on and so forth." And that's what they called "anti-Soviet conversation."

The general carefully tries to take back my "case." I won't let him.

"I won't leave this."

He says softly, "Agnessa Ivanovna, you know what? You are rehabilitated—rehabilitated. And this," he waves his hand, "let it go. Why do you need it?"

Mikhail Davydovich was already back home from his own Gulag, and he also said to me, let go of it, let them live. How do we know, maybe they were forced to say those things about you?

So I never got in touch with them.

But sometimes I wake up at night, as if a current is running through me. Karavaev, that gorilla, who groped me under the blanket; Genina, who wheedled the kerosene stove from me; Sinyavskaya, whom I covered with my plaid! That current runs through me and a thought gnaws at me—can it be that they went on to enjoy life?

Well, they certainly paid me back for everything.

And that's how it turned out—I was arrested for a kerosene stove.

View from the Outside: Maya

The next time Masha and I met, I already knew about the denunciation. Masha Sinyavskaya was so happy to see me: "Maya, dearest Maya." I look at her and wonder, does she know or not? I understand, I feel that she knows nothing. She was a calm, even-tempered, principled person. She wasn't ashamed of her drunken father, she pitied him. In 1943, when all the girl students were demobilized (she was a history student), she turned it down. "We are in such a terrible war," she said. "This is not the time to study, but to fight." And she went off to the front. But before that, she brought me home to her parents. Her mother kissed me, "Mayechka, Mayechka!" and she asked me, "And how is Agnessa Ivanovna doing? How amicably we all lived together." She was just about singing, a honeyed expression in her eyes. I might have said something about whose hands were dirty, but I just couldn't. I was ashamed for her, uncomfortable. I kept still and pretended that I didn't know anything. Masha and I never met again. Even though none of this was Masha's fault.

When Papa found out that Agnessa had been arrested, in his despair he began "to beat his head against a closed door." He wrote everywhere—to the procurator, to Beria himself, and actually got a meeting. Wherever he was able to get a hearing he tried to prove that this was a mistake, that she could not possibly be guilty of anything. He wrote to Beria that if she was guilty then "I too am an enemy of the people." He was beside himself, he was blind, Later my husband Nikofor Zinovevich said to me that Papa was selfish: "Didn't he think about his children, about you and Brusha? Why did he jump everywhere, press so hard, and write those letters to Beria? Didn't he understand that if they arrested him that would be a terrible mark against his daughters, or his grandchildren? How could he not think about you?"

But Papa was incapable of thinking about anything else. He was possessed by Agnessa, he saw her and her alone and was prepared to pay any price to rescue her: "If she is guilty," he wrote, "then arrest me, too."

And they did.

Figure 1. Mirosha (undated photo, mid-1930s)

Figure 2. Mironov and Agnessa at resort (no date)

Figure 3. Agnessa and Agulya (1932)

Figure 4. Agnessa and Mironov's marriage certificate. Translation:

Registry Office of Zhovtnevii Region of the City of Kiev
Marriage Certificate No.1399
Zhovtenii Region of the City of Kiev
September 13, 1936

Citizen Mironov, Sergei Naumovich and Citizen Agripopulo, Agnessa Ivanovna entered into the state of matrimony. The marriage is entered into the civil registry of marriage on September 13, 1936.

Figure 5. Agnessa and Agulya at a Mongolian shrine, 1937

Figure 6. Agnessa and Mikhail Davydovich, 1959

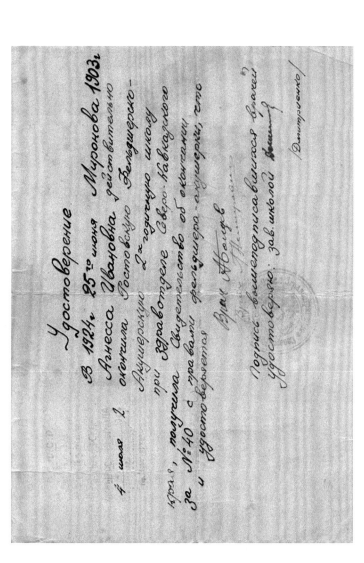

Figure 7. Agnessa's medical certificate. The document reads, in part:

CERTIFICATE

Novocherkassk. July 4, 1932

This is to certify that on June 25, 1924 Mironova, Agnessa Ivanovna (1903) completed a two-year course at the Rostov Feldsher [Paramedic] and Midwife School of the Department of Public Health, Northern Caucasus Region.

Figure 8. Agnessa in 1963

Figure 9. Agnessa, 1977

Figure 10. Agnessa and Lena, 1977

Figure 11. Mira Yakovenko and Olga Yakovenko, 2002

Part II

Who Will Repay?

Slavery

From the Kuibyshev jail they took me—an important state criminal—to Moscow. Three officers of the Ministry of Defense took me to the train station in a Black Maria carrying my dossier. Everywhere you looked there were armed soldiers. Three strapping men standing guard over one woman who was guilty of nothing while a horrible war was on, the enemy already in the Caucasus. This was 1942. In the Lubyanka, just as in the Kuibyshev jail, the windows were boarded up with planks, a little peep-hole at the top through which the light could scarcely penetrate. In the day the cell was dark, at night it was lit with the brightest possible lamp.

I was wearing a red knitted jacket with a fluffy white seagull on my breast. Suddenly at night there was some clatter and a woman guard pounced in: "Rise." Everyone jumped up, pulling the little rag from their eyes—you couldn't sleep without one because of the lamp. The crazed guard made straight for me, yelling what a nerve, you blank-blank, to sleep in red. It is too irritating! And I had to take off my jacket. And do you know why it irritated her? Red—this is the color of blood and she was responsible for making sure that no one hurt themselves. On another background blood was visible, but not on a red background. She had probably looked through the peephole, seen a red spot, and was horror-stricken—blood! Blood all over! Of course, she then saw that it was a jacket, but she took her shock out on me.

I had not yet even looked around at the Lubyanka when a tiny, hysterical woman was pushed into the cell. She sat down on an unoccupied bunk and looked around in the half-dark to see who else was there. Finally her eyes grew accustomed to the dark. Seeing that we were all looking at her, she whispered "Vlasova." At first her name meant nothing to me (by this time I can't remember her patronymic and surname). She had a bag of dry bread bits and she passed it around to all of us. We took as much as we wanted until the bag was empty. She didn't care. She wasn't hungry then and she didn't eat dinner either. That is, she didn't want to eat *yet*. In the first days after arrest most people feel that way. I was like that, too. The newcomers don't know that soon they will be starving. And if they know, they don't care. That's how strong the shock of arrest is.

The newcomer told her story. Her husband was the well known general, that very one that we had heard of before we knew the names K. K. Rokossovskii and G. K. Zhukov, two outstanding generals, especially in World War II. In evacuation she had to live with her relatives on a kolkhoz. She was not suited to the work. But she had brought a lot of money with her, so her relatives were utterly obsequious and she was free of responsibilities. Her husband sent lavish packages of food and wrote often. Suddenly the gifts and letters stopped coming.

Then a wagon with two officers came over the slushy rural roads. Is the wife of General Vlasov here?"

"I'm here."

"Get ready, we're taking you to Moscow."

"Why?"

"Your husband has asked us to bring you there safely."

She rejoiced: that means he is alive, healthy and they would soon be together.

Then they say to her, "Bring all your things. You will not be coming back."

They traveled through the mud to the station and boarded a train. When the train stopped they brought her jam, chicken, and buns. How did they find those things? The officers were very nice to her, they couldn't do enough for her. She took it as her due, after all she was the wife of an important general. She was accustomed to that kind of treatment.

But the closer they came to Moscow, the more their behavior changed At first they were as nice as could be, then cold and indifferent, and then rude. At the Moscow station they sat her in a Black Maria. The Lubyanka, search, fingerprints, and so forth and so forth. Then they locked her up with us.

She was hysterical, helpless. She was a spoiled, beloved girl-wife of an esteemed general. And now—this.

They called her up for interrogation.

When she returned she told us that interrogators had a pile of letters that had been taken from her in the search.

Interrogator: "Where did you hide that letter?"

"What letter?"

Interrogator, mockingly:

"You know which one."

"My husband hasn't written for six months, he stopped writing a long time ago."

"You are lying! Confess! Did you destroy the letter? What did it say?"

"What letter? I don't understand."

"Don't play the fool. Of course, you destroyed the letter, but you will tell us what was in it…"

That's how they tortured her. I don't know what happened to her. Was she shot? Did she rot in a camp? I myself didn't understand anything then, and in the prison we had no news. I thought then that Vlasov has been arrested like Mironov and all the other husbands. Later, when I was already in the camp, I met two prisoners and asked who they were. They answered "Vlasov's people." That's how I began to understand something.

They interrogated me only two or three times. The investigator in charge of my case asked some trivial questions. Maybe, like the general who rehabilitated me, he was confused about why I had been arrested. But when he looked through the case and discovered that I was Mironov's wife—aha!—it seemed to make sense to him. At that point he began to yell at me, but I had no idea what he wanted.

Then I was called in again. The peephole opened just enough for the guard to be heard: "Who is there with a name that begins with "m"?

"I am."

"Your surname?"

"Mironova."

"Come out."

I leave the cell. And I am led... not to the office of the investigator, not along those corridors. We pass a descending staircase—thank God, we're not going to the basement. We mount the stairs and enter wide corridors, the floors covered with carpets. Quiet, clean, beautiful. It was like the place that Meshik had called me to. No, even more splendid. We go into a large office. A life-size portrait of Stalin on the wall. Further back, someone sits at a table, but I can't tell who it is, except that everything is grandiose and extravagant. And I—a pitiful little grain of sand in the sea—insignificant. And suddenly a gentle voice: "Agnessa Ivanovna, if I am not mistaken. Come closer to the table, please. Please, sit down."

A miracle! I don't believe my ears. After all the frisking and searching. The back passage, the front passage...

I approach. A nice-looking man is seated at the table. He is leafing through documents on the table as if to verify something.

"Your surname, name, and patronymic."

I tell him. He silently consults the documents again, muttering "Hmm... OK... hmmm."

Meanwhile, I looked around. Through the half-open door to the next room I see a table covered with a snow-white tablecloth, and on it appetizers. You can only guess at them! To see this after two months of prison slop.

I sit with the sunlight in my face, so that I can't see very well. The man at the table begins to question me, how, when, why was I arrested. I answer that I don't know why, but I tell him how, when, and where. I tell him in great detail (he demanded the details, or more precisely, he did not demand, he respectfully requested). Then again, he wants to verify something.

"Who was your husband? What was his position? I mean Mironov."

"He was the head of the second section of the Commissariat of Internal Affairs [NKVD]."

"Aha... hmm... Well..."

He picks up the telephone and dials a short number. Speaking softly so that I won't understand, he says something, I hear Mirosha's name. Well, I think, now he will question me about Mirosha, he will begin to torment me. But he says, "Excuse me please. You are free to leave." He pushes a button and I am taken away.

To this very day this is a puzzle. I have thought about it so often, I have tried to sort it out. And, finally, I think I have figured it out.

I remember the man with the same name, Mironov, the chief of the economic department of the NKVD, who was our guest in Novosibirsk and who was subsequently arrested. I think they mistook me for that Mironov's wife. Her name was Alla. That means, A. Mironova. And I too am A. Mironova. She was a beauty. And more than that, she was like Messalina.[1] There were many cruel conflicts among men on her account.

Beria loved women and probably knew that there was an A. Mironova in the Lubyanka. He asked his closest helpers to find out whether or not that A. Mironova was that woman. The table was laid for a feast with her, if it turned out that it was she. Beria, after all, was a hedonist.

Then my interrogator let drop the following phrase: "Well, you have now been interrogated by the People's Commissar himself."

What did he mean by that? It is certain that it was not Beria who sat at that table. Possibly the man who sat there called Beria. In fact I'm sure now that he did. And perhaps Beria had looked me over without my knowing it? When I was in prison I looked terrible. For some reason I was so yellow that my nickname was "the Japanese." I probably didn't please him.

And finally, perhaps my interrogator made a slip of the tongue. It was not that "the Commissar himself examined me" but that the "Commissar himself had been interested in me." That is how I was in a "beauty parade" in the Lubyanka.

03 80

I was sentenced to five years of corrective labor. They took us away in a "Stolypin train."[2] There were twenty-three people in our compartment. Can you imagine? The upper berths, the best for lying down, were already occupied by women sentenced for criminal acts. We "fifty-eighters," women sentenced for anti-Soviet speech, had to cram and squash together on the lower benches. For eighteen days we traveled like sardines in a can, sleeping in sitting positions or however we could. They gave us salted fish, some kind of

---

[1] Messalina (c. 17/20–48 A.D.) was a Roman empress, the third wife of the Emperor Claudius. She was a powerful woman with a reputation for promiscuity.

[2] Introduced by Pyotr Stolypin, prime minister under Nicholas II, these were ordinary train cars specially refitted for transporting prisoners. They were designed to allow the guards to see and hear the prisoners. The prisoners' comfort was not a goal.

disgusting herring. We were so inexperienced that we ate them in one gulp, and then, oh how we dreamed of drinking our fill. "Drink, drink!" We called to the guards. The guards played deaf.

In the morning the commandant of the convoy passed by our car. Fat, yawning, in trousers held up with suspenders over a crumpled shirt. A stupid, self-satisfied snout. The criminals fawned on him, calling out obsequiously, "Dear Citizen Commander, we need something to drink, please order them to give us something to drink. We ask and ask and they don't bring us anything." "Ah, go fuck your mother. I'm sick of you. Fuck all of you."

From morning till night we were subjected to that kind of unrelenting obscenity—loathsome and wretched. At first I felt as if I were up to my neck in vomit. Then I got used to it. They just didn't know any other language.

Among the women criminals was one who stood out for her incredible insolence, Vlasova she was called. I had been able to salvage a blue kettle, in our situation a very valuable object. In the morning I could fill it with water and drink from the spout during the day. From the upper bunk they began to plead, "Give us something to drink. Come on, just a drop. Fuck your mother, how dry my mouth is!" I was repulsed. After all, one drank from the spout, but if someone asks for a drink, how can you refuse? I passed the kettle up. Vlasova grabbed it and announced, "Now it's mine." I was terribly upset. At that moment the commander was passing in the corridor and I turned to him, "Citizen Commander, the women on the upper benches have taken our kettle..."

Vlasova dropped her vulgarity for an ingratiating tone. "Citizen Commander, that's not true. Back there in prison she gave me the kettle in return for a bread ration." From the lower bench we began to argue, to protest. From above they responded with obscenities, shrieks, yells.

The commander: "Sort it out for yourselves, mother-fuckers."

Vlasova lowered her shoes right in my face, her companions howling with laughter. I covered my face with my hands, humiliated, powerless. I could not fight with her.

Our thirst grew so intense that when we transferred from one train to another, one woman snatched at a piece of ice blackened with coal and soot and began to gnaw, suck, lick just to somehow freshen her parched, puckered mouth. "Give it here, give it here." It passed from mouth to mouth, everyone feverishly licking it.

Our escorts were on a spree for the entire journey. They would booze up, stuff themselves with food, and go to the women's compartments to choose women. The commandant picked our compartment. He comes, he stands at the grill, he stares from one face to another for a few minutes. He jabs his cigarette at one young woman: "Hey, you. What are you in for?"

"I don't know myself... I was a teacher..."

Like it or not, he has the power. He could do something for her.

"Maybe you'd like to wash my floors."

All the women: "Go, go, they will give you bread."

Keys jingle, the grill opens, the chosen one leaves. Time passes. Night. Everyone sleeps somehow, legs contorted every which way. In the middle of the night the keys jingle again. She returns, squeezes into her place among the legs and the bodies. Under her coat—a loaf of bread. We can sense it with our noses. And, softly, in the darkness: "He gave her bread!"

"The commandant promised to do something about my case," she whispers to me. "He will petition for me, only for me."

Power—who cares at what cost. We all clutch at straws. We arrive at Dolinka.[3] An austere place, sand, desert, low barracks and wire barriers hidden behind the dunes.

No sooner had we descended from the train than we threw ourselves on the sand, stretching our legs, straightening our bodies tortured by eighteen days of sitting upright and immobile. I thought about the young teacher and I watched—will the commandant separate her belongings from everyone else's? Not yet! He barks out, "Fall in!" He walks in front of us carrying a pile of our possessions. When he gets to the gate he hands over our things all together, as if he had never promised her anything. The convoy had fulfilled its task and returned to the train to go back for more prisoners. And that's how she remained—as if he had spat on her. What good is she to him now? Another train, another enormous choice of pure, modest, cultured women who wouldn't give him a look under other circumstances.

At Dolinka they registered us according to our training and experience. I identified myself as "medical personnel," stating that I had completed two courses at a medical institute. I worked in the hospital only a short time before they transferred me to the clinic, a huge barracks for 300 people. It wasn't really a clinic. It was simply a place for patients who were too weak to walk.

Next to the clinic was the "wasting-away" room. It was completely white—the walls, the sheets, the tables, the doors. Only the hands of the patients were a ghastly yellow. They could no longer eat. They lay inert, their faces vacant.

It was winter. Every morning six or seven corpses were removed. They soon froze. The frozen corpses were stacked upright beside the toilet. Then the corpses were transferred to a small barn that had been emptied, but it was too small as well, so they spilled out of the exit onto the terrace. The corpses were naked but for whatever available rag had been carelessly thrown over them. Such a great number of them accumulated that it was difficult to close the door. To enter or leave one had to press them even closer together. Some lay bow-legged, a leg sticking out here, an arm there. If you didn't want to brush up against them, you had to step over them.

---

[3] Dolinka was the administrative center of Karlag (Karaganda Camps) in Kazakhstan. Within Karlag there were more than 200 camps in an area roughly the size of France.

We quickly grew accustomed to the sight. Once I left the barn, squeezing the corpses against the door and I think, "What's happened to me? These are corpses, and I fear them about as much as I would pieces of wood." I step over arms and legs and I walk on as if it were nothing. I think, "In normal life I would never have believed that I could live like this. And here, I pay no attention."

And I survive. I will bear everything and I will not die. I will not die, I will not die. I will survive!

ଓଃ ଓ

In the clinic they gave us an "enriched" diet: besides soup, they gave us three-fourths of a glass of milk and "vitamins," consisting of two table spoons (and no more) of vinaigrette: a few potatoes, cooked beets, onion and a drop of sunflower seed oil.

It was my job to dole out the food.

When I came to the barracks, my predecessor Tamara taught me—"when you pour milk, hold back a tiny bit and that way you'll always have a bit." I tried to do that, but you have no idea how closely they scrutinize you.

I lived in a cubby with four other women, one of whom was sleeping with the captain of the guards. Her name was Klava. Of course, that was strictly forbidden, but people were able to secretly live together. On the day I arrived, my predecessor Tamara assigned me my housekeeping duties.

That day Klava turned to her in my presence and said, "Aunt Tamara, is there anything left for me to eat?" Tamara gave her milk.

Tamara went off to her new duties. Everything went well at first. Then, one evening that Klava came up to me—"Is there anything left to eat?"

I had nothing to give her. I never learned how to keep a bit of milk back for myself. And anyway I would not yet have known what to ask in return. I was still so ignorant.

One evening, I remember, I had washed my hair and wrapped the towel around my head like a turban. I washed my underwear and calmly went to sleep. Suddenly—two o'clock in the morning—a call came for Mironova—collect your belongings! What's happening? Where? Why?

It was dark outside; we were gathered into rows of 6 people and "Left, right. Left, right." The convoy could shoot without warning and "left, right, left, right" and off to the station. There they looked at our documents, but mine was missing. That means that the whole business had been so hastily decided, that they had not received them yet. They went off to look for them. We all wait. They find them.

They stuffed us all in a freight wagon that was waiting on the track in a dead end. The wagon had no benches. We were squeezed in on the floor and the wagon was locked from the outside. The train was on its way.

☙ ❧

We arrived by morning. The door opened and before us was brilliant sun, a green steppe, red tulips. It was April, when the steppe is all in bloom. It was warm.

They took us a short distance to a one-room Ukrainian mud hut in the middle of the steppe. "We will live here for the while," said the security guards and ordered us to build bunks in the hut.

It was a small room for forty-five people, but we built the bunks and squeezed ourselves into it.

The first day the guards gave us only bread. We were so upset that the next day they gave us millet, onion, and a bottle of sunflower seed oil. That was supposed to last forty-five people for three days. These food stuffs were right on the base. The evening before I had noticed a small addition to the hut, probably a small peasant barn for fowl. But at the moment there were no fowl. A small, skinny shabby woman lived in it. She had served out her term, but when the war began there was an order to keep all freed prisoners in the area until the war was over. She had established herself as a kind of "purser." When she gave out food she said to us "Good people, choose two women who will be the cooks."

We were a motley crew. Among us there were educated people, simple peasants, girls from western Ukraine, and boys from fifteen to seventeen years old from the Factory Vocational Schools, imprisoned for falsifying ration cards or petty theft because they were hungry.

Two peasant women were chosen to do the cooking. They cooked out-of-doors in clay ovens under a canopy like they have in Ukraine for cooking in the summer. But hardly anyone had dishes to eat from. To have one's own dishes was extremely important in the camps. If you have your own dishes, you get the first portions and of course the fat rises to the top. The last portions were nothing but the dregs. The other prisoners have to wait until you are finished with your dish. You eat, you pass your dish to the second, who passes it to the third, and so on. But you'd better keep an eye on the second and third so that your dish doesn't "vanish." Unhygienic? Filthy? Who cares about filth, hygiene? No one cares about that in the camp?

I already understood what having one's own dishes meant. Not long before I had exchanged a bell-shaped, half-liter enameled jug for bread. I'm telling about this in detail so that it becomes clear how I saved my own life. When I had the jug, I was always among the first to be served. Also, I made a pin cushion. I cut off a piece from the lining of my squirrel fur coat from which I was never parted—not in the winter, not in the summer, not for a second. It hardly looked the way it once had, but it served me faithfully. Anyway I cut a piece of the pink silk lining with a little pocket knife which I had managed to hide away during a body search. Then I plucked blue, yellow, other colors of threads from wherever I could, from a skirt, from my tights, stuffed in a piece of cotton and embroidered a very bright and pretty "flower" with six petals on it. When the pincushion was ready I knocked on the door of the addition to our hut. The door opened a sliver and I heard the coarse voice, "What do you want?"

I showed her the pincushion. "Isn't this something you can use?"

As soon as she saw it, her expression changed. Women in the camp longed for something that was even a bit beautiful, some illusion of domestic comfort. The "purser" relaxed:

"What do you want for it?"

"Bread."

"I don't have bread. The convoy guards have bread."

"I can't give it to you if you have no bread. I'm hungry."

"I understand. And if I can give you millet?"

"I'll take it!"

She poured out a half mug of millet. I asked her for a pinch of salt.

People were cooking gruel on our stove, and I offered to watch the fire. I threw in wood chips and bits of straw and carefully put my millet in the mug, filling it to the top with water. I placed it there and wondered whether the others would say anything. And what if they chased me away from the stove?

The millet boiled and began to spill over from the mug. I grabbed it in time, let it cool a bit and began to eat it with the stump of a comb. I didn't have a spoon. I ate it, it is hot and thick. I ate it all. In the meantime, the gruel was ready to eat and my mug was among the first. Everyone noticed, but no one said anything. I ate that as well and felt heaviness in my stomach—I was full. It had been a long time since I had gone to bed full.

There is a story by Jack London called "A Piece of Steak," about a boxer who could not buy a piece of meat before a fight, and he lost the fight. True, in my case it was not a piece of steak but a half-cup of millet, a half-cup that saved me.

In the morning—it was April 23, 1943—they pushed us to go further. It was sunny, but the head wind was so powerful that one could barely walk against it. I said to the convoy guard, "This wind is knocking us over."

"We have to go, mother-fucker."

"But not in this kind of weather, we could stay here a bit longer."

"We have our orders."

It was hard to walk, and it was hot. I was wearing every warm thing I had, including, of course, my fur coat. They said roughly, "Whoever is hot should put their things on the cart." Everyone began to put things on the cart and I did, too. It was a relief, but not for long. The wind increased, dark clouds appeared, and it began to rain. The road disintegrated into puddles and soon it was like a dirty lake. The mud was like dough and we were perspiring. Then the rain turned to hail, stinging the face and the spine. The temperature dropped, our clothes, wet from the rain, began to freeze; icicles sprouted on my fur coat. If it were not for the hurricane wind, one could have heard them jingle. Then a thick snow began to fall. It was such a blizzard that you couldn't see a person who was three steps in front of you. We couldn't make ourselves out, we couldn't make out the convoy. Our younger prisoners walked ahead, the older ones lagged behind, and I was someplace in the middle. Nothing could be heard over the howling wind (was someone crying out?), there was no air to breathe. The wind blocked our breathing. We had to move, we had to overcome the wall of snow—our only salvation lay ahead. But there was no strength.

People around me are already falling and not getting up. We had a robust Polish beauty with us who had left behind four children. She was wearing only cotton trousers and a quilted jacket over her naked body, for she had exchanged the rest of her clothing for bread. Her cotton pants were wet through and through and had started to freeze. She was walking not far from me. I saw how she fell. Stop and help her? One must, one must! If you don't, later it will torture you. At the same time, I think—if I stop to help her, I will not be able to get up either.

Go, go, go! And I'm dreaming about a barrier between me and the wind and storm. I would lie down behind it, I would snuggle down and hide from the storm, I would swoon, I wouldn't budge. It's a good thing that such a barrier did not appear. Were I to lie down, I'd never stand up again.

And then there was a moment when the torrent of snow diminished. Out of the corner of my eye I could see that on the horizon there was a narrow strip of bright sky under the black clouds. It was like that very sunny day on which we had left. I couldn't believe it, so I looked at the strip of sky again. I prayed to it, as if God were there. Can it be? God, if you exist, please let me reach it.

And I did.

Like an animal I suddenly sniffed the smell of smoke and I crawled, dragging myself toward that odor, pushing through a new onslaught of snow. And before me I thought I was seeing a huge whirling fire. And walls! But the snowdrift was melting. I found myself in a rude clay shepherd's hut that was meant to shelter sheep. A fire was burning in the middle of the floor, the smoke escaping through a hole in the roof. Around the fire sat our convoy, the dogs, the girls from western Ukraine, and the pupils of the factory vocational schools. They had abandoned us to save themselves.

A screen divided the room in half. One half was probably for the sheep. The people were breaking up the screen and putting the pieces in the fire. They also threw in rotten straw.

I didn't yet feel or understand exactly what was going on, but I crawl to the fire, to that wonderful savior of humanity—fire. I sat close to it and stretched my hands to it. I was saved.

Then I took off my fur coat. It was dry on the inside. I hung it to dry on a pole. Icicles that had penetrated the fur melted and dripped. I turned my feet to the fire. My boots had disintegrated and simply fallen off my feet. By the end of the march I walked in the snow in my socks. But my feet were alive; they could already feel the heat of the fire.

The guards were bickering about who should go back to fetch the stragglers. "You go, mother-fucker," "Fuck you, go yourself." This was the sullen dialogue between them. They were in hats with earflaps, sheepskin coats, and gloves.

"Senya—where's Senya? He was right alongside of us," the girls from western Ukraine cried excitedly. They implore the guards to go out and look for him (nobody cared about the older people). But their requests met with the most evil obscenities. Then the girls, young and strong, decided to go themselves. Now the guards were generous with advice. "Take a piece of wood that's glowing from the fire and wave it from the door. Hey, it's night, it's dark out there."

The girls paid no attention.

"You don't have to go out. He'll see the smoke from the hole in the ceiling."

The girls left. So strong they were, they found Senya, but he was motionless. Were they too late? Had he frozen to death? They placed him near the fire and massaged him. In a short time his eyelashes fluttered and he awoke.

I had wrapped myself in a woolen scarf. Suddenly I felt that someone was tugging at me. I looked around and saw that a man in wet underwear was trying to push his way under my scarf. I released one end of it and he wrapped himself, embracing me with one hand on my left breast. I didn't care. We sat there side by side, nestling up to each other under my scarf, motionless, without any desire. I don't even know his name. We did not speak to each other. We couldn't. We were like two miserable animals, drawn to the warmth, saved by the warmth of our bodies.

Half-dead, we spent the night like that. The bonfire was dying down, but someone stoked it. All the wood from the room divider had gone up in those flames.

In the morning a bright sun rose over the pale steppe. The grass and flowers were under the snow and ice. More guards appeared on carts, not clear from where. They were yelling. I don't remember about what. They went out to collect the fallen and they brought back fifteen corpses. The robust Polish beauty in felt boots—the one I didn't help—lay on the cart. Her hands lay over the side of the cart, shuddering with each jolt.

Someone in our group became very agitated. The guards calmly—phlegmatically—answered, "This happens every year." The dead frozen corpses didn't bother them. The important thing to them was that the convoy arrived on time. The responsible authorities then crossed the dead off their lists. If a prisoner escaped, they were blamed. But dead—they just yawned.

Why do I go into such detail about the mug, the needle, the fur coat? Well, they saved me. The mug, the pincushion, the fur coat. I was full, I regained some strength, and my coat kept me dry. I talk about material things, but I also prayed, fiercely, passionately. "God, if you exist, if only you exist, let me survive."

And I did.

Mama taught us children to pray, to believe in God, to attend church. I am a believer even if I don't go to church. There is a God, there is something—believe me.

And the things we had put on the cart? Gone. They told us that the cart had turned over in a snow drift and no one was interested in retrieving our things. They were surely lying. They took the things for themselves. That's how I lost my cup.

03 80

Again, we walked. We didn't make much headway after yesterday's walk. I had to wrap my feet in underwear and over that, felt house slippers that I found in the bottom of that rucksack that never left my side.

We walked for a very long time. By evening we came to the Aratau Hills in the southern Urals. It was a sheep herding center. They didn't ask what anyone knew how to do, we were just all expected to work. But the majority of us, including me, couldn't do anything.

We were supposed to weed the grain fields, to pull out the weeds with our hands. We had to weed the vegetable gardens as well, but at least there we had hoes. Then came the harvesting. We had mowers, but we had to weave the sheaves and put them into haystacks. In the winter we looked after the sheep. We got the hay for them under the snow, fed them, milked them, cleaned the stables. It was so hard to do the milking. The milk was used to make cheese (not, of course, for us). Sometimes the sheep were chased out onto the steppe to find feed under the snow by themselves.

We were terribly hungry. If they found last year's potatoes (starch was retained in the potatoes' eyes), they threw it into our gruel to thicken it. It was more nourishing.

I was like a skeleton. They called me grandma. My nose began to bleed from hunger and filth, so I was put in the hospital. After I recovered I was lucky enough to stay there, although not immediately. At first they send me to work as a paramedic on one of the farms. All the farms were in the steppe. There the barracks for the prisoners were larger and had Russian stoves. The military guard lived in separate barracks.

In the summer they send groups of ten prisoners out to the steppe to look after the sheep. These are called the summer farms. The summer shepherds try to position themselves against a hill. The hills are not high, but they shield the shepherd from the wind. They build a fireplace and smear clay on a pot for cooking. The prisoners are not guarded. The guards only come by to check up on them and to bring them enough food for several days at a time.

After hungry winters and springs everyone wanted that job. And the shepherds could drink sheep's milk; it wasn't possible for the guards to keep track of the amount. Sometimes they secretly slaughtered a sheep. They cooked it quickly at night and ate their fill, beginning with the innards. Of course, they couldn't eat the whole sheep at once, so they hid the remains of the first meal. This is how they did it. They hid the meat in a hole that they dug next to the fireplace, placed planks over the hole, and covered them with clumps of topsoil. It looked like an undisturbed swampy spot, and they declared that a wolf had taken the sheep. When the guards hurried over to inspect, we saw their carts from afar, but the prisoner on watch on the hill warned the others. Before the guards could get there, the prisoners had obliterated all traces. Noise, swearing. The guards knew that they were being deceived, but they couldn't find a thing. All the shepherds swore that a wolf had eaten the sheep right down to the bones, and they showed the guards gnawed bones that they had spread around and even spilled sheep's blood on the ground. The dogs threw themselves on the bones and on the fireplace, but nobody took any notice because, of course, that's where food always was cooked. The guards found the usual prison fare, not a hint of meat. The prisoners hung together. So the guards had to leave with nothing. The prisoners hung together, it all went smoothly.

It was even easier when the sheep were giving birth. The guards knew more or less how many were pregnant, but not precisely. So it was easy to grab a lamb. Of course, they could only do this once in a while.

The sheep herders liked me and waited for me to come, sometimes they greeted me with whoops, "Doctor lady, come quickly, we saved the heart and liver for you." I began to gain weight. No one called me granny any more as they had in the spring.

ଓଃ ଃ୦

Once I went to one of the summer pastures and found a man lying under the bushes. He look haunted, skinny, almost a skeleton. He lay motionless. The prisoner who did the cooking whispered to me, "He's the bird catcher."

This prisoner caught birds with snares and brought them to the authorities. Several days ago he disappeared. Was he lost? The rumor was that he was not so innocent, that he went out further and further every day. And finally he just didn't come back. They considered him to be a runaway and announced a search. One day a guard came to the summer pasture. Suddenly, the bird catcher came out of the bushes, probably because he smelled the smoke and was hungry. He saw the guard, but there was nowhere for him to run, so he just fainted.

At that time the gruel was being cooked. I said to the cook, "Feed him."

"Oh, I'm afraid."

"Well, I'm not afraid!" I said calmly. I took my bowl to the cook, she filled it and I approach the bird catcher. The guard saw me:

"What are you doing? He's a fucking runaway."

"We don't know that yet," I answered calmly and pushed the bowl at the bird catcher. The bird catcher opened his eyes, shuddered, came to life and began to hungrily lap up the gruel. The guard kicked the bowl out of his hands, but said not a word to me. They yelled at me less than at others.

The cart was arriving, coming for the runaway. Guards jumped out of the cart and began to beat him. They were enraged. They hate escapees because it is always a bad mark on their record. They kicked him. They were killing him. He was barely breathing. For a while he moaned, but then fell silent. And they keep kicking, beating, beating.

I felt as if they were beating me. I couldn't watch. I went into the hut, but the others watched with completely dumb indifference, as if to say that's how it should be. They beat him to a bloody pulp, then they tied him to the back of their cart, upside down like a child in the mother's womb. They tied him to the cart in such a way that he was almost trailing on the ground and all the obstacles on the road beat him, stones, bushes. And the guards sat and urged on the horses. Later I was told that when he got to the farm he was still alive, but they beat him again, this time to the death. It was in the normal course of events to be beaten to death, to be shot. And one had to be grateful for it. But if you tried to escape, you unleashed a storm.

০৪ ৮০

On the farm I lived in a tiny room that was separate from the barracks. Men slept in the barracks. The women slept in a separate part, enclosed by planks. There were only a few women, perhaps fifteen. And then there was the little room for me. The stove was meant to heat the barracks, but there was a connection to a little burner in my room. This was to enable me to sterilize the instruments. But you can imagine what the instruments were like. I didn't even have a syringe with a needle. There were no medicines: potassium magnate, iodine. There were no powders for headaches that weren't too old to use. That's it. How was I supposed to treat people? Oh, yes, there were thermometers so that I could issue permission for prisoners to take off work.

One prisoner slept in a space separated from my little room by a thin plywood wall. He was constantly trying to win my favor, he was something like in love with me. He fixed my stove for me, he stole for me the dung bricks we used for fuel. And he wanted something for himself—to stay in the warm room by my side.

He managed to steal some grain, which I cooked. We were full. Then suddenly—a search. A guard beat him fiercely. He returned all bloody, but he laughed scornfully and swaggered, as if to say—did he think he could humiliate me? Like a real man, he spit on the whole business.

But what joy to come in from a winter storm to a warm barracks; city people will never understand that. That barracks, filthy and smelly, seemed like the finest palace. Once I went to another farm, and when I started out to come back I could barely make out the road. The wind whistled. I hurried along, because if it were to storm, I'd soon be dead. The snow drifts were swept along by the wind. Hurry, hurry, I'm perspiring and completely exhausted. The wind is pummeling snow right into my face. I cannot catch my breath. I won't make it. And suddenly—the storm twists around and ends. And I was almost there.

Something dark before me—a wall. I pushed the door. My God, it was as if I had entered another world. Two lamps were burning, it was light, or at least after the dark it seemed very light to me. People were already asleep, two Russian stoves glowed.

I was covered with snow, and there to greet me was an eighty-five-year old man who slept by the door. He had waited for me, worried.

"Oh, good. Agnessa Ivanovna has returned, Agnessa Ivanovna has returned!"

I'm so lucky to be alive. How nice it is to have someone waiting.

He, that old grandpa, was very attached to me. I always feel sympathy for elderly people, something I didn't understand when I was young. The grandpa had five sons and two brothers on the front. They fearlessly fought for the old man's release, but it was like talking to a deaf wall.

03 80

I have a copy of the magazine "Around the World," no. 2, 1978. On the third page there's an article about Maikop and about Captain Petrovsky. He was my first love. When the Red Army was approaching Maikop, its commanding officers proposed to the Cossack ataman General Danilov and his closest aide Captain Petrovsky that they surrender the town of Maikop. Danilov and Petrovsky agreed under the condition that the Reds allow the Whites unhindered passage to Georgia.

Why did the Whites give up the town? I think that they understood that in any case the Reds would take the town, but they wanted to avoid unnecessary bloodshed. Further, Danilov had a family in Maikop and he didn't want to put them in danger. And why did Petrovsky agree? Well, I think it was because of me.

To explain: several White officers courted Lena. One of them arranged for her to go horseback riding, and we learned how to do it. There were four of us. First, Lena and her admirer and Captain Petrovsky, and then they began to take me. I was sixteen years old, in the third class of gymnasium. Lena had already graduated from gymnasium—all eight classes—and was studying for a certificate to teach children in the lower grades.

They took me to make two couples. Although I was too young for him Petrovsky began to pay attention to me. He was about thirty years old, already a mature person from a noble family. Before the war he had graduated the physics-mathematics department of St. Petersburg University. He was so interesting—well built and well groomed, in a military tunic with an ornamental braided loop on the shoulder; he was, after all, in a Cossack division.

I was insanely in love with him. You know how it is when you are young. Poetic, uninhibited. I rarely saw him, probably because he was often busy and did not want to encourage our romance. He had no intention of marrying me, and to seduce such a young girl—well, he was a very ethical person. That was probably why he was somewhat restrained and, well, cool. But I, all I could think about was meeting him. I looked incessantly for excuses. And Lena knew because I told her how much I was in love with him.

When Lena got married she held "high society receptions." On her birthday she invited officers, including Petrovsky. I dreamed of seeing him there. But Lena—as always, insensitive—said to me, "Don't come because it will be too crowded at the table and we have to invite my in-laws (her husband's parents lived in Maikop). That makes twenty people, where would I put you?" I didn't go. Instead, I wept all evening.

Now, when I remind her about it, she says nothing of the sort happened, it didn't happen. She doesn't remember.

Despite that, Petrovsky and I began to meet. First, in the park as if by accident. How proud I was, what insane happiness, as if I had thrown myself into a fairy tale. Imagine! I am walking with my classmates, girls from the gymnasium. And suddenly I see him in the distance. He approaches us, and it's clear to everyone that he's coming to me, like a magic prince to a young girl. Tall, shapely, interesting, in his long, tight-fitting military tunic. He politely greets us all, but he is looking at me. We go off together and stroll along the paths through the park and we talk gaily, and everyone sees us together. When it grows darker and I have to go home we find my girlfriends and accompany them to their homes (oh, they were so jealous!). Then he accompanies me home and in the dusk, he kisses me at the gate. That's how we began to meet.

Once on a stroll we found ourselves in the cemetery where there were gravestones of White officers who had perished. Petrovsky said, sadly, "What will the Reds do with these monuments?"

"What could they do, they won't do anything?"

"Nothing? They will destroy everything, stone by stone."

"Are they coming here?"

"I hope not."

Another time I went to a picnic with him in the countryside. He lay on the grass looking up at the sky. I saw his face so clearly. Very, very fine wrinkles and clear blue eyes.

When we didn't meet for a long time I was lonely, I pined for him. Finally, when a long time passed, I wrote to him—why wasn't he coming to see me? I told him how much I missed him. He answered with a little note appointing a time that we should meet in the park. We sat side by side on a bench. He didn't say a word about my letter (although I knew for a certainty that he had received it), but he asked, "What have you been doing. Were you bored, did you miss me?" And he embraced me tenderly, gazing into my eyes.

Another time, at one of Lena's parties, we sat close to each other, side by side on the couch. I could feel his holster and pistol at my side. I carefully and surreptitiously unbuckled his holster and took out the pistol. I opened it (I knew how to do it, he had taught me and Lena how to shoot in the countryside), and found seven bullets in the magazine. I took two out and put the pistol back in the holster. Petrovsky never noticed. I took them to remember him by.

The Whites still hoped that the Reds would not come. They hoped that they could force the Reds back. But we could see from the little red flags of the Front on the map that they were closing in. I didn't see Petrovsky for a long time. Again I wrote him, but this time there was no answer.

Then, one day I went to the baths and came out in a kerchief and plain, everyday clothes, not the way I liked to dress for him. And there he was—Petrovsky. Not in his military tunic. He wore a light grey overcoat with epaulets. He saw me and laughed.

"Who do I see, who is this?"

I was embarrassed to be seen in such clothing and I would have slipped past by him, but he turned it into a joke. "Who is this, I don't recognize you! Ah, you're coming from the baths?" Then he turned serious.

"Listen, this is what's happening. The Reds are getting closer. We would like to hope that there won't be a confrontation. But anything could happen."

He humorously saluted me and hurried off. That was the last time I saw him. Now I understand. It was probably at that time that he and Danilov began to negotiate with the Red commanders to avoid battles in the city. He really didn't have time for me. When the Whites left, my girlfriends asked me if he had said goodbye to me.

I lied. "Of course we said goodbye. He rushed over on a horse, said farewell and left."

But he did not say goodbye to me.

The Whites did make an agreement with the Reds. The White officers who wanted to remain in Maikop stayed, gave back their guns, and lived peacefully. There were soldiers who were from Maikop and they were tired of war. The Reds promised not to touch them. Lena's husband was also from Maikop and deeply loved her. He could not leave her. For a time the Reds honored the agreement. Then they rounded up all the former White soldiers, took them north and shot them.

Did those two bullets that I took from Petrovsky's pistol have harmful consequences? Fortunately, no. Petrovsky survived. When Mirosha and I were in Mongolia, among the old foreign journals there was one from Belarus in the 1920s. I came upon a photograph in which Petrovsky is on a camel next to Danilov. The caption under the photo was: Cavalrymen sitting on camels. Russian officers serving in the French foreign legion."

To verify that I wasn't mistaken I showed the photo to Lena and asked: "Who is this?" She exclaimed, "Oh, that's Petrovsky!" That was a quarter of a century ago.

On the gulag farm the guards lived separately, but they frequently burst into our barracks. We could hardly wait for them to leave, so that we could cook up something to eat (if we had succeeded in getting something). Among them was one Denisov, no longer young, perhaps fifty years old or so. He was married. Middle height, slightly hunched over with clear blue eyes and a finely wrinkled face. The first time saw him I almost fainted, he looked so much like Petrovsky, but of course older. True, in my memory Petrovsky was tall, but perhaps it only seemed so in comparison with the short little general. The years lay heavily on Denisov, bending him over. But his facial features were exactly like Petrovsky's.

I noticed this guard because of that amazing resemblance. I tried to draw him out. At first he was contemptuous of me. I was an "enemy of the people." Gradually he began to relent, to thaw, to talk about himself more and more openly. He would come to my little room, sit on a stool and talk, for example, about the fact that he had no education and that he was now learning alongside his children; when they had homework he did it with them.

He talks and from time to time I look at him, probably with a certain kind of expression. Can it be Petrovsky? No, of course not, it is simply an irresistible illusion.

And then one day the guards came to us to make a search. Simply an unexpected "shake down," as they say in the camps. There was a woman prisoner to whom people came with things to hide, and she hid them. Pronina was her name. Undoubtedly, she took some kind of recompense for this service. It turned out that she had hidden something that was not permissible in the camps. When they found it, they gave us hell and put her in a cell.

Prisoners brought things to me to hide for them as well, because my little room could be locked. The guards found them.

"What's this?"

"That's not mine."

So, let them yell at me. Who cares? The head guards yelled and Denisov was obsequious. From his tone of voice he was clearly trying to please them: "Well, she's like Pronina," he says. "Maybe she wants to be in a cell as well."

I don't believe my ears; to do this for such a trifle? And if it had been something more serious, he probably would have deceived me more shabbily, more despicably.

Well, they yelled and hollered, took all the things I had hidden for others, but they didn't put me in a cell. The next day I went outside. There goes Denisov. Usually I greeted him, "Good morning," and he would answer me. This time I said not a word, I didn't even look in his direction. Of course, he noticed and I'm sure he knew why.

Later that day I was in a nearby summer pasture. There was Bynchuksha, the head guard's wife, rushing towards me.

"Oi, Ivanovna, hurry, hurry up. Denisov shot himself."

I couldn't believe it. "Denisov? That can't be."

"Oi, I don't know anything. Just hurry, hurry."

He was lying in the bachelors' barracks. He had shot himself in the mouth with a pistol, the back of his skull was shattered and everything was covered with blood.

"Well," I say, "there's nothing for me to do here. There is nothing to say about death—just a cold corpse." And I left.

I felt as if I had been shot. I was shaken and puzzled. To this day I don't understand that death. Could it have been because of his cowardice the day before during the search. Or maybe it coincided with something else?

I don't know. Sometime I am haunted by the thought that it really was Petrovsky—impossible, supernatural. It's a strange story.

ఇ ೞ

The last year before I was released I was already working as a nurse in the Aratau hospital. There I became friends with the prisoner Valya Shefer.

Her husband's father was that minister of the Provisional Government, right after the October Revolution in 1917. He is the model for a character in *Flight* by Bulgakov. The son took his father's surname—Korzukhin. He and Valya had a son Kolya, who also took that surname. Valya kept her maiden name, Shefer.

During the war her husband fought on the Front and disappeared without a trace. That's why Valya was arrested. She simply could not get used to camp life, and if you can't, you sink. They gave her the heaviest work. One time in winter they sent her to the woods to collect kindling wood. She was ordered to search for it under the snow, cut it, and bring it back on a sleigh pulled by oxen. But a storm blew up and in the morning she was found unconscious and covered with snow. However, she gave some signs of life and was taken to the hospital. Her feet were completely numb. Although she regained some feeling she was left with serious polyarthritis.

She was already in the hospital when I began working there and whenever there was talk of releasing her, our doctor-prisoner Andrei Andreevich and our hired nurse Panna (she was not a prisoner) objected. "No, she is not ready," they said. And in that way they saved her life; they understood that in the barracks she would perish. They kept her in the hospital for two years, and when they were ready to let her get up she could not walk. Her joints were seriously deformed. Somehow she was able to creep along with crutches. Andrei Andreevich told me later: "If we had let her walk earlier her joints would have recovered somewhat, but then she would have been sent back to work."

What should have been done? The question was—life as an invalid or death. They chose life as an invalid for her. Valya and I are still friends. Now she is unable to move at all, even with crutches. She is chained to her bed and needs complete care.

At that time there was a Latvian writer in the hospital, En V. En—that was really his name and that's what I'll call him. He had a very advanced case of an acute form of tuberculosis. There was little chance of survival. He loved to talk with me. Once he said sadly, "Tomorrow is my birthday and no one will remember…"

I was on call that night with a nurse's aide. She had been the wife of the Party secretary of the Odessa region and now she was overjoyed to be a nurse's aide. She was always saying to me, "Ah, Agnessa Ivanovna, before I didn't appreciate how well we lived!" I said to her, "Tomorrow is En V.'s birthday. We have to give him a present. Please ask the cook for my bread ration for tomorrow." She brought it to me and we wrote a note to En that said "Happy birthday, dear En V. We put the bread and the note on a branch. I sent the nurse's aide to call En. It was one o'clock in the morning, but the patients were not sleeping. The nurse's aide told En, "The nurse wants you to come." He got dressed and came to me. I said, "There is something for you on the window sill."

He went to the window, read the note and he was so moved that tears ran down his cheeks. His voice shook, "Whose portion is this? Whose is it?"

"It doesn't matter," I answered. "It's not important. Sit down, please, and tell us how you used to celebrate your birthday at home. Tell us all the details. We'll relive it with you."

We sat together until the morning. An order came to the hospital to move all the chronically ill patients to a barracks built especially for them. Our patients were upset and depressed; they were sure the authorities were transferring them to hasten their death, to destroy them.

Then I got a farewell letter from En. "Your sentence is finishing and you will soon be released. Could you take my manuscript out with you? It is a play. I have no hope of taking it out myself." He knew that death was not far off. There was another request in the letter. "I know of course that this may be unpleasant for you, but I decided to ask anyway. When they take us to the new barracks and we say goodbye, I would be so happy if you would kiss me. If this is so unpleasant, I suppose it might be, then let us just say goodbye with a handshake."

It really was unpleasant for me. But the next day as I made my rounds of the patients I bent over him and whispered, "I read your letter and I'll be happy to fulfill your request." When they brought the patients out into the yard and it was time to say goodbye, I went over to him. I could feel him freezing, his entire body straining. To kiss him or not? I embraced him and kissed his cheek hard.

I hid his manuscript.

ఴ ෴

Our head doctor was Andrei Andreevich Ovanesov. He was from Ossetia.[4] He was temperamental, his dark eyes were very intense. In freedom—in that other life—he had a wife and children. But here, in our life, he was single, as we all were.

With us he was sensitive and nervous and he spoke very openly. He told us that when he was arrested he was glad, or more precisely—he felt very relieved. Before then he expected to be arrested. He waited in terror every night, living, as they say, under the sword of Damocles. So when they arrested him all that anxiety stopped, the sword had fallen, and everything was simple. He no longer had to wait, frozen with terror.

One day it snowed very hard. It had to be swept. I had just received a parcel with mittens that had cuffs. They were very fashionable. I put them on and began to gaily dig away, when who should just be passing through the heavy snow? I threw a snowball at him, as a greeting. He stopped and said "I didn't know that you are such a flirtatious woman."

We spent New Year's Eve in the hospital's annex. We rustled up some spirits to add to the water, we asked everyone to bring whatever food they could. Valya Shefer knit me a wool sweater and we dyed it a mellow green that suited me very well. Everyone admired me.

Andrei Andreevich more than everyone else. The expression in his dark eyes was torrid. "I want to sit next to Agnessa Ivanovna," he said. "Only next to her." Everyone laughed and sat us next to each other.

In the spring a nineteen-year-old girl came to the hospital with dysentery. She was from western Ukraine, where she had been arrested for participating in a youth demonstration against the Soviet Army. It was some kind of a rebellion. All the young people were sent to camps—in Siberia and Kazakhstan.

I notice that Andrei Andreevich went out with her to the steppe. They were gone an hour and a half. Oh, that didn't please me at all. When they returned I said to Andrei Andreevich, "What do you need with a nineteen-year-old girl?"

---

[4] Ossetia is an ethnolinguistic region located on both sides of the greater Caucasus Mountains. The language is related to Iranian. Physically, Ossetians resemble all other inhabitants of the Caucasus.

He tries to justify himself. "She wants to be a nurse's aide and I was just explaining to her what the work is like."

"Well, look out!"

He reacted warily. "Does that bother you?" He looked straight at me and said quietly, "Only say the word… and I'll drop her."

I laughed. Well, a joke is a joke, but I let him know that it was not entirely a joke. Of everyone in the camp, Andrei Andreevich was the only one who appealed to me that way.

One night that very spring several doctors, including Andrei Andreevich, my colleague Augusta, and I were sitting around in the hospital barracks. It was already a lovely evening. We sat and joked, and I sparred with Andrei Andreevich. When Augusta went to do her shift, I went to my room. I had barely lain down when there was a knock at my door. Andrei Andreevich.

"You said that you suffer from insomnia."

"True. I have trouble sleeping. Can you get me some phenobarbital?"

He left and quickly returned with phenobarbital. He put it on the table and suddenly began to embrace me.

"What's the matter with you, Andrei Andreevich?"

He let me go, narrowing his eyes. "Well, your behavior…"

"That was all in joking."

"Ah, joking?" he said angrily. "I'll show you joking."

And he grasped me again.

We started keeping company. When Augusta was on duty, he would come to me. Other days, when the doctor with whom he lived was on duty, I would go to him.

When I married Zarnitsky I didn't want children and I had several abortions. And then I didn't get pregnant again, not with Zarnitsky and not with Mirosha. And now I was nauseated in the morning and, scarcely believing it, I knew I was pregnant.

What to do? I really had no choice. I could not, I must not bear a child. How in the world would Mikhail Davydovich have reacted? No, it was not possible. In other words, an abortion. But we had no appropriate instruments in the hospital and no gynecological department.

So, no instruments—what to do? Picture this. Night. Dark. Only a candle burns in my room, flickering, casting shadows on the wall. The two of us, two slaves, with whom they could do whatever they liked, vigilant, expecting that at any moment there would be a bang on the door announcing an inspection. Andrei Andreevich is trying to give me an abortion with his hands, smeared with iodine, without instruments. But he was so nervous, so agitated, that it just didn't work.

I couldn't breathe from the pain, but I bore it all without a moan, so that nothing could be heard. Finally, I said "stop," utterly exhausted. We tried for two days. Finally it all came out, a clump and a great deal of blood.

Thus, I never bore a child.

‌‌‌‌‌‌‌‌‌‌‌‌‌‌‌‌ ⊂౩ ୧౨

My term was almost over, I was counting the days to my release. My soul was already in freedom.

But where should I ask to go? I would not be allowed to return to Moscow. Lena was living in Lithuania in Klaipeda and Agulya was with her. Andrei Andreevich was very gloomy.

"Agnessa," he said, "How can we part like this? Maybe, when I'm released…"

"No, no, Andreika, please don't. You have a family, children, and I have a husband. You are a man of the Caucasus; you'll find a place for yourself here."

"Oh, Agnessa, that was all before I knew you, and now… I'll write to you."

"No, no, don't write. We'll part calmly, amicably, we'll part like friends."

"I will write."

"Don't write. I'll do whatever you ask of me, but we must not write to each other."

These are conversations we had on the eve of my release. They had already said to me, "Tomorrow your term is over." That's how it was done. The next day they lead the liberated person to the barbed wire gate—"Leave!"

I left for the last time on a cart strewn with junk. Panna arranged it for me. I had sewn En's manuscript into a pillow wrapped in woolen sweaters which I had knitted in the hospital. The guards had barely inspected my things and I was already on the cart when one of the chief guards started following me, all in a sweat.

"Stop. We have to search Mironova properly. She's coming from the hospital, and she's taken a white laboratory coat." Two more guards came after me.

I explained to them that the lab coat was from my student days and that I got it from home. But they wouldn't listen. The chief guard grabbed my pillow and kneaded it.

Panna and Andrei Andreevich had followed after me. Andrei Andreevich had the right to sometimes walk outside the camp without a guard. Panna could not contain herself. She snatched the pillow from the guard's hands and threw it back into the cart.

"That's enough," she screamed furiously. The wagon driver clicked his tongue and the horses set off. Panna and Andrei Andreevich walked on either side of the wagon and then ran. Panna took one hand, and Andrei the other. His face was wan and in the dusk looked almost yellow.

Later I saw Panna again, she came to the station. I never saw Andrei Andreevich again. He was a slave. He was not allowed to come to the station.

The barracks for released prisoners was a den of inequity—cursing, cards, thievery, lice. I was advised to rent a bunk in the village and I did so with another recently liberated woman. We paid five rubles a day for the two of us. The captain who signed off on all the papers talked to me in a very friendly way and suggested that I go somewhere not far from Moscow, for example, to Petushki, or Maloyaroslavets or Aleksandrovsk, just over 100 kilometers from Moscow. We were not allowed to live any closer.

How lucky that I declined: everyone who went to those towns was rearrested.

I asked to go to Lithuania because my sister was there. He opened the map and turned it so I could see it. "Not allowed," he said, pointing to Lithuania. "But look, you can go here, showing me with his finger a village on the border of Lithuania. I agreed.

We got our passports in the barracks before release, they had been made out for us even earlier. A Cossack with a pockmarked face came to the barracks and began to call out surnames. When he called mine, I took the passport and read: This passport is issued for half a year on the basis of this and that, article 39." I read it and I remember that this is not a passport, it is a blacklist. I said this to the Cossack. He said: "Well, you shouldn't have committed a crime."

This self-assured, pockmarked freak is lecturing me. This is what had been stuffed into his head.

I couldn't stay in Moscow more than three days. I stood at the railway counter and thought—I'll risk it. I ask, "Can I go to Klaipeda without a pass?"

"I don't know. Ask at that counter over there."

"That counter" was closed. A relative who was with me was horrified. "What are you doing? They'll catch you on the train and you'll be sentenced again."

"And I'm telling you that I'll say that I was robbed of everything."

At that moment I could have convinced anybody of anything.

The next day I went to the cashier's counter that was closed the day before.

"I'd like a ticket to Klaipeda."

"Certainly, a reserved seat?"

And they gave it to me. In the course of the whole trip there was not a single inspection.

Return

When I got to my sister Lena's I was aghast at how poor they were. Now it was clear to me that my "Mongolian" things had gone to keep them alive. In the camps I couldn't understand why they didn't send me parcels. And other things had been left in Moscow. We had left two trunks with the mother of one of Mikhail Davydovich's colleagues and with Nadya, the wife of Mirosha's drunkard of a brother, the one that so embarrassed Mirosha. I had gone to them in Moscow, but alas my things were no longer there. The colleague's mother screeched that the things had been stolen and Nadya almost attacked me: people are starving and you think we should guard somebody's things?

Agulya had been living with Lena. She had grown up, of course, and she was estranged from me; at first she wouldn't have anything to do with me. Just before he was arrested Mikhail Davydovich had succeeded in taking her to Lena in Rostov. That left Lena alone to protect the children from the air raids as best she could, expecting to die at any moment. They made it through to Kislovodsk, but the Germans came. Finally the war moved to the west and Lena returned to Rostov with the children. Vasya, the man from Maikop that had been in love with her—and who later fathered her daughter Nika—was demobilized. Their house had been destroyed by bombs. She was allocated a little house whose owner had died. But the tenant's son appeared with documents proving that the house was now his, threw their things into a space that was really a corridor, and he occupied the rest of the house.

They almost starved. Pavel, our brother Pukha, who had also lived with them at one time, went to Lithuania with his new wife and took Agulya with him. Agulya wrote them that there were potatoes and lard in the market. They all moved to Lithuania.

They found a place to live, but it was very crowded. Lena, her daughter Nika, Agulya, Lena's husband Vasya, and Lena's first husband as well. Sukhotin—remember, Lenya, Vasya, and Sukhotin had lived together in Rostov—had served out his sentence in the camps and he came to live with them. Lena's son Borya had studied to be a tank driver and he went to the Front—to Germany, in fact. He had been wounded there and now was also living with Lena. They were all very hungry; Borya was the only one working and his earnings were small. Sukhotin turned out to be a very inadaptable person and Vasya was already ailing.

I immediately began to look for work. I went to a hospital and boldly asked whether they needed a nurse. Yes, we do but—"first you must register." And right there you have the vicious circle; to work, you need to be registered, to be registered you have to have work.

And me with a blacklisted passport "issued according to paragraph No. 39." I would never get work with that passport and I wasn't even allowed to live in Lithuania.

But this is what I learned in the camp: you must always act boldly and decisively—one might even say insolently—otherwise you're finished. Only then will you get what you want in this country. I am not afraid of anything, not even death. And no matter what, I must keep my head. That's what I told Agulya: fear nothing, act bravely. Only then will you achieve something.

I asked Lena's husband Vasya to fix up my passport. He drew well, he was a real artist. And this is what he did: using a razor he erased the words "Article No. 39." And he substituted exactly what was on his passport, something like III, II, III and something else. It was perfect, that is, you could only see the erasure in a ray of bright light.

And I went again to the militia for a passport. The first time, the chief wasn't there. I felt such relief, because I had been so agitated before I went. I knew the reception hours. So I went again. I foolishly went just before November, even though I knew that when the holiday approaches everyone is busy and distracted and no one is interested in visitors; they even round up some "anti-Soviet" people and arrest some of them for several days until the holiday is over.

I dressed up in Lena's dress, her hat with the little veil, gloves, and under my arm, proof of my address. I think—what if the boss looks at my passport under the light?

I went to the snack bar, ordered one-hundred grams of vodka, drank fifty and poured out the rest. (I had brought something from home to munch on.) I felt sure of myself, "I don't give a hoot and plunge into sea up to my knees" and off to the militia.

A young girl sat at a typewriter in front of the chief's office, probably his secretary. I say to her, ingratiatingly, "Dear young woman, I've just returned from evacuation to join my daughter and I have to register."

There were masses of "dark" people in Klaipeda—the evacuated, the deserters, thieves, bandits, unknowns of all sorts. But I was able to make myself delightful to the young woman, and she said kindly, "Please wait, the director is busy just now." I was relieved—at least I wasn't immediately turned down. She asked me for my house registration, my passport and placed the information on the director's desk. She didn't close the director's door. I could see everything. Some sort of military officials and the director were arguing about something. I sensed that the conversation was coming to an end and I felt that he was in a hurry: his attention was wandering away from the table. He turned to the receptionist.

"Is anyone waiting for me?"

"Yes, for a registration."

"Show her in."

I entered his office and began to tell him about evacuation, but he impatiently interrupted me. "Why did you come here?"

I repeated that I had been evacuated to the Karaganda region and I had come here to join my daughter. He seemed to think that the daughter was an adult.

"Do you have a place to live?"

"Yes, and I have work."

He picked up my application, barely glanced at the passport (rushing!), and signed without even looking: Registered! I sat stony-faced as if it could not be otherwise, but inside I exulted. I took my house registration and went home.

My brother-in-law dealt with everything else in the housing department so that I could be as invisible as possible. Now that I had passed the militia, the housing, department, everything else followed automatically. And that's how I got registered in Klaipeda

And that's how boldly one must act.

The passport was valid for six months. Then it had to be renewed, and again, and again, and each time I was a wreck. Finally I decided that I had to try to get a real passport. So I went to the militia and again turned to the employees, "Dear girls, I'm sick of having to renew all the time. Isn't there some way to get a real passport?"

"Do you have a birth certificate?"

"No, but all you have to do is ask in Maikop where I was born."

They inquired and were told that all such documents had disappeared during the war. At the militia they said bring whatever you have to ZAGS. There I got the girls on my side again. They conferred, vacillated and doubted, but finally said, "Well, come back tomorrow."

The next day they gave me a document that said: according to the information from ZAGS, this person was born at that time in Maikop, etc. And I got a real passport! Without any "caveats" and without any erasures. You cannot imagine how happy I was! Valya Shefer with her blacklisted passport was so envious. And then there was the registration, it came up again when I moved to Bogorodskoe near Moscow, and then to Moscow. I have to say, I got everything there, too.

But I've run ahead of my story.

While I was busy settling the problems of passport and registration and work, I was neither here nor there and I didn't answer any of the letters I got from the camp. And the letters kept coming. I was happy and afraid at the same time: after all the return address on the envelopes was the camp. Then, when everything was settled, I wrote to explain why I couldn't answer. My friends there had been very worried, afraid I had been snatched up again. Andreika even sent a telegram to ask what was happening to me.

Everyone in the camp missed me. Augusta wrote me that after I left Andrei Andreevich pined for me. He would come to her when the new nurse's aide was on duty and would sit until late at night, reminiscing about me. He told her of his grief: "I have lost a friend…" He often repeated how unhappy he was in the camp and that he wanted to find another place. That wasn't so easy, but it was easier for doctors. He was so lonely.

He developed a pain on the right side of his stomach. Everyone thought it was his liver and were even able to arrange a good diet for him. The pain became so sharp that he was put in hospital, where an operation was performed. "Just save my life, please save my life," he implored. When they opened his abdomen they found a perforated ulcer, the result of nerves. Peritonitis had already set in. Two days after the operation, Andrei Andreevich was dead.

Poor Andreika.

ଓ ଞ

I found work in a hospital. There was a rigid separation between the Russian doctors and nurses and the Lithuanians. The Russian doctor operated only with Russian assistants and nurses, the Lithuanians with theirs. I, of course, was in the "Russian camp."

I worked very hard, I came early and left late, sometimes working beyond my shift, substituting for anyone who asked me to replace them. I shared with my colleagues what I had learned in the camp hospital. Andrei Andreevich had taught me a lot.

Then the head nurse—everyone knew she was passionately devoted to the Party—approached me, saying: "You see, Agnessa Ivanovna, we are supposed to recommend two people for Party membership. I don't want any Lithuanians. I've decided on you, I'll recommend you."

I equivocated. "I'm very grateful to you for your faith, it is a great honor for me. But, you know, it's my age. In my youth I was in the Komsomol, but now I don't deserve it, I don't feel ready for such a big step"—and on and on. I barely squeaked out of it.

I had been planning to go to Moscow, but Vasya died before my departure. Before he died he told Borya, "Now you will be the only man in the house."

Translator's Note: In 1944, two years after Agnessa was arrested, Mikhail Davydovich was arrested. In the following letter he is explaining to Agnessa about the period between their two arrests, i.e., 1942 to 1944, when he was in Moscow.

Later Mikhail Davydovich wrote me about that time and how he advocated for me in Moscow: "In your heart you were critical of me. You assumed that I was rejecting you, that I'd forgotten you. You don't understand what was happening. I tried to do something. I don't want to speak about my feelings, about how I lived then, about my wish to die. But I never forgot you and I regarded our separation as a misfortune. I was even relieved when they "called me up." I was freed from the terrible burden of pretending to be someone I was not" (July 14, 1955).

In August 1944, Mikhail Davydovich was arrested. The investigator "pinned on" him the accusation that he had participated in the Gamarnik plot, and a Special Conference sentenced him to five years in a Work Rehabilitation camp.[1]

First he was put to work in a mine, but he fell ill for a long time. Then they assigned him to the camp club. When he finished his sentence he was sent into exile in the village in the Yavlenko-Leningrad region of northern Kazakhstan.

He had already written from the camp that his daughter Maya had sold the dacha in Krasovo and that part of the money was designated for me.

In the autumn Agulya enrolled in an institute in Moscow and was given a place in the dormitory. Maya sent me my share of the dacha sale, and I decided to live with Mikhail Davydovich in Yavlenko. In 1950 he wrote me how much he was waiting for me: "There would have been a roof over my head, warmth, and you."

I was all prepared for the trip. I had purchased everything on the list, reserved and paid for a ticket, and sent Mikhail Davydovich a telegram: "Arriving on such and such a train, car number such and such. Please verify receipt."

No answer. Why? What's happening?

I send another telegram.

I get an answer this time: "Korol has left Petropavlovsk."

The word "left" explained everything.

This is what happened. Mikhail Davydovich lived in anticipation of my telegram. And suddenly a man in a KGB uniform appears: "You have been summoned to Petropavlovsk." With terrible anxiety and a bad premonition Mikhail Davydovich went—and was re-arrested there.

Arrested. Mikhail Davydovich was like a madman for several days. He could not make peace with the idea that everything was gone. Later he wrote me about how he felt at that time.

---

[1] Yan Gamarnik was head of the Political Administration of the Red Army. In 1937, along with most of the Red Army high command, he was accused of espionage and of a plot to assassinate members of the Party and the government. The alleged plot was called by his name. He either shot himself or was shot in his home in June 1937.

July 8, 1955
My Dearest Friend, Aginka,

Three days ago it was a year since the unforgettable day that I was swept away by an avalanche and thrown into the abyss. This is a terrible anniversary.[2]

I lived in the hills in profound isolation. I was surrounded by murk, nonsense, greed, stupidity, and much cruelty. The only link I had to life on this earth, to the real world, to actuality was her. I waited for her because she promised to come to me. The entire meaning of dreary life was concentrated in one desire: to see her. I don't even think a starving person yearns for food the way I was yearning for her

I counted the days to her arrival. I rented a charming, clean little house with a spacious kitchen and a typical Russian peasant stove and one sunny room with painted wooden floors. I immediately paid for two months in advance and had a celebratory drink with the owner in honor of the sacred day. I bought an axe and a poker, and borrowed tongs. I prepared pots and the small wash-stand shone with its humorous coloration. The cold cellar in the kitchen, the mud room, and the pantry were empty. I thought up various decorations to make my little house artistic for her arrival.

Oh dear, where can I find flowers for her? I'll buy them in the town. One bouquet for her at the train station, the other I will give to the driver to hide. When we come home in about eight hours the bouquet will be on the table. And the bathhouse will be heated. And the duck roasted.

I ascended the hill to where the path ended. I breathed in deeply the fresh air and I saw her. That great happiness roused me and I stepped lightly, I sang, I smiled and... I don't know how this happened but I flew down. A wind swept me up and threw me into an abyss. I looked about with dimmed eyes, I heard words but I didn't understand their meaning. My ears buzzed from the violent fall—but I was not afraid. I lost her, she will not come again. I was overcome by desperation over the impossible, mourning for the crucifixion of man, for life's peculiarities. And I thought of the poet's words:

Farewell, the candles are burnt out
It is not strange to walk out into the shadows
To wait all my life for a meeting that never comes
To remain alone in the night.[3]

---

[2] Mikhail Davydovich's reference to "three years ago" is not clear. The text that follows describes how he waited for Agnessa to join him in his exile in Yavlenko in 1950.

[3] This is a verse that the popular singer A. Vertinsky added in 1927 to the famous poem by S. Esenin "Dosvidaniia, drug moi, dosvidaniia." Mikhail Davydovich misquotes the second line, which should be "How I fear walking into the shadows."

For four days after my fall I lay alone in the abyss. Somehow, my fall had not entirely crushed me. A doctor, a very kind woman, nursed me, trying to bring me back to myself. Then another doctor tried, too. I felt the fall and the concussion for a long time. But I began to understand what had really happened to me: waiting for her I reached the limits of emotional intensity and I was cast into a frozen state. I fainted.

CB 80

This is what Mikhail Davydovich was accused of this time: sometime at the end of February 1950, Mikhail Davydovich was in a cafeteria in the village of Yavlenko with his housemate Sinitsky and an unknown tailor, where he engaged in an anti-Soviet conversation.

Mikhail Davydovich never ate in cafeterias. At that time he was ill, he could barely move, he lay in the hospital. Who, finally, was that tailor? In Yavlenko there were only four tailors. It was not a problem to find them, but no one actually looked for them. The procurator mockingly said to Mikhail Davydovich, "How can we find him if you don't even know his surname?" The regional procurator was called Zhigalov. He either conducted the investigation himself or determined how others would conduct it.

The whole affair was crudely concocted. Mikhail Davydovich said that if in Moscow the secret services were virtuosi in fantasy, in the provinces the accusations were so obviously trumped up that by the first examination the outcome was already clear: the fakery was as clear as the nose on your face. Here is one example: interrogation of a "witness" — a librarian. They press her:

"The accused engaged in anti-Soviet agitation?"

Terrified, she babbles, "I don't know..."

They squeeze her harder.

"He knows foreign languages?"

And suddenly she sees the light: "He told me that he was a friend of Hitler's."

Well, you can't go much further than that. The judge was embarrassed. "Sit down, sit down, witness!"

That was the kind of comedy that took place at the trial. A long time ago Zarnitsky, my first husband, was able to triumph over all foolish accusations with his intelligence and his logic. Now, whatever idiotic accusations are screamed out, there is no way to overcome them. Mikhail Davydovich had to be railroaded. Even before the trial began his fate was decided. Ten years in a strict regime camp.

CB 80

Winters in northern Kazakhstan are brutal and the winds are terrible. On December 14, 1957, Mikhail Davydovich wrote in his diary:

December 14—it is a notable date in my life. On that day they mutilated me and brought me to my present condition. Angina and hypertension have worked me over. After six and a half months of incarceration, starving and freezing in damp cells, I was taken in a Stolypin train to Karaganda. The train arrived on the night of December 11.

In the morning they took us in a Black Maria to the camp—Novyi Maikuduk—and put us in intensified regime barracks which were barely heated. Three days later they took us from the camp and stuffed us into an open truck. I don't know exactly how cold it was, but it was not more than minus 30 degrees centigrade. It took at least three hours to get to Spassk. When we got there I was unable to get out of the car. They carried me out on a stretcher. I spent the night in the bath house and thawed. But I was "ruined" for work.

I lay all the time in the barracks. I just couldn't get warm. The medical technician who made the rounds of the barracks noticed me and took me to the clinic. My blood pressure was 240/120.

Mikhail Davydovich spent a long time in the clinic. I know very well what "clinic" means in the camps, how many wasted people lie there, how many corpses are taken out every morning to be packed in piles. I've seen it all and I can easily imagine it.

As soon as Mikhail Davydovich could write, he sent a postal card. It began "My Dear." It was addressed to me, but I read it to Maya and Brusha as "My Dears," so that their feelings wouldn't be hurt. It contained the phrase "Now I will be able to write you again only in six months." According to camp regulations one could send and receive letters only twice a year.

03 80

I am thinking about my friend Valya Shefer, about how the doctors saved her life at the expense of her life and how she paid for her freedom with her useless legs. Well, Valya had a relative who had a dacha in Bogorodsk about 100 kilometers from Moscow. She lived there because her blacklisted passport did not permit her to live any closer to Moscow. The dacha had several rooms, and I visited her there in 1950. Agulya was already studying in Moscow and living in a dormitory. So I decided to remain with Valya in Bogorodsk. I found work teaching music in a kindergarten. The pay was next to nothing, I scarcely had enough for bread.

The winter of 1952 witnessed the beginning of the "Doctors' Plot." Hearing about the "Kremlin poisoners," our mood plummeted.[4] So, we thought, here we go again, they will rearrest us and send us to camps with double zeal.

---

[4] Shortly before he died on March 5, 1953, Stalin accused nine doctors, six of them Jews, of plotting to poison and kill the Soviet leadership. It was an episode of blatant

And suddenly we learn on the radio that Stalin is ill! If they had actually told the public about it, it must be... no, we didn't dare believe it. He—the father of all progressive humanity, the great leader of the world proletariat, the great scholar, the greatest genius. Didn't we all think he was eternal? But Levitan mournfully issues a bulletin. We couldn't turn off the radio, greedily grasping at every announcement: "Fall in cardiac activity. Periodic breathing. Irregular breathing!" Is it possible?

Finally! "The Central Committee mournfully informs that today at 5 a.m. and so many minutes, because of profound cardiac insufficiency..." and so forth. He had died!

I grabbed a broom and began to dance the Can-Can. If Valya had feet, she too would have danced. But she clapped and sang in ecstasy.

A knock at the door. I open it. Our next-door neighbor with eyes red from weeping. "What a misfortune! What a tragedy for our country. What are we going to do? How can we live without him? Everything will fall into ruin, our enemies will vanquish us. Our dear one, our beloved..." And lots of tears.

We put on our saddest faces and echoed her lament. Thank God, our window was high above the ground. She could not have seen how I danced.

c3 80

After that, letters from Mikhail Davydovich came in torrents, floods of letters. The regime had fallen, now one could write as much as one wished. Suffering, silenced for years by the camp regimes, Mikhail Davydovich rushed to tell everything, to share everything with us. Sometimes he wrote several letters in one day and most often the censor didn't even look at them.

Mikhail Davydovich lived in a barrack with invalids who, like himself, were not able to work. He was ill, but the joy of the coming happiness overcame his pain.

The joy of expectation! Could we have dreamed then that it would turn into torment? That for three years freedom would only tantalize without ever actually happening? And everything bad that could happen, did happen.

In principal, prisoners unable to work were certified for immediate release. Mikhail Davydovich was certified and then the certification was withdrawn. In 1954 he wrote to the General Procurator of the USSR; Brusha wrote as well at the same time. The reply was that Mikhail Davydovich's case had been considered. He was granted amnesty and his sentenced reduced to five years. This kind of decision meant immediate release. But the decision

---

anti-Semitism, which had been building under the guise of anti-Zionism, alleged Jewish separatism, and alleged Jewish lack of allegiance to the Revolution. The doctors were arrested and tortured. On March 5, 1953, just days before their trial was to begin, Stalin died. A month later the doctors were released from prison, all the false charges dropped.

seemed not to have reached the Spassk camp. Only at the end of the year was Brusha informed that a decree of the Superior Court of the Kazakh SSR annulled the accusation of participation in a group of agitators and the ten-year sentence was reduced to six years. Why Kazakhstan, when the Moscow had already decided the question? And why reduced to six years? Did that mean that Mikhail Davydovich did not receive amnesty and that he had to sit out more than another year? And what then? Again exile? Again Yavlenko?

Then a decree was issued that all the prisoners who were ill or invalids were to be freed and sent to nursing homes. But, thank God, he was sent instead to a state farm.

He was rehabilitated for the first accusation (participation in the Gamarnik Plot). For the second accusation ("stupid and illiterate provocation") there had been no trial.

Mikhail Davydovich wrote me:

To tell the truth, my liberation has tortured me, has exhausted my heart and my nerves. Liberation has become odious to me. I consider life in arrest to be normal. But still, I long for you, and this is so difficult. Because liberation is turning out to be a torture, I no longer write you the kind of heartfelt letters I wrote you before. I am sure that the minute I'm with you I will once again find that peace of soul, regain my ability to work and the joy that had always supported me. But, my God, it is so hard to bear this. They say that we will have a trial to sort things out. I don't believe it. They can do whatever they like with no rules. Sometimes they ask at the trial if the person acknowledges his guilt. If they ask me that, I'll never be released.

Mikhail Davydovich saw the schemes and intrigues of the regional procurator Zhigalov as the reason for his problems. The uncouth, ridiculous Zhigalov, sensing his own inadequacies, could not forgive Mikhail Davydovich's intellectual superiority, his humor during the interrogations.

And finally...

January 10, 1956

My darling Agochka. I am coming to Moscow. The Superior Court informed me that they have released the documents, that "this case has been reconsidered because of the absence of proof of criminality." I have my passport. I have my photographs.

I had been expecting to be sent back to Yavlenko under convoy, and suddenly such a reversal. I will be embracing you within a week, my beloved, and I will never be parted from you again. I believe that we will begin to live together anew and we will take care of one another. But not to indulge myself in joy—I restrain myself and await new complications and changes.

On January 19, 1956, we met Mikhail Davydovich at the train: Maya, Brusha, his brothers, nephews, relatives, and friends. The snow fell in large clumps. We waited by his train car, people streamed off the train, they kept coming—and no Mikhail Davydovich. Everyone but him. Then I lost patience, pushed my way through the exiting people and into the corridor. I looked in the first compartment, the second: they were empty. And, then, in the third compartment there was a very old man with a sunken mouth, the angle of his lips woefully pulled down, an old misshapen sweater, an old quilted jacket, a deerskin cap that Maya had sent him; one could see at once from what beautiful distant land he had come. In an instant I understood: he was terribly agitated, he couldn't master his emotions, his chin trembled. He could not bring himself to initiate the embrace and in his eyes there was a frightened question. My expression didn't reveal the impression he made, and I immediately embraced him and kissed him repeatedly.

"You—first," he whispered and leaned into me.

Later he told me how he had deliberately stayed behind, praying that I would find him first. He hoped I would.

For a time after his return Mikhail Davydovich let himself rejoice in being home with us. He wanted nothing to set off his nerves. Wishing to banish everything he had been through, he wanted only to live, to live among his loved ones and his friends.

Mikhail Davydovich had dreamed that once free he would do serious writing. But he understood that the 15,000 rubles he was given at rehabilitation would not go very far. No serious offers came his way. Although he had contempt for the kind of utilitarian scenarios he was offered, he couldn't stand sitting around and doing nothing. So he took contract work. writing a scenario entitled "Safety Techniques for Agricultural Power Stations."

Mikhail Davydovich's Party status was immediately restored, but he never achieved the rank of general. "You have been too long out of service," the military authorities told him. His pension, therefore, was very small and the queue for apartments was impossibly long. Maya went to live with her husband and gave us her room.

But Mikhail Davydovich did not despair. He got new teeth—the mournful droop at the corners of his mouth was corrected. He was joyful and hopeful.

In the camp he had been loved and by the end of his term he had made many friends. They visited with us often. Whenever they came to Moscow we happily put them up in our one room. We did what we could for them, fed them, found clothes for them, and gave them money—when we could.

In the beginning it was we who gave. Later the gifts began to come. Packages with smoked sturgeon and caviar came from Astrakhan, for in the summer there was plenty of sturgeon in the rivers. I remembered my time with Zarnitsky when he had a barn where we could hang the fresh sturgeon. Now we had no such place to store the fish, so I distributed it among relatives, friends, and neighbors.

Whenever we went to the Models', friends from the camp, or when camp friends came to visit us, there was a lot of reminiscing. And it was cheerful. Now, from afar, that life did not seem so terrible. In fact, camp life was not remembered as it had really been: the forced labor, the barbed wire fences, the control towers with shotguns, the guard dogs howling from cold in the dark mornings, cutting trees or clearing snow in this fierce cold in tattered jackets. No, no one reminisced about that.

They reminisced about "saucers." This is what had happened. One of the prisoners was supposed to have a meeting with his wife and he searched all over the camp for little saucers, because his wife apparently liked to drink her tea from a small saucer. But his wife found a boyfriend, a soldier on the train, and never made it to her husband. From then on the prisoners made fun of the guy, asking "so what about the little saucers?" Recalling this, Model, that prankster Model, even to this day bursts out laughing.

Or they make fun of how often the prefix *spets* (special) was used as a kind of euphemism: "*spets*-contingent" meant prisoner; "*spets*-housing block" meant barracks; "*spets*-cargo" meant corpse; "*spets*-box" meant coffin. They seem to have forgotten the corpses often did without the luxury of a coffin.

Mikhail Davydovich recounted the conversation he had just before he left Spassk. He walks through the prison camp and hears a woman, the wife of a guard, cursing about the cost of electricity. Mikhail Davydovich asks her who she was so angry at.

"Oh sure, you'll be fine. They'll release you and you'll go right back to where you worked before, but what will my husband do for work? Where can he apply?"

Mikhail Davydovich shrugs his shoulders. "In this case I'm afraid I have no sympathy for you."

Yes, it could be light-hearted, but once in a while it made me angry.

Mikhail Davydovich was forbidden to drink even a drop of liquor, but his friends constantly encouraged him to drink and they wouldn't listen to reason. He willingly yielded to their insistence. Nor was he supposed to be agitated, but everything that happened touched him deeply. I remember once we were spending an evening with a family of our acquaintance. Our host was defending Stalin, saying that now that Stalin was dead it was easy to criticize him, and Mikhail Davydovich argued with him. They had a falling out. The next day Mikhail Davydovich called and when our host answered the telephone Mikhail Davydovich didn't even greet him. He simply asked to speak with the wife. He said to her, "I apologize for spoiling the evening."

But when I began to berate a woman friend for breaking off our friendship as soon as Mirosha was arrested, Mikhail Davydovich took her part.

"Be forgiving," he said to me. "She's not to blame, that was such a dangerous time and so frightening to small people. They just couldn't separate right from wrong."

He wrote in his diary:

> Hate should not rule one—love alone should rule. Love should bring people together. Even in the name of fighting oppression, one should not give way to hate. That is only substituting one kind of oppression for another. The victorious oppression will become even more onerous than the first one and will demand recompense for its victory; it will demand struggle and self-sacrifice. I expunged from my soul my hate for my oppressors, my offenders, my executioners. They are miserable souls, and I have achieved spiritual peace and equilibrium.

But his "equilibrium" didn't last long. At first Mikhail Davydovich saw everything through the rosy haze of his return. But soon that haze took a back seat to the barbarous details of our existence. He didn't find work that suited him. Again, as when he had returned from America, he just sat home. But then he was full of strength and energy. Now he could barely drag himself down the stairs from the third floor, and physical debility undermined his moral condition.

I was working as a nurse in a polyclinic. Mikhail Davydovich tried to help me with the housekeeping as much as possible. Sitting at home he involuntarily became immersed in housekeeping trivia: trying to return bottles when no one would take them; something goes wrong with the toilet and it is impossible to get a new one through the housing administration, so he goes around to the neighbors and tries to buy a "stolen" one from the maintenance man; some wiring goes wrong, he has to pay the electrician with vodka... it took him out of himself.

His only escape was his diary. While he was in the camp, when the regime eased up, he had written:

> After so many years I—an old man—sit in a concentration camp like a criminal against society which I love, against a government to which I gave all my strength without regard for my life, like an enemy of the party which was my "holy of holies."

Now his entries changed:

> I bless the day I was arrested. It began my purification and preparation for a new life. I bless my eleven years of prison and camp—that is how my resurrection began. Without these experiences I would live lived my life in a spiritual void, in a fog, with muddy thoughts and erroneous precepts.

But he did not find enlightenment.

On October 25, 1957, the fortieth anniversary of the October Revolution, Mikhail Davydovich wrote:

> For a year I have lived with two nails pounded into my head, and I can't get rid of them. It's time to finish with them.
>
> The first: how can it be that millions of people, guilty of nothing at all, were subjected to torment and suffering because one man had a horrible character and no regard for law? Was this actually lawful and inevitable? Or is it that under socialism this phenomenon rushes in from the outside? Or is it the consequences of the system? The 20th Party Congress and the Central Committee courageously exposed and abolished it. But that is not enough for me. I must know why that happened in the first place. This is not about me, it is about socialism. If this can happen under socialism, then what is socialism?
>
> When I was in the rehabilitation camp I was sure that I was in the right and those who had imprisoned me were in the wrong. I was convinced that my imprisonment and the suffering of millions of people was because a few leading figures abandoned the foundations that remained the essence of my world view. And I lived to see my convictions validated. That was done by the 20th Party Congress and Khrushchev.
>
> Well... in the last year I have started to question my former convictions. I am no longer so sure that my previous convictions were right.
>
> The second nail: anti-Semitism.

Finally Mikhail found satisfying work. General Khrulev, the chief of our home front area during the war, had written his memoirs. He was having difficulty writing, so Mikhail Davydovich began to help him. They were very interesting memoirs. Mikhail Davydovich told me all about them.[5]

Khrulev knew a lot, including a lot of scandal. For example, there was a complete absence of home front authority at the beginning of World War II. The lack of preparation was so extreme that the home front was organized according to rules established by a tsarist general under Nicholas II before World War I. And this was for the world of 1941!

In addition, Mikhail Davydovich began to collaborate with Sanevich on a book about Frunze.[6] His enthusiasm for this project was partly drowned in

---

[5] General Andrei Khrulev (1892–1962). General Khrulev was a talented administrator and made significant contributions to the reorganization of the home front during World War II. He narrowly escaped the fate of fellow generals in Stalin's purge of the Military High Command.

[6] Mikhail Vasilevich Frunze (1885–1925). Frunze was an important Bolshevik leader in the 1905 Revolution. He played a significant military role in the 1917 Revolution and the civil war. He was a member of high rank in the Soviet leadership, but he took a position antithetical to Stalin's in the intrigues of the 1920s. In 1925 he reluctantly

the humiliation that he was soon to experience. The contract with the publisher was made in the names of Gamburg, Khoroshilov, Sanevich, Struve, and Bragilevich, who were listed as the authors.[7] Mikhail Davydovich was, as they now say, their *negro:* that is, the fruits of his labor would be attributed to them. Mikhail Davydovich's surname was not to be found among the authors. Of course, Sanevich promised some kind of remuneration. Mikhail Davydovich felt so bad about having no wages (he was tormented by not being able to provide for his family) that he swallowed his pride and agreed. But it was very difficult for him. The work helped to take his mind off of these problems, but still he felt that life was passing him by, that he had been cast out onto the margins of life. He wrote in his diary:

January 23, 1957

Yesterday A. I. Binevich paid me a visit and he asked for my advice about the difficulties he was having with his pension. He told me that he had discussed it with a member of the Party organization of the Ministry of Agriculture. That man answered, in the presence of two more comrades, that there was no reason to make a fuss about his pension and that he should get out and not go down that road. But then one of the men who was present said, "Where should he go? He is a pensioner, he can't work anywhere."

The Party man said, "Well then, he should just die." I couldn't believe Binevich and I questioned him in detail. He swore that the answer was exactly that: he should just die. It seems to me that the Party bureaucrat said aloud what a lot of others are thinking. Slavin told me almost the same thing. They said to him, "You are just hot air from an old steam pipe. Get out and stop whistling." I have also heard the same thing from a flunky with a sinecure in a no less vulgar form. So what is it? Is it the official line or is it the independent behavior of individuals? I know that many people consider our liberation to be a mistake, that we should have died there, that we should not be making a new life among the living. They believe that it is natural for the next generation to replace ours, that resurrection of the dead and their reentry into life was not a useful thing to do. The dead should be in the cemetery.

In 1958 Mikhail Davydovich went to Kiev to see relatives and to visit Babi Yar, where his dead parents lay.[8] However I tried to divert him from such

---

underwent an operation and died on the operating table. It is generally assumed that he was one of Stalin's early victims.

[7] The book came out in 1962 as I. K. Gamburg et al., *M.V. Frunze: Zhizn' i deiatel'nost'* [M. V. Frunze: Life and work] (Moscow: Izd-vo Politicheskaia literatura, 1962).

[8] Babi Yar, a ravine near Kiev, was the site of a massacre perpetrated by the Nazi occupiers in September 1941. Groups of men, women, and children were led to the top of the ravine, shot, and dropped into the ravine layer upon layer. Almost 40,000 Jews were killed in the course of two days. In addition, Soviet POWs, Communists, Romani,

distressing thoughts, they tortured him more and more. His memories of the trial in Petropavlovsk, of the procurator Zhigalov cut through like a knife. He began to search for information about him to find out whether or not he had been punished. He did not succeed. Greasy oafish mugs responded to him with indifference: "It was a violation of socialist legality." Mikhail Davydovich should probably not have raked it all up, it took too great a toll. But he couldn't do otherwise. That thorn in his flesh was tearing him apart and that ceaseless torment overrode his original conciliation and equilibrium.

In the summer of 1959 we rented a dacha in Kratovo for the entire season. His brother Mitya with his wife Maria Vasilevna and daughter Tanya lived with us. We tried to live happily and sometimes we even danced to the gramophone in the evenings. Mikhail Davydovich was a very good dancer. He invited Maria Vasilevna to dance and jokingly reminded her how he learned to dance when he was being "groomed" to go abroad. How long ago that was! Mikhail Davydovich danced with his "lady" with confidence, but watching them I noticed that he was overdoing it, trying to hide his shortness of breath. Suddenly it struck me that he was dancing for the last time. I was terrified and banished the thought, as if by itself it could bring harm to him.

Then En came to the dacha, that En, the Latvian writer who I met in the hospital in Aratau when he was ill with tuberculosis. He had asked if he could kiss me when we parted. When I returned from the camp I sent his manuscript to his sister. He was a bachelor and his sister, thinking that we were lovers, wrote me very friendly letters inviting me to visit in Latvia. But I explained to her that I had a husband, because I wanted to dispel that illusion. En had survived and returned to his native land. I had just written his sister to ask whether he was still alive and En himself answered. His letter expressed passionate feelings.

Mikhail Davydovich didn't like the letter. I tried to convince him that there had been nothing between me and En but friendship. En, it seems, took it for something more. And so he came to us when we lived in the dacha in Kratovo. We drank and toasted with cognac. En and Mikhail Davydovich had a wonderful conversation, so all jealousy disappeared. They were comrades in grief, two former camp prisoners who had experienced exactly the same things. They developed an open and intimate friendship. En was a playwright and Mikhail Davydovich was an editor; they agreed that Mikhail Davydovich would edit his play, because in its original form it wasn't quite right.

Mikhail Davydovich came out of his shell. He was so enthusiastic and content now that someone still needed him. He bounced back, he felt his strength and his talent.

03 80

Ukrainian nationalists, and random civilians were massacred. Between 100,000 and 150,000 people lost their lives at Babi Yar.

For several days Mikhail Davydovich was in a good mood, but then he was once more overcome by thoughts of Zhigalov. He began sending claims to the General Procurator of the USSR; he was anxious, he lost sleep. His shortness of breath grew ever worse, he panted more and more often, his lips were cyanotic, and he often spoke about dying. He said that he didn't fear death; death was unavoidable and it would come to him soon. He was calm.

The procurator sent a reply; Zhigalov had been relieved of his position and received the punishment that he deserved. Mikhail Davydovich didn't believe it; maybe they fired him from that work, but they sent him elsewhere and now he lives in clover and maybe even gets a pension—maybe the highest—or a military or personal pension and shamelessly shows off his medals.

Even though other rehabilitated prisoners told him that not one of the former persons in the court, neither the procurators nor the investigators, was left there, Mikhail Davydovich didn't believe it. But this wasn't enough for him. He believed that we should have a second Nuremburg court for these criminals.

Again and again he brought up the question—how could this have happened? In his tortured way he was looking for explanations, some kind of sense to it, a justification of the past. He threw letters at the Central Committee, with these words written at the top: Pass this on after my death. He formulated a theory that camps were created because we were a poor country that needed an army of slaves for the ambitious construction that had been undertaken, cheap slave labor. Beria (of course Beria, one could not have said Stalin) used the experience of Ancient Egypt and Rome and divided our entire population into prisoners and Red Hats (employees of the NKVD and State Security wore red bands on their hat). But as the Red Hats class grew more numerous, that system would become economically disadvantageous.

ଔ ଓ

In the last months of his life Mikhail Davydovich fell into a state of profound pessimism. He had frequent strokes. The week before his death Maya came and told how she had been with a mutual friend who had a photograph of her mother Fenya. Maya asked if she could have the photo and brought it to her father. Fenya on the beach in a bathing suit, so alive.

December 1, 1959, Mikhail Davydovich died.

I could not bring myself to look at his archive for three years, it was too hard for me. I only looked at the cover and opened his diary. And suddenly I see that photo on the first page: Fenya, the sea, the beach. It was literally a stab in the heart: *this is what I took him away from.*

Some time later I told this to Brusha. I could talk to her about anything.

"I was never jealous of your mother, but..."

Brusha tried to convince me that I wasn't guilty of anything: "No, Aunt Aga. The picture is there quite by accident." But I know better.

A very large crowd accompanied Mikhail Davydovich to the cemetery; many from the journal *Red Star*, and colleagues from the cinema, but most were friends, former camp inmates. At the memorial (at Maya's apartment) everyone wanted to speak about Mikhail Davydovich—what a wonderful friend he was, a reliable comrade, an unselfish person who could get along with people of all nationalities, of every stratum. Mosei Iosifovich Model was there. He raised a glass and said, "Dear Misha, I am older than you, I should have died—not you." And he burst into tears.

Here is the obituary in *Red Star:*

M. D. Korol

Mikhail Davydovich, one of the workers in the Soviet military press and a cinematographer. He passed the entire imperialistic war as a soldier in the tsar's army and then was an active participant in the Civil War. Mikhail Davydovich worked in the political administration of the Red Army until 1922. From the first edition of *Red Star* he was the head of the editorial department and simultaneously the editor of the journal *Red Crocodile*.

Later the Party sent Mikhail Davydovich to work in cinematography. As the vice-chairman of the editorial board of Sovkino [Soviet Cinematography] Mikhail Davydovich Korol dedicated great efforts to putting out films about the Civil War and the heroism of our people. Especially notable is that he participated in creating Soviet masterpieces like Chapaev.[9] In the last years of his life Mikhail Davydovich was associated with the cinema studio Multfilm.

Everyone who knew Mikhail Davydovich will forever remember him as a superb organizer, a talented publicist, and a modest and deeply devoted party comrade.

And not a single word about how he had been repressed. Not a word about how he had cruelly suffered. Not a word about the real reason for his death.

View from the Outside: Mira Yakovenko

Agnessa and I were friends until her death—more than twenty years.

In that time her hazel eyes, as I first knew them, turned into cloudy blue-grey with a sclerotic glitter. Wrinkles appeared; she began to dye her graying hair a gold color. No matter how age changed her, her former beauty shone through everything. Her trim figure and her proud posture, her great sense of her own worth—all attracted attention. In these last years she had many

---

[9] Vasily Chapaev, born a peasant, became a Red Army Commander and a hero of the civil war. He was an icon of Soviet bravery. The film was enormously popular in the Soviet Union.

admirers. Someplace in the list of friends a dignified elderly man, looking at her, said with a bow: "You were obviously very beautiful in your youth."

No, she did not want to capitulate to her advancing years. From Mongolia she had brought a special motorized chair that she used every morning in all seasons, standing naked before an open window and getting a full body massage. Then came her exercises. Then after a light breakfast she took a walk, often to the other end of Moscow to take care of some matter or other. She considered this morning routine obligatory. She never allowed herself to lie in bed for a minute, saying that the secret of youth is that you must never allow yourself to let go for a single minute, never give in to the desire to weaken, you should never slump or sit incorrectly in a chair. Everything had to be tucked up, otherwise the bones take the form of an elderly person, and can never be corrected.

Agnessa admired beautiful women of the past. She felt solidarity with them in their beauty. Long before many people began to justify and rehabilitate Natalya Goncharova, Pushkin's wife, she was always on her side. She told me that it pained her to see the kind of disdain people exhibited at Natalya's grave. The grave was unkempt. On the gravestone only "Lanskaya" (the surname of Natalya's second husband) was written without a word about how she had been Pushkin's wife. Agnessa understood her behavior and approved of it.[10]

Having lived her life as a beautiful woman, she found an analogy to herself in the past.

Agnessa read a great deal. She especially loved historical literature. In Leningrad Agulya's husband found the memoirs of Witte and put it on a shelf without reading it.[11] *Agnessa dreamed that when her son-in-law went away on business, she would take the book away to Moscow with her to read. She recited to me the contents of the historical novels of Dmitry Merezhkovsky which she had read in her youth.*[12] *And when the memoirs of Prince Dologurukov were published she could not tear herself away from them for*

---

[10] Pushkin's wife, Natalya Goncharova, was a famous beauty and coquette who reputedly had many affairs after her marriage to Pushkin. Pushkin died in a duel with one of her alleged lovers.

[11] Count Sergei Witte was an influential and gifted figure in economics, industrialization, and diplomacy in the reign of Nicholas II. His expertise in railways brought him into Nicholas's circle of advisors, and he oversaw the construction of the Trans-Siberian Railway. He was forward looking and liberal, guiding Nicholas through the 1905 revolution to accept a semi-constitutional, elected legislative body.

[12] Dmitry Merezhkovsky (1865–1941)—novelist, poet, religious thinker, and literary critic—was a major figure in Russian cultural life. His passionate and mercurial political enthusiasms managed to offend political activists of all stripes, and in 1920 he fled to Paris. He was nominated for the Nobel Prize many times.

several weeks: they recounted the fate of Peter II's young wife and other historical figures of the Byron era.

She was deeply affected by Mikhail Davydovich's opinion that Russia should have a second Nuremburg trial: she had copied out the entire text of the 1946 agreement in her notebook.

Many rehabilitated prisoners who had suffered from denunciations and interrogations were afraid of any public visibility. Agnessa feared nothing. She was a passionate agitator. On the Metro, the street car, standing in line, if someone began to justify Stalin or to be censorious towards the repressed, she would immediately intrude and with her eloquence and passion, more often than not beat down her opponents: she, after all, had herself been in the camps and she knew the truth firsthand—not from hearsay.

I loved being in her apartment on 4th Tverskaya-Yamskaya. Mikhail Davydovich did not live long enough to get a separate apartment. He came to her there after his release and she remained there in the communal apartment after he died. The neighbors came and went, Agnessa remained.

You walk into the entrance, go up a steep staircase to Apartment 13. Agnessa, waiting for you, opens the door, always welcoming, always cheerful, always well-groomed, lightly made-up, her hair delicately tinted—fully presentable. In the winter she wore a pale pink wool sweater. I loved that sweater; everything she wore was always beautiful. It made me want to dress that way, too.

Then clip-clop, a whisper, the rustle of a bamboo curtain—and I am in the room. The large window to the right is still sunny, the sun soon moves on. Evening falls.

The cakes I've brought sit on the round table in the middle of the room. Agnessa is delighted and dismayed. "What are you doing to me, dear Mira, I'm getting fat even without these cakes!" But she can't restrain herself, she loves these cakes. There is food on the table, not much but varied. Sometimes, however, there is just toast. And we always drink tea.

Oh, that round table. A bright oilcloth covered its age. So many stories told around that little old table.

08 80

You know, I want to marry again and I don't hide it. I always believed that a woman should be married. As it says in the Gospel, "A man shall cleave to his wife." Those are very wise words. Agulya has a girlfriend with a graduate degree. She was married, divorced, and has had many temporary lovers. What's that about? She was a married woman and now who is she? Just a tart!

I don't approve of that. And especially at my age, one needs a friend. I very much need a person like Mikhail Davydovich to whom I can speak from my heart with mutual understanding. How lonely some of my evenings are. Ah, in a carriage to the past you don't get very far.

For a long time I corresponded with the director of a conservatory in the city. He once served under Mirosha and he was very much in love with me. But we broke it off—he suddenly married a very young girl. Well, it seems that I must live out my life alone. But, you know, I never whine. I don't have a special male friend, but I have so many friends around me. I'll survive.

But life, of course, is not easy. I got a pension. I was so afraid that they would ask: why is there no mention in your passport that you were sentenced to incarceration or released on Article 39? Well, Vasya erased that for me when I needed to be legitimate in Lithuania. None of my documents tell that I was in the camp. But at the Social Security they never asked, they took my application for rehabilitation and only said, "Add the length of your term in the camps." That's all. At least that proceeded smoothly.

Fifty rubles. It's so hard to live on that. Remember, Mikhail Davydovich helped General Khrulev write his memoirs. If only they had been published! Khrulev would have shared with me, or given me something from his honorarium. But the memoirs were not published because now everything has to be hidden-hidden-hidden. How many mistakes were made at the beginning of the war! Now we are only heroes, victorious. They need lies, and Khrulev wrote the truth. Some time after Mikhail Davydovich died, he called me. He wanted to meet with me. I wait and waited—and then he died. Now the memoir will certainly never be published. The book about Frunze came out in 1962. The authors: Gamburg, Khoroshilov, Sanevich, Struve, Bragilevich.

Sanevich gave me a copy and wrote a long grateful message praising Mikhail Davydovich on the title page, indicating that this or that chapter really belonged entirely to him. But his name is still not among the authors. How much of his soul he poured into that book!

And look what's happening now.

I went to see a play, and this is the dialogue: a boy says, "But your father sat for eighteen years."

"Well, so what if he sat," merrily answers the young son. "He was rehabilitated and he gets a pension."

Or: "Just think, 200–300 people were arrested. So what!?"

And further: "Let's not irritate old wounds."

Whose wounds? The wounds of the executioners? I just can't hear that calmly. All lies, lies. Everyone wants to whitewash, to shut up, as if nothing happened.

Think about *Journey into the Whirlwind* by Evgenia Ginzburg. Now I'm afraid to keep *samizdat* around, I've accumulated so much.[13]

---

[13] *Samizdat* is an abbreviation of the words meaning "self" and "publish," meaning the form that the dissident movement was forced to take in the 1960s and into the '70s and '80s. Stalin's successors rarely permitted criticism in any form, social, political, or liter-

I've destroyed it all, but I cannot part with that manuscript—with Evgenia Ginzburg. Let them put me away again. That book is about all of us, about people like me.

Of course, wherever I can, I try to earn a bit. Not just for the necessities. I so want a piano. Let it be an old one, cheap. I don't get enough music in my life. Ah, the radio—no, that doesn't quite do it, it feels like something inflicted on me. But to sit down at the piano and play whatever your soul needs at the moment.

True, not long ago it was if my thoughts had been heard. I was cleaning up my room. I stood on a chair to wipe the dust from the top of the chest of drawers with a rag. My eye fell on a record player that lay neatly covered up. I thought about taking it down and putting on my favorite record—*Valse Triste* by Sibelius. But no, I left it there. I was too lazy to take it down, unwrap it and turn it on. Later, at about midnight I was getting ready for bed. I turned on the bedside lamp at my head, I put on my night dress. The radio was off, silence. And suddenly I heard a chord. I recognized it immediately—Sibelius! A violin sang softly, sadly and then the entire orchestra. The tender mysterious waltz spread through my room. And again—memories of my life.

Now I have found work that will probably last for a long time. Charlotte, a relative of Mikhail Davydovich's, has asked me to look after her. She is chronically ill and can't take care of herself; I will be like her nurse-companion, I'll take care of her. She has no one else in the entire world.

"Don't abandon me, Agnessa!" she pleaded with me. "You won't leave me?"

"I'll never abandon you," I promised. "Not until you or I breathe our last breath."

I don't know which of us will die first, I don't know. We are both seventy-seven years old.

ଔ ଞ

I have a piano! Now I can play whatever I like when I like. Beethoven and Chopin—these great musicians have accompanied me through my life. The piano. How did I get it? I am rich! Yes, it's awfully sad of course. Charlotte died, peacefully, without torment. And she left me her savings. I actually got an inheritance! I did not stuff it away in a savings account. If there's money—one must live, life is so short!

Life is short. It passes by like an hour.

---

ary. Dissent was therefore expressed in works that were written and circulated clandestinely in manuscript form: typed and endlessly copied and recopied. It included such major works as Evgenia Ginzburg's *Journey into the Whirlwind* and the poetry of Joseph Brodsky.

First I gave everyone close to me 100 rubles: Agulya, Tanya, Maya, and Borya. Nika, and all the rest. And then. After all, I have so long dreamed of making a "trip to my youth." I've dreamed of going to my dear places—Maikop, Rostov, the beaches of the Caucasus.

I found my Verochka, my Maikop girlfriend, in Sukhumi on the Black Sea. I took my niece Nika and her son and Agulya with her children. Verochka's relatives asked only a bit from us for our lodgings. We had a room on the second floor and the use of the kitchen below. We ate out-of-doors under the sky, it was so warm there. My young people spent whole days on the beach. I didn't go to the sea, I sat in the garden. I swam only early in the morning before it was hot and while the beach was almost empty. It is now hard for me to tolerate the heat. Once I so loved it. The south, the sea, the sultry weather. That's my native element.

Verochka's family had been very rich, and after the Revolution, during the requisitions they hid the really valuable things. They buried them under a big flowering bush in the garden. The men who came to take our things were meticulous; they examined almost all the flowers, but miraculously they didn't touch the bush. They were probably sick of the whole business. With the hidden valuables Verochka's family was later able to buy several houses and they gave one to her. It was not large. Whitewashed, it sat shining between the blue sea and the blue sky. Magnolias were blooming in the surrounding garden. Paradise! "Do you remember that we had pink bushes in Maikop?" my girlfriend laughed and pointed to the house. "Here is one of them."

She saw that I was confused, so she revealed that family secret to me—fifty years later.

In Maikop I looked for old streets and houses, acquaintances that were dear to me from childhood. But I scarcely recognized the places, everything is so changed. I couldn't find Mirosha's and my precious poplars, and I couldn't even find the little path to the river.

ଔ ଓ

Mirosha was not given rehabilitation. The procurator answered me that it was not possible because he exceeded his powers in Mongolia. But everything Mirosha did was ordered by Moscow. Stalin brought Choibalsan to power; every one of our people who goes to Mongolia now visits Choibalsan's grave and brings flowers. And Tsedenbal, who is venerated, he was Choibalsan's successor.

Mirosha, Mirosha! How often I reminisce about him now. My dreams haunt me. I dream of Rostov in the time of our "Underground Apprenticeship"; how we quarreled, parted, and again threw ourselves into each other's arms.

In my dream I am running to a rendezvous with Mirosha. I see poplars, the path to the river—but no Mirosha. I look for him, hoping, believing that he will come. I try to force the dream to conjure up Mirosha—to see him alive as before, to touch him. But merciless reality intrudes on the dream, poisons it, and I am clutching at a phantom whose wispy outlines slip through my fingers and melt away.

In another dream we are driving in a car together, we come to the station, wait for the train, but Mirosha disappears. I search, search. No Mirosha.

The fruitless searches of my dreams torture me. My mouth is parched and I cannot slake my thirst. I awake. There is no joy in remembering the dreams. Rostov, sunlight spilling onto the street, my youth. All this I have in my dreams. But no Mirosha.

Perhaps he can't come to me in my dreams because he has no grave. There is no place I can go to talk to him.

In spring, on the Day of Remembrance, when I visited Mikhail Davydovich's grave, I came across the grave of Zinaida Raikh, the wife of the great theater director Meyerhold. His theater was liquidated in 1937 for being "alien" to Soviet art. In 1939 he was arrested, allegedly dying in prison in 1940. Although no one knows where Meyerhold lies, he has since been rehabilitated, and now there is a large black obelisk with his profile carved at the top, with his name, birth date, and the approximate date of his death. Lots of people do that now: erect tombstones to rehabilitated victims, even though no one knows where the murdered bodies are really decaying. They do it so that the dead won't fall into oblivion.

If Mirosha had been rehabilitated, I would do it too: we could put his name on the Korol family tombstone. And there would be a place on this earth for Mirosha, a place I could find him in my thoughts.

When I discussed my own burial with Maya and Brusha, Mikhail Davydovich's daughters, they said that of course my urn would be buried beside Mikhail Davydovich's.

"No, darling girls, no. Let Mikhail Davydovich rest with Fenya, your mama. She came for him, she took him to her."

"Auntie Aga, you're jealous," the girls answered.

"No, dear girls, I'm not a bit jealous, but why should I be a third wheel there? Fenya—your mama—was Mikhail Davydovich's wife. Mirosha was my real husband, and if we can't be together then bury my urn in the Vagankov cemetery so that you don't have to go to two separate cemeteries on the Day of Remembrance. If Mirosha and I can't be together, I'd rather be completely alone."

Of course, one could simply engrave Mirosha's name on the family tombstone without waiting for rehabilitation. In that case, he would not be listed in the cemetery's registry, but who cares? The truth is that the Korol family doesn't want the name of an *executioner* on the family grave stone. Oh, yes. Now I understand well the real reason that he cannot be rehabilitated.

But was Mirosha an executioner? I can't believe it. "I am just Stalin's cur; there's no way out for me," he once said to Mikhail Davydovich. Once he fell into that dreadful machine, he could not worm his way out, and only I know what that cost him. However he suffered, he had no choice but to give the orders for executions. Stalin, that "Greatest Genius," was insatiable. The Moloch needs blood, blood, blood. To save himself, Mirosha had to spill it.

And that blood is on Mirosha.

In what communal grave are buried the men who were shot at Lefortovo? In what dump do they lie? I don't know. I know only that there will never be a place for me to weep for Mirosha.

That is his posthumous punishment.

The Last Party

Agnessa never missed her birthday, not once in her life even in the most difficult prison and camp conditions. She celebrated it always and everywhere in any way she could. Of course she would not miss it here in Moscow. And no matter how small her pension she celebrated it lavishly, even more so now that she had a small inheritance. She baked the traditional Napoleon, she made potato pirozhky, herring "in an overcoat," and other delicacies.

Irrepressibly sociable, Agnessa had made friends with her young neighbors, who usually helped her prepare for the traditional celebration. But this time they were both busy and she prepared everything herself. She told a hilarious story about how she rustled up fresh fish, almost coming to blows with an arrogant fellow who thought he could take her turn in line. She was seventy-nine years old.

This party was exceptionally gay, fifteen guests and an elegant table, better than she had ever set before; such a jolly party. Normally Agnessa drank a half a glass of cognac, this time she permitted herself three. Then Agnessa danced with her nephew Lev. They danced an old-fashioned tango, but Lev did not come up to Agnessa's standards. So she taught him how to do it. In an elegant form-fitting black dress she drilled him — twirling him around, arm outstretched, hands entwined, she danced forward proudly and artistically. The rest of us could not tear our eyes away from her.

The next day I came to visit Agnessa. There was an ambulance at her entrance.

Agnessa died two weeks later. It was 1982.

Epilogue*

Agnessa and Mira met in 1960 as mature adults. Agnessa was fifty-seven and Mira forty-three. Agnessa's adventures were behind her. Mira's fulfillment was still ahead of her. Dramatically different as were their backgrounds and life experience, each had in her own way lived through the same "painful and difficult years—world wars, hunger and devastation, the Stalin years and unrelieved fear." Everyone who knew them recognized that they had a special kind of relationship. Agulya tells me that "Mama [Agnessa] often spoke of Mira, they were very close friends. Otherwise Mama would never have opened up to her as she did."

Mira Mstislavovna was born into several generations of dedicated medical professionals, both men and women. Her grandfather, Vladimir Ivanovich Yakovenko, was a pioneering psychiatrist who established the Moscow Regional Psychiatric Hospital 2, which bears his name to this day. Her father was a physician, as were her two aunts; her uncle was a biologist. Mira's childhood dream to be a person of literature and letters was not encouraged. "In the family this was not considered a serious profession. Her parents said, 'You learn to write by yourself, like Jack London, but your real profession can be only technical or medical.'" Mira dutifully became a physicist and took her work seriously. She worked in various laboratories and defied the age limit of thirty-five by beginning graduate studies at age thirty-eight and finishing with high marks. But physics was her day job—writing was her enduring, consuming passion.[1]

---

* Except where I indicate otherwise, the information in this epilogue comes from the following sources: "My Family," an unpublished account of the Yakovenko family going back two generations written by Olga Yakovenko, Mira's daughter; a day-long interview I conducted with Olga Yakovenko in 2009, as well as many subsequent meetings, conversations, and letters; a three-day interview with Agnessa's daughter Agulya in St. Petersburg in 2011 and many subsequent letters.

[1] Mira's published works include a biography of her grandfather, *Vladimir Ivanovich Iakovenko* (Moscow: Rossiiskoe obshchestvo medikov-literatorov, 1994); *"Kuda ushla moia zhizn'?": Povestvovanie v pis'makh, dnevnikovykh zapisiakh, vospominaniiakh, i ofitsial'nykh dokumentakh o zhizni i trudakh Aleksandra Alekseevicha Vanovskogo* ["Where has my life gone?": A narrative in letters, diaries, memoirs, and official documents on the life and works of Aleksandr Alekseevich Vanovskii] (Moscow: Memorial, 2009), a biography of her Aunt Vera's first husband; *Zoia Ge: Dokumental'naia povest'* [Zoya Ge: A story in documents] (Moscow: Memorial, Zvenia, 2006); and *Pavel Al'bertovich Ivenson* (Moscow: n.p., 1994).

In 1938, twenty-one-year-old Mira spent a summer holiday in the northern Caucasus. She was enchanted by the history of the Khevsury, a tiny tribe native to the Caucaus Mountains with a dramatic, bloody, and romantic history. Among her early writings were two novels about a beautiful Khevsury princess and her melodramatic and tumultuous love affair with a prince. Olga Yakovenko, Mira's daughter, calls them "women's novels." They were, she says, "lurid, gothic, flamboyant and exaggeratedly romantic." The novels remained unfinished, but "life on the roller coaster of Soviet History" provided Mira with plenty of drama for her subsequent serious writing and she did not have to make up a bit of it. She found Agnessa—a real-life beautiful, romantic, flamboyant heroine.

In 1956 Mira met a man who played a pivotal role in her life. Mosei Iosifovich Model, a Party member since 1905, was arrested in 1936 and sentenced to Vorkuta, an immense Gulag 150 kilometers north of the Arctic Circle. His wife was exiled to Kazakhstan, where she met Mira's Aunt Vera (Vanovskaya).[2] Released from the Gulag, Mosei Iosifovich and his wife opened their apartment to other "enemies of the people" who came for advice and support in their quest for rehabilitation. They asked Mira to help her Aunt Vera negotiate the intricacies of rehabilitation.

Mira went to work on her aunt's behalf. She haunted the reception rooms of the KGB until Aunt Vera was rehabilitated and compensated for the Moscow apartment and belongings that had been confiscated when she was arrested.[3] "In these visits to the KGB's offices Mira Mstislavovna saw with her own eyes and heard with her own ears the stories of people who had so suffered... She got to know many of the innocent Gulag victims and she was utterly selfless in her efforts to help them."

Mira filled notebook after notebook with their life stories. She wrote feverishly. And, in 1960 Mira met Agnessa in the Models' apartment at what Agulya remembers as a "meeting of old Bolsheviks." Thus began twenty years of friendship, more story-telling, and more note-taking. Before the dis-

---

Zoya Ge, niece of the famous Russian artist Nikolai Ge, went to prison for her work with Vera Figner and the People's Will in the late 1880s. The story of her life was entwined with that of many families who experienced the upheavals in Russia in the late nineteenth and twentieth centuries. She died cold and hungry in Moscow in 1941.

Pavel Ivenson was an extraordinary engineer. He was arrested in 1935 because of his "foreign origins," although his Scandinavian family had lived in Russia since the eighteenth century. He spent five years in the Solovetsky Gulag.

[2] Aunt Vera's first husband, A. A. Vanovsky, was a Menshevik and a leader in the 1905 Revolution. He left the Soviet Union for a life in Japan, where he abandoned his politics to become a teacher of literature and a philosopher of religion (see n. 1). Vera's second husband perished in the Magadan Gulag.

[3] Between 1947 and 1954 the NKVD underwent several changes of name. In March 1954 it was renamed the KGB and remained so until the disintegration of the Soviet Union.

integration of the Soviet Union, nothing Mira wrote could have been published, including Agnessa's story. She wrote, as they say, "for the drawer."[4]

In 1989 the Memorial Society was founded.[5] "This was really what Mira Mstislavovna had been waiting for all her life," says her daughter. "Memorial became more important than anything else: more important than the family, than everything. Her work there was the main thing to her. She lived for it."

I met Mira in 1997 in the Memorial offices shortly after *Agnessa* was published. She was eighty years old and no longer writing. During the day she took care of her ailing, housebound husband. Every evening she took buses and the Metro and went on foot, arriving at the Memorial offices from her apartment on the far side of Moscow. She stayed until the last Metro and last bus ran at midnight, doing whatever needed to be done so that the researchers and administrative staff could do what they needed to do: "I love being here, I love the staff, I love the work they do." The work was its own reward.

Other rewards followed. *Memorial* recognized Mira's talents and the amazing story she had to tell. "But," Mira told me, "before they decided to publish *Agnessa*, there was a lot of conflict. Not everyone wanted to publish it. Some Memorialtsy thought it romanticized Mironov."[6] True to its mission of facing the past, Memorial did publish it and held a book party in the Memorial offices on Mira's eightieth birthday.

Agnessa's fifteen years with Mirosha—six years of "underground apprenticeship" and nine years as his wife—were her halcyon days. She cared nothing for politics or the Party, except insofar as Mirosha's successes thrilled him and gave her the life they both relished. Indeed, she had contempt for both ideology and for the culture of the Party. Insisting that she only began to glimpse the nature of his "men's work" around 1937, her utter lack of guile in describing her life strongly suggests that she chose not to "know." But whether she learned gradually or because in 1937–38 the nature of his work was thrust upon her, they both ultimately paid for their life of excess, luxury, and privilege. Mirosha paid with his life and Agnessa paid with the enduring pain of justifying Mirosha, if not to the outside world, then to herself. "The truth is that the Korol family doesn't want the name of an *executioner* on the family gravestone." Was Mirosha an executioner?

---

[4] Mira left behind unfinished works based on the oral histories she took from the survivors of Stalin's repression. Olga believes that her mother suffered a kind of "survivor's guilt" for not having endured the Gulag, and she believed that Gulag survivors were somehow superior to her. When Mira was very old, Memorial offered her a place in a sanatorium catering to survivors of repression. She turned it down, for she sincerely believed that she did not deserve it.

[5] See Appendix B for a description of the Memorial Society.

[6] Probably for that reason, lest I fall under Agnessa and Mirosha's spell, Arseny Roginsky made sure I had the document in Appendix A. Please read it.

In her explanations, scattered through the book, Agnessa begins with Mirosha's devotion to the Party. As Maya, Mikhail Davydovich's daughter, pointed out, "It is just as Agnessa says of Mirosha. Mirosha was just like Mikhail Davydovich. The Jews had suffered from anti-Semitism, from pogroms, and humiliation. The Revolution had put an end to anti-Semitism. It was *their* revolution." But by the time she is narrating her life to Mira—and after five years in the Gulag—Agnessa can no longer claim to be ignorant of the terror inflicted on Soviet citizens in the name of the Party. So Agnessa patches together a narrative to suggest—or demonstrate—that Mirosha was nonetheless deeply distressed—sometimes—by what he was forced to do. When Agnessa and Mirosha went to Karaganda in 1932 they found that the exiled kulaks had all died off and that their children were eating each other to survive. "At that time he suffered greatly about things like that, I could see it. But he was already beginning to push them out of his head, to dismiss them. He was so dedicated to the Party, he always believed that everything the Party did was for a purpose."

Perhaps that is what Mirosha believed. What about what Mirosha actually did? Was he complicit? Here is one of the few NKVD insider accounts of how the NKVD elite acquired its privileges—in a country racked by famine, dislocation, scarcity, substandard housing, medicine, terror, and repression:

> [T]he head of regional branches of the NKVD at their discretion had the right to shoot hundreds of people without trial. "Over fulfilling" was encouraged with bonuses, medals, and promotions... Thus, inside the penal machine this led to a logically coherent and well thought out system of stimulus and rewards. The results of this system lead to only one thing: to killing for the sake of killing.[7]

Mirosha was no less a sybarite than Agnessa, nor does Agnessa hide Mirosha's delight in their luxuries and in his success for the sake of success. If she is to live with what she still grudgingly admits he might have done, she has to transform Mirosha the perpetrator of inhumanity into Mirosha the victim of inhumanity. They were both victims, she of petty jealousy and rivalry. Both could be traced back to Stalin. Mirosha was a victim of Stalin's machine. Once entrapped, he had no choice but to carry out his orders. "Kill or be killed." Yes, he loved his life—bonuses, lavish resorts, luxury, professional success, power. But, in the end it was "Kill or be killed." Agnessa is helped, in a peculiar way, by the fact that ultimately the Revolution that had "liberated" Mirosha also killed him. Or, more precisely, it was Stalin as the spokesman for that revolution: Stalin, the "Moloch needed blood, blood, blood." For Agnessa there is no ideology, no history, and not even complicit

---

[7] Mikhail Pavlovich Shreider, *NKVD iznutri: Zapiski chekista* (Moscow: Vozvrashchenie, 1995), 1.

intermediaries to be examined; first Stalin's cur, then Stalin's victim. Not even after she had undergone the agonies of the Gulag.

The Gulag was an indelible and piercing experience for Agnessa. It opened her eyes wide to the worst that the Soviet state could inflict on its people. It pushed the boundaries of her natural generosity and concern beyond her family to embrace the community of Gulag victims. But it did not define her. She did not have to deal with the wrenching betrayal experienced by thousands of true believers in the Soviet State and the ideals that allegedly guided it, the sense of betrayal experienced by the Evgenia Ginsburgs and, closer to home, her third husband, Mikhail Davydovich. She had been betrayed not by the failure or distortions of Communism or by a calculated system of terror, but by wicked, small-minded neighbors. She was guilty of nothing. She had put no one to death and she had done nothing to deserve her denouncers' venom. She had only taken the bounty that life heaped upon her and she felt no shame for that.

As Mira Mstislavovna shaped Agnessa's story, she made plenty of room for Mikhail Davydovich precisely to emphasize how profoundly damaging the Gulag was to people like him, the dedicated sons and daughters of the Revolution—in contrast to Agnessa, the intellectually and emotionally uninvolved bystander. Unlike Mirosha, there was no blood on Mikhail Davydovich's hands to justify his punishment and suffering. He had not been seduced or forced to do terrible things. He had devoted his service to the Soviet Union in honorable ways. He was highly critical of Mirosha, because he knew that Mirosha was an executioner. "Why don't you just shoot yourself," he tells Mirosha in disgust. He was not the great love of Agnessa's life, but she loved him and suffered with him. Again, in the end, it was all Stalin's fault and fault of the atmosphere and policies that Stalin created.

The last character in Agnessa's story of her life and times is Agulya, the daughter of Agnessa's brother Pavel, whom Agnessa and Mirosha adopted and brought up as their own child. What happened to a Soviet child whose fairytale life was snatched away from her when her father was shot and later revealed to have been an executioner, whose mother had spent had spent five years in a Gulag?

After Mirosha's arrest when Agulya was eight years old she lived as many other children did in the immediate pre-war years through World War II and into the 1950s. First, she was evacuated with Agnessa and Maya from Moscow to Kuibyshev when the war broke out. After Agnessa was arrested in 1942, Agulya was handed around from one household to another, from Moscow with Mikhail Davydovich to Mirosha's brother—twelve people in one room—then to "Uncle Pavlik" (her biological father), then to Agnessa's sister Lena in Rostov, and finally to Lithuania to live in a communal apartment with six people in one room because in Lithuania "there was milk to be had there and potatoes and suet." Agnessa joined them in Klaipeda after her release from the Gulag in 1947 and, says Agulya, "I had to get used to Mama again."

Further, she adds, "I never suffered, not when I lived with Aunt Anna, not when I lived with Aunt Lena, or with Uncle Pavlik."

I spent three days with Agulya in 2010. Agulya was eighty, trim and lively, and happy to talk about her past. Many times in the course of our meetings Agulya said, "We have never had means. But everyone was poor. Here it's always been like that; then and now, always." The opulence of her first eight years is entrapped in photographs. The consequences of that life followed her into her adult years. In this way as well, she was like thousands of other Soviet citizens. She knew that her stepsister Maya lived under the cloud of Mikhail Davydovich's Gulag record: she and her husband did not marry officially because her husband feared Maya's family history would cost him his job. Outside of the family Agulya spoke to no one—she emphasized, to no one, never—about either Mirosha or Agnessa. "And you know what? No one ever told me not to, I felt it myself." Agulya wanted to study chemistry—but the application to a professional institute required her biography. Her name and patronymic identified her as Mirosha's daughter. So, first she was advised by Maya not to apply to a chemistry institute, but to a certain textile institute that was not likely to closely scrutinize her background. By that time Agulya knew that Uncle Pavlik was her biological father. She had learned by accident when she was in her late teens. Agnessa advised her to substitute Pavlik's biography for Mirosha's and to use her biological sister Tanya's birthday as her own. Agulya has no regrets and few complaints. She worked in textile chemistry her entire working life and enjoyed it. She was happily married and lived with her husband and two children in Tashkent until 1960, when they moved to her husband's home town, Leningrad. Her relationship with Agnessa grew stronger and stronger over the years.

Agulya now claims that she never spoke directly to Mira and that everything about her in *Agnessa* came through Agnessa. By the time Agulya and I spoke, thirty years had passed. Today her version of Mirosha's role in her life is not exactly as Agnessa, through Mira, presented it: "*I could not forget about Papa. We all dreamed that he would return.*" She was reluctant to speak much about him and was clever about dodging the subject: "I suppose I was attached to him, he was my Papa. But I only knew him for six years. I was almost two when they adopted me and I was eight years old when he was arrested." Nor does she speak of his arrest and disappearance with much affect: "They didn't explain anything to me, but I understood something was wrong. I didn't pay any special attention to it. I didn't suffer... I had Mama with me, I had Babushka with me. Thank God Mama was not arrested, but I knew she was very upset and that she also expected to be arrested any day."

This is how Agulya remembers her mother. Like everyone else, she found Agnessa charming, lively, charismatic. She admires Agnessa's pride in her appearance. She did not speak of it as vanity. She could laugh at Agnessa's love for her material possessions. "You know, Mama always had a lot of suitcases and trunks." She thinks of Agnessa as an educated woman who read widely and spoke three languages. From Agulya I learned that Agnessa and Lena had three years of Greek school before they entered gymnasium in Maikop. They learned French in gymnasium—"In those days, if you went to gymnasium you really learned the language." Agnessa and her sister Lena used both languages in their conversation and in letters.

She admires Agnessa. The mother she knew best was a hardworking, generous, life-loving person. A few months after Mirosha was arrested, Agnessa went to work for the All Union Agricultural Exposition. In Klaipeda, by means of courage and cunning, she found a position as a nurse, supporting her sister, her sister's children, her sister's former and current husbands, and Agulya for three years. "She always said don't be afraid of anything," Agulya says proudly. Between 1950 and 1955 Agnessa lived in Bogorodsk with her disabled friend from the Gulag, Valya Shefer. She cared for her friend and taught music in a conservatory. When Mikhail Davydovich was finally released from the Gulag, they lived in Moscow and Agnessa worked there as a nurse until she retired. After her retirement she cared for a relative of Mikhail Davydovich for a short time.

At one point in a conversation with Agulya I referred to Mirosha as her father. She interrupted sharply, "Pavel Ivanovich is my father."

I was taken aback. "And Mirosha?" I asked.

"I only know Mirosha from photographs, I was almost two when they adopted me. I only lived with him for six years. Maybe if he were alive it would be different. Pavel Ivanovich, in my heart he is my father."

In general Agulya was evasive when I brought up Mirosha. Finally, she reluctantly said, "What do I think about his guilt? Well, I don't know, maybe he committed some kind of atrocities, yes, I suppose in some ways he was guilty. But he was forced to do as he was told, kill others, or kill himself, or give himself up to be killed. That's what he did in the end, gave himself up. That's what Mama thinks, and that's what I think, too...."

Then Agulya took me by surprise. "You know, as he said, he was Stalin's cur. And he was not the only one. There were many like him. *But still worse—in Stalin's time there were after all so many who perished because they were denounced.*" It is easier for Agulya to fully acknowledge a common evil in Stalin's time when it was inflicted on truly innocent people. It is less complicated. One does not have to wonder about whether the object of inhumanity perhaps had done the same thing to other people. Agulya points out that Agnessa had not mistreated anyone. "Those denunciations, they were treachery. Envy. If a person bothers you—well, it was easy to just take revenge by denouncing. And nobody (among the authorities) ever bothered to check whether the accusation was true. A denunciation is made, well, fine, just go ahead, do what you like. Did Mama have a trial? It was purely arbitrary and lawless."

Agulya's children loved Agnessa. They found her fascinating and endlessly amusing—when they were children. But Agulya worries that when she dies her two children, now grown with their own families, who have no interest in their grandmother's time, will just throw away her memorabilia like it was junk. I promised Agulya to find an archive for her documents and photos, and I did.

A Last Word from Agnessa

Among Agulya's memorabilia is a short diary left by Agnessa. It is fourteen pages, written on both sides of each page. It is dated sporadically, the first date is 1969, the last date, 1980. The first eight pages are about this:

"I have long been aware of my gift for sometimes foreseeing events.... When I try to tell those closest to me, they don't believe me—it's only coincidence, they say." She then gives many examples of her clairvoyance, some of which Mira included in the book, like seeing Zarnitsky for the first time and having a premonition that they would marry. The remaining pages are filled with dates that are important to her: the dates of the deaths of Beethoven and Chopin—"I need to know these dates because these great musicians have been my life's companions." There are quotes from her reading and entire verses often about love and death: George Bernard Shaw, Sergei Esenin, Pushkin. She copied out a discussion between Tolstoy and V. V. Stasov about whether some notion of God is necessary for human compassion and justice. I cannot resist this fragment of prayers from the Koran: "Woman is like a camel that must carry Man on herself through life's deserts."

The last entry is dated January 18, 1980. "Everything can be forgiven… but shedding innocent blood cannot be forgiven." She does not provide the source.

Appendix A

Stenographic report of the meeting of the heads of operational points, operational municipal and regional branches of the UNKVD of the Western Siberian Region, conducted by the head of the administration of the NKVD of the Western Siberian Region, commissar of State Security 3rd rank.
S. M. MIRONOV[1]

July 25, 1937

[...] Until we have conducted the entire operation, this operation and its results are a state secret. When I acquaint you with the entire plan, all the figures that you will hear today, to the extent possible, must remain buried in your head until you have expunged them. The individual who is responsible for the minutest divulgence of the general figures will be subjected to a military tribunal. Because the figures are somewhat unusual for the region, I consider it necessary to acquaint you with them so that you can orient yourselves to the scope of the operation.

[...] After I have acquainted you with the order and the plan for the region as a whole, don't hesitate to ask questions. We wish to resolve all misunderstandings now, because after the meeting we must adjourn the meeting so that you can catch your trains.

[...] If you have secret interrogations of witnesses and orders for arrest, then the plan begins with that.

This order does not have to be checked by the procurator.[2] We will send the procurator only the list of arrestees [...]. You will give the lists to the procurator after the operation is over without indicating which of them belongs to the first and second categories.[3] In the lists you are to indicate only

---

[1] First published in V. N. Uimanov and Iu. A. Petrukhin, comps., *Bol' liudskaia: Kniga pamiati tomichei, repressirovannykh v 30–40e i nachale 50-kh* [Humanity's pain: To the memory of the citizens of Tomsk, repressed in the 1930s, 1940s, and beginning of the 1950s] (Tomsk: Upravlenie KGB SSSR po Tomskoi oblasti, 1999), 5: 102–03m, 110–11. See facsimile reproduction on p. 216.

[2] "The procurator, like the Soviet court, conducts the struggle against [...] enemies of the Soviet Power, spies, saboteurs and other agents of the foreign bourgeoisie." From *Uchebnik "Sovetskoi Konstitutsii"* ["Soviet Constitution" manual] (Moscow, 1951).

[3] In 1937 the Politburo issued the infamous Operational Order No. 00447. It divided arrestees into two categories. The first category consisted of active "enemies of the people," who were to be arrested and shot. The second category described people who were active but less hostile. They were subject to sentences of eight to ten years in the

Из стенограммы совещания
начальников оперативных пунктов, оперсекторов, городских
и районных отделов УНКВД Западносибирского края,
проводимого начальником Управления НКВД по
Западносибирскому краю комиссаром Государственной
Безопасности 3-го ранга С.М. Мироновым

25 июля 1937 г.

[...] До тех пор пока мы с вами не проведем всю операцию - эта операция является государственной тайной со всеми вытекающими отсюда последствиями. Когда я буду Вас знакомить с планом по краю в целом, то всякие цифры, о которых Вы услышите, по мере возможности должны в Вашей голове умереть, а кому удастся, он должен эти цифры из головы выкинуть, кому же это не удастся, он должен совершить над собой насилие и все-таки их из головы выкинуть потому, что малейшее разглашение общей цифры и виновные в этом пойдут под военный трибунал. Поскольку цифры достаточно любопытны по краю, я считаю необходимым познакомить вас с ними, с тем, чтобы вы могли сориентироваться с масштабом операции.

[...] Когда я вас ознакомлю с приказом и оперативным планом по краю в целом - у кого какие будут вопросы - не стесняйтесь, с тем, чтобы все недоуменные вопросы были решены, так как после совещания первыми же поездами все должны разъехаться по местам.

[...] Если имеются секретные допросы свидетелей и ордер на арест, то с этого и начинайте дело.

Постановление с прокурором не согласовывается. Прокурору мы посылаем только списки арестованных, причем списки придется составлять начальнику оперсектора в 4-х экземплярах - один оставлять у себя, один посылать в край для рассмотрения на тройке, один направлять начальнику РО при ГО и один прокурору.

Операция проводится сначала только по первой категории - отбирайте наиболее активных.

Вы посылаете на тройку готовый проект постановления тройки и выписки из него. То, что мы откорректируем на тройке будет перепечатываться в крае.

Page 1 of the "Stenographic report of the meeting of the heads of operational points, operational municipal and regional branches of the UNKVD of the Western Siberian Region..."

Gulags or prisons. For the entire text of the order, see J. Arch Getty and Oleg V. Naumov, *The Road to Terror: Stalin and the Self-Destruction of the Bolsheviks, 1932–1939* (New Haven: Yale University Press, 1999), 473–80.

whether the arrestee is a kulak or a criminal, the code by which he was arrested, and the date of the arrest. In the beginning we are concerned only with the first category—cull out the most active.

We can now detain prisoners in the KPZ [Pretrial Detention Facility] for two months [...].

Do not schedule face-to-face confrontations with the arrestees. It is sufficient to interrogate 2–3 witnesses. As for group cases, in exceptional circumstances you may conduct face-to-face meetings if some among them will not confess [...].

The limit on the first operation is 11,000 people. That is, you must arrest 11,000 people by July 28. Or, arrest 12,000, indeed even 13,000 and even 15,000. In fact, this number is not fixed. You may even arrest 20,000 in the first category with the proviso that later you can pick out from among them those who belong in the second category. The limit on the first category is 10,800 persons, but from among them the more interesting must be culled [...].

You must pull out and crush everything in the organized underground. The task before you is to uncover the organized underground [...]. This business is not diminishing. On the contrary, the struggle with the organized counter-revolution expands and expands [...]. We must not allow our attention to weaken, and some part of the apparatus—if it discovers cases of organized counter-revolution—must remain strong. I think this operational-political task is clear to all of you.

Now, some technical questions. If we take the Tomsk sector and several other sectors, then the average for each of these sectors should be 1,000 people sentenced, and for some sectors—2,000.

What should the chief of the operational sector do when he arrives? There must be a place where the sentences are carried out and places where the corpses are buried. If this takes place in a forest, then the turf must be prepared earlier and then the turf must cover the place so that the area cannot be used later by contras or by religious groups as shrines to religious fanaticism. The bureaucracy of the sector should not have the slightest knowledge of either the place where prisoners were sentenced or the number of sentences that were carried out. The bureaucracy should know absolutely nothing, because our own bureaucracy may become the vehicle for spreading these facts.

Appendix B

MEMORIAL: International Historical, Educational, Human Rights And Humanitarian Society

The international society "Memorial" was created in 1988 on the wave of a broad social movement involving people of various generations and experiences, differing political orientations, and, of course, people who had been politically repressed and their relatives. It was a movement of all who supported the creation of a democratic and just state and who understood that this was possible only if Russia reckoned with the communist past. The first head of Memorial was Andrei Sakharov, who had just returned from exile.

For many years, indeed decades, the political repression of the Soviet Union had been entirely excluded from Soviet public discourse. One of Memorial's main tasks was to form a *cultural memory* of that repression. We had to move quickly to find and preserve material evidence of the arrests, exile, murder, and the Gulag that had been inflicted on hundreds of thousands of Soviet citizens. The call went out and a flood of people surged into the small room that Memorial occupied at that time in Moscow, bringing handwritten recollections of the camp—either their own or those of their relatives who had died in the camps. They brought photographs, documents, handicrafts, embroidery, and other objects made by the prisoners. They brought clothing, sketches, and pictures created by camp artists. Young historians went out on expeditions to the sites of former camps to collect every remaining fragment of camp life that had survived so many years of silence and oblivion. For the first time in Soviet history former prisoners and their families felt the social and historical significance of what they had silently endured for decades. Thus emerged Memorial's archive and museum.

Memorial's museum now contains more than two thousand items, the largest collection of objects and artifacts used and created in the Soviet Gulags. Every artifact of camp life—every kerchief or cap, old quilted jacket, or raggedy camp slippers on wooden soles—is preserved. The museum has also preserved a large collection of applied art, created by the prisoners, especially women. Anything discarded—pieces of wood, aluminum wires, or scraps of fabric and leather—was refashioned into the most varied objects: holders for eyeglasses, cigarette holders, powder compacts, and many other such things. These things would be given as keepsakes on holidays and birthdays. For many this was not just a way to be creative, but also a way to survive.

Memorial's museum has the only collection in Russia of paintings and graphics created by camp artists.

In 1992, on Memorial's initiative and with its participation, a law was passed that finally opened to the public the secret archives holding all documents connected with the Soviet political repression. And now after two decades of intensive research we can compare the two kinds of memory: the repressive system's memory and the private memories of the repressed. Do they contradict or support each other? What the secret archives contained, of course, is what the Soviet system considered necessary to preserve. That is to say, the archives contain the memory of the system. But what we learned from the archives was mainly how the system functioned. Only then did it become clear why that system carefully preserved everything that related to the repression. Because to destroy the evidence of its crimes would be to destroy the system itself.

Further, the archival evidence reinforces the conviction that individual memory is of paramount importance. In the official documents the real person disappears, disintegrated into "Gulag dust." In the Stalin epoch approximately four million people were arrested on political charges. The majority of arrests followed searches during which NKVD personnel destroyed all the personal documents of the arrested—diaries, letters, notebooks. Thus, many documents and works of art disappeared without a trace. All the more valuable, then, are the contents of Memorial's archive—housed in a small building in the center of Moscow—the only repository in Russia of people's memories of repression.

Memorial's archive has fifty thousand dossiers pertaining to the fate of concrete individuals: Soviet and foreign citizens, party and state officials, and the most ordinary Soviet people. One finds in these dossiers a "snapshot" of the time just before the arrest: family photographs, memorabilia, and personal papers that provide a picture of Soviet daily life from the 1920s to the 1950s. This includes official documents pertaining to the arrests, documents about rehabilitation, information contributed by relatives, and sometimes copies of transcripts of interrogations. These dossiers also contain personal papers related to prison camp and exile that have been donated to Memorial, mainly by the relatives and children of the represssed: letters written by women prisoners to their small children who were either put in orphanages or housed with relatives; children's letters to their parents in camp written on bits of paper torn from school notebooks, often in childish handwriting. Excerpts from camp newspapers, the programs of camp performances, worksheets, and certificates of merit from competitions in the Gulags illustrate the absurd attempt to reproduce so-called "free" life.

Memorial further contributes to the cultural memory of the terror by publishing memoirs and collecting and publishing the names of Gulag victims. We have compiled lists of victims found at the sites of mass burials. For the last few years, on October 29, the eve of the Day of Remembrance, Memorial has held an event during which anyone who wishes can read aloud the names of several of the forty thousand Muscovites shot during the Communist terror. For many, this serves as a substitute for the unknown graves in which the victims are buried.

Memorial's work is not limited to recovering the past with the Museum, archive, research projects, and books. It also provides medical and social services for elderly Gulag victims, as well as for the children of Gulag victims who were consigned to orphanages or placed in KGB homes. We advocate vigorously and publicly against the mythologizing and falsification of the Great Terror. Indeed, we are equally present in present-day Russia's struggle against human rights violations. We work for equal rights for national minorities in several regions in Russia and former territories of the USSR, giving legal support and other assistance to refugees and victims of human rights violations. We document and publicize these human rights violations wherever they occur. And we actively participate in current discussions about social problems, all the more since in Russian society discussion about how to evaluate Stalinism continues.

Memorial actively participates in forming international associations that deal with the problem of historical memory, organizing international conferences dedicated to research on Stalinism and conducting seminars and roundtables in collaboration with international research centers. This endeavor includes initiating dialogue with Ukraine, the Baltic countries, and Georgia on the problems of memory and historical politics.

Finally Memorial is deeply concerned not only with the mechanisms of how memory is transmitted from one generation to the next, but has actively stimulated this transmission. For the last twelve years Memorial has organized an all-Russian historical competition for high school students to engage in their own historical work. The project is called "The Person in History: Russia in the Twentieth Century." Memorial considers its educational outreach program to be one of the most important means of expanding the scope of historical memory. That is why our archives and collections are open to all researchers.

Since the birth of Memorial the struggle to expose the truth about the Communist past has not only continued but has become even more important. Over the past decade the authorities have increasingly sought to shift the direction of what one might call "historical politics" in order to create a *positive* image of the past and *pride* in Russia, to shift the image of the past in a positive direction and promote pride in the past. This has led to tremendous confusion, especially among young people, and the image of Stalin as an "effective manager" sometimes coexists peacefully with patchy knowledge about the repressions even in the minds of those whose own families have been affected.

In this connection Memorial played an active role in organizing the program "Preserving the Memory of Victims of the Totalitarian Regime and Promoting National Reconciliation," which was presented in 2011 by the Council on the Development of Civil Society and Human Rights under the auspices of the President of the Russian Federation. Its proposals have sparked an extensive and ongoing discussion in Russian society. This has shown once again that the tasks Memorial set before itself at its founding have not lost their urgency and that the historic work of overcoming the totalitarian past must continue.

Irina Shcherbakova, Director
Youth Education Program, Memorial

Suggested Reading

Since the demise of the Soviet Union the student of that period has had previously unimaginable access to archives, as well the no less unimaginable freedom to speak with people about their lives. This is a suggestion for works in English for the reader who may wish for a wider context to Agnessa's experiences and for a comparison with the lives of her contemporaries.

Adler, Nanci. *Memories of Mass Repression: Narrating Live Stories in the Aftermath of Atrocity*. New Brunswick, NJ: Transaction Publishers, 2009.
Applebaum, Anne. *GULAG: A History*. New York: Anchor Books, 2004.
Cohen, Stephen F. *The Victims Return: Survivors of the Gulag after Stalin*. Exeter, NH: PublishingWorks, 2010.
Conquest, Robert. *The Great Terror: Stalin's Purges of the Thirties*. New York: Macmillan, 1968.
Figes, Orlando. *The Whisperers: Private Life in Stalin's Russia*. New York: Metropolitan Books, 2007.
Fitzpatrick, Sheila. *Everyday Stalinism: Ordinary Life in Extraordinary Times. Soviet Russia in the 1930s*. New York: Oxford University Press, 1999.
Ginzburg, Eugenia Semyonovna. *Journey into the Whirlwind*. New York: Harcourt Brace Jovanovich, 1967.
Goldman, Wendy Z. *Terror and Democracy in the Age of Stalin: The Social Dynamics of Repression*. New York: Cambridge University Press, 2007.
Hochschild, Adam. *The Unquiet Ghost: Russians Remember Stalin*. New York: Viking Press, 1994.
Lewin, Moshe. *The Soviet Century*. London: Verso, 2005.
Mochulsky, Fyodor Vasilevich. *Gulag Boss: A Soviet Memoir*. Translated and edited by Deborah Kaple. New York: Oxford University Press, 2010.
Paperno, Irina. *Stories of the Soviet Experience*. Ithaca, NY: Cornell University Press, 2009.
Scherbakova, Irina. "The Gulag in Memory." In *International Yearbook of Oral History and Life Stories*, vol. 1, *Memory and Totalitarianism*, edited by Luisa Passerini, 103–15. Oxford: Oxford University Press, 1992.
Solzhenitsyn, Alexander. *The Gulag Archipelago, 1918–1956: An Experiment in Literary Investigation*, 7 vols. New York: Harper & Row, 1998.
Vilensky, Semen, ed. *Till My Tale is Told: Women's Memoirs of the Gulag*. Bloomington: Indiana University Press, 2001.